The Author of This Book
Was Once a Skeptic...

By 1980, popular late-night radio personality Joel Martin had made headlines by exposing several psychic hoaxes, including the famous so-called Amityville Horror. So when Patty, a young production assistant on *The Joel Martin Show*, begged him to meet the renowned channeller, George Anderson, Martin warned her—

"I'll expose him as a
phony in a minute!"

"Just see him once," Patty pleaded. And Martin did. And that was just the beginning . . .

. . . because George Anderson knew intimate details about Joel Martin's life that no stranger could have possibly known . . . without being in contact with the other side.

WE DON'T DIE

As seen by millions on:

DONAHUE!
GOOD MORNING AMERICA
SALLY JESSY RAPHAEL
LARRY KING LIVE
THE MORNING SHOW

WE DON'T DIE

DIE

GEORGE ANDERSON'S
CONVERSATIONS WITH THE OTHER SIDE

JOEL MARTIN & PATRICIA ROMANOWSKI

B

BERKLEY BOOKS, NEW YORK

This Berkley book contains the complete
text of the original hardcover edition.
It has been completely reset in a typeface
designed for easy reading and was printed
from new film.

WE DON'T DIE

A Berkley Book / published by arrangement with
the author

PRINTING HISTORY
G. P. Putnam's Sons edition / March 1988
Berkley edition / March 1989

ISBN: 0-425-11451-1

A BERKLEY BOOK ® TM 757,375
Berkley Books are published by The Berkley Publishing Group,
200 Madison Avenue, New York, NY 10016.
The name "BERKLEY" and the "B" logo
are trademarks belonging to Berkley Publishing Corporation.

PRINTED IN THE UNITED STATES OF AMERICA

10 9 8 7 6 5 4 3

Acknowledgments

We are deeply grateful to each of the individuals named in this book, as well as to the dozens whose anonymous public conversations with George are included and the countless others who have helped us in varying ways. Though we cannot thank them each by name, they have our deep gratitude.

We also wish to acknowledge collectively the following for their contributions to our work:

Rita Allen, Charles Ambrogio, Vincent T. Apicella, Howard Stephen Berg, Bryce Bond, Sri Chinmoy, David Cintron, Jon Connelly, Constant Listener, Mary Crowley and family, Dennis, Renée Dorr, Warren Eckstein, Robert C. Gottlieb, Karl Grossman, Frank G., Harry Hepcat, Muriel Horenstein, Bernhardt J. Hurwood, Patricia Ippolito, Dr. Leonard Jasen and Mary Jasen, Roxanne Salch Kaplan, Jim Knusch, Donald Lapore, Tom Lechner, Guy Levaillant, Lewis Lorenz, Dorothy Maksym, William Marshall, Mary and Stephen Matejov, Patricia McIlvaine, Howard Metz, Rick Moran, Ed Peterson, Dr. Richard Resua, Richard Ruhl, Kristina Rus, Tom Santorelli, the Reverend Douglas Scott, John Smith, Renée Stanley, Lloyd Strayhorn, Neil Vineberg, Paul Zalasin.

Special thanks to those who have kindly consented to being subjects and have allowed us to identify them by their true names: Lauren Fremer, Dr. John Gschwendtner, Ph.D., Barbara and John Licata and their family; and Dr. Brenda Lukeman, Ph.D.

Our sincere appreciation and thanks to our literary agent, Sarah Lazin, for her enthusiasm and support, and to everyone at G. P. Putnam's Sons who has worked so closely with us and made this a wonderful experience: our editor, Faith Sale; Jennifer Barth, Gypsy da Silva, Marilyn Ducksworth, Suzanne Herz, Mary Kurtz, Benjamin McCormick, and Fred Sawyer.

Joel Martin and George Anderson wish to extend their special thanks to Patrice Ann Vohs. Thanks to Stephen Kaplan for many years of friendship and expertise; Max Toth for generously sharing his vast knowledge with us; the management and staff of Viacom Cablevision of Long Island—Eric Kronen, Gary Zelamsky, including Jean, Sandy, Jeanne, Barry, Tom Demarinis; and all the *Psychic Channels* crew members, and producer-director Jill Teichner.

In addition we each would like to note those special people in our lives whose unwavering support helped see us through.

I would like to thank Robert and Rochelle Bashe, Danielle Karmel, Mary Longo, Dianne Parker, Elisa Petrini, Lynn Romanowski, Richard Romanowski, and Mr. and Mrs. H. P. Whiteside. My sincere gratitude goes to Joel Martin and George Anderson for their trust and friendship. And, as always, to my husband, Philip Bashe, whose thoughts and feelings helped shape my work. His experience showed me the true meaning of George's gift. Finally, to my late parents, John J. and Marjorie Maxine Romanowski for literally coming through when I needed them most.

—P.R.

I would like to thank my parents, George Sr. and Eleanor Anderson, and my family—Alfred, Dolores, and James Anderson—as well as Janice Goldberg, Donna Koopman, and Donald Walker, and my many other relatives and friends here and in Europe. My deepest thanks and appreciation go especially to Eileen Maher for her confidence in me in 1978, when she encouraged me to move toward working with the public. And my sincerest thanks to Monsignor Thomas Hartman for always being there when spiritual counseling was needed, especially regarding the psychic experience and ability.

—G.A.

My thanks always to Elise, whose encouragement in my research never wavered, whose knowledge enlightened me, and whose love and spirit strengthened me. Special appreciation to our families, Charles and Sadie Cohen, Evelyn Moleta, and to the memory of Shirleyann. Finally, to Christina Martin for her loyalty, patience, and belief in me through all my years of broadcasting and research for this book.

—J.M.

This book is dedicated to each and every person to whom we have brought comfort, and to everyone who may find that comfort in the future.

—J.M.

To Mary Kay and Johnetta Marie, for listening to the other side.

—P.R.

Contents

FOREWORD   1

INTRODUCTION   5

We Don't Die: George Anderson's   15
Conversations with the Other Side

APPENDIX I: Glossary of Psychic Symbols   261

APPENDIX II: A Selective History of   265
    Mediumship

BIBLIOGRAPHY   285

Foreword

By the time I began hosting radio talk and news programs in 1972, I had worked as a New York City public schoolteacher, a college instructor, and producer of television and radio programs and written materials for educators. Though I had traveled extensively throughout the United States and Canada, I brought to my professional life the skepticism that seems to come from being born, raised, and educated in New York. I was always looking for the truth, whether my guest was a politician, actor, author, rock star, or an average person with a story to tell. My programs covered a wide range of subjects, some—such as the nuclear power industry or the true story of Billy Hayes, which became a book and film, *Midnight Express*—very important to me personally. Generally, the shows were planned with the listening public's interests in mind.

I knew my audience and learned early on that the general topic of unexplained phenomena was always popular. Over the years I had the pleasure of interviewing such leading writers in the field as Lynn Schroeder, Elsie Seachrist, Ruth Montgomery, John G. Fuller, Elizabeth Fuller, Charles Berlitz, Dorothy Allison, Fred Lenz, D. Scott Rogo, Ruth Mattson Taylor, John White, and Herbert Puryear on various topics, some related directly to mediumship. I did my research for each show but never took any position on the paranormal, unless you consider publicly exposing frauds taking a position. As much as I might have admired some of my guests' work, I had no particular opinion on the possibility of life after death, or discarnate communications. It wasn't that I didn't "believe in" them; I just never thought about it.

That—and countless other things—changed when I met George Anderson in 1980. What has transpired between then and now is the story of *We Don't Die*.

In those seven years we have conducted countless tests and he has performed thousands of public and private readings. Invariably the results are the same: George reveals to his subjects information—about events, experiences, trivia, even nicknames—for which the only possible source is the living consciousness, the spirit, of the deceased. In some cases, the spirits give forth information about events that occurred during and after their own physical death, or that will occur in the future.

George and I have kept records and notes on both public and private readings, in addition to the audio and video tapes of our broadcasts, from the day we met. Shortly thereafter I became convinced that George's story would be of great interest, and so we continued working together, with George telling me of special readings that he believed would help me in my research. Though in some cases names have been changed to protect the identities of those involved (and in the instances of criminal cases, circumstances, descriptions, and other identifying facts were altered), the readings—the words spoken by George and the subjects—are real. Each reading presented here was taken verbatim from audio and/or videotape recordings. The transcripts have been edited where necessary for clarity and brevity (repetitions and irrelevant asides were deleted); however, the words in each reading are presented in the order that they were spoken. In the few cases where the readings were not recorded, the subjects and George were interviewed independently. The contents of only one reading, the one George did for a suspected murderer, are taken from his memory alone, with certain details later corroborated by the police.

Within a short while after we first met, I had collected literally dozens of boxes of research material on George. It was time to write the book. In 1985 I explained to Patricia Romanowski, whom I had known for several years, about my experiences with George. Much to my surprise she was far more open-minded about discarnate communications than I had been, and agreed to be my co-author. I am indebted to her. This book is the result of the original research on George, our further research, and many hours of discussion.

It's just the beginning. The fascinating years since 1980 represent only the very first steps toward our understanding that death is not a termination but a transition, that as human beings we have capacities and abilities far beyond our imagination. We don't die. That making this discovery—and seeing its proof—has changed our lives, eternally, goes without saying.

JOEL MARTIN
Long Island, New York
July 1987

Introduction

In the United States a person dies every sixteen seconds—or doesn't die. Who among us has not speculated about what we generally refer to as "life after death"? What happens when a young man claims—and repeatedly offers evidence through thousands of readings and many scientific tests—that he receives communications from those who are deceased? What do we learn after he spends years under intense public scrutiny, and successfully demonstrates these abilities for thousands of listeners and viewers, countless anonymous callers, and dozens of others, among them scientists, physicians, psychologists, law-enforcement officials, parapsychologists, theologians—even magicians and self-appointed debunkers? What case can be made for proof of life after death by the incontrovertible evidence gathered and presented as a result of this young man's extraordinary gift?

We Don't Die—the true story of psychic medium George Anderson, Jr.—answers these questions.

Regardless of our personal religious beliefs—or lack of them—death fascinates and frightens us. We come into this life knowing, at least consciously, little or nothing about death. We must *learn* to fear death, and we do, with the result that we fear not only death but the dying. Our feelings about death are rarely clear. Though we live in an enlightened age, the subject of death remains taboo, and our words and actions express many of the same superstitions and fears our "backward" ancestors embraced.

But why is this so? Is death really the end? Most ancient civilizations, nearly all major religions, and the majority of people alive today view death as a natural *transition*. Most of us would speak of those who have died as being "at rest," or having "passed on." We remember them through prayers, we name our children after them, and we inscribe tombstones with words beseeching them to remember us in turn. Cynics might conclude that we simply cannot accept death, that we deny its existence and reject its presumed finality through our words and rituals. But maybe in those words and rituals we are really saying something else, expressing not denial but truth. After all, doesn't describing someone as being "at rest" or "asleep" suggest that one day he or she will "wake up"? Doesn't the term "passed on" suggest that there is something to pass on *to*? And of what use are the messages—our thoughts and prayers—if we truly believe that death is the end and that our loved ones no longer exist, not even as spirits? Do we know, deep inside, that we don't die?

Dr. Elisabeth Kübler-Ross's work with dying patients revolutionized our thinking about death. Her later studies—and those of Dr. Raymond Moody, Jr., and others on the so-called near-death experiences (NDEs)—opened yet another door. Though there have been countless references to what we now recognize as the NDE in both religious and secular texts throughout history, the phenomenon has been seriously studied only in the last two decades. As a result of those published studies and many public opinion polls, we know that tens of thousands of Americans have had near-death experiences and report—despite suffering clinical death (defined as the absence of heartbeat, respiration, brain-wave activity, or muscle response)—being drawn out of their "lifeless" physical bodies and moving through a tunnel toward a dazzlingly bright light. Though the details of individual NDEs vary, most people who've been clinically dead and report such an experience claim no longer to fear death. Does the near-death experience verify what many of us feel strongly deep inside—that in fact we do *not* die?

No one can say with any certainty what "causes" the near-death experience or the so-called deathbed visions (instances where a dying person reports seeing deceased loved ones "coming for" him), but they are too common to be dismissed. Of Americans polled by the Gallup Organization in 1981, 15 percent reported having had a near-death experience. And 42 percent of those polled claimed to have had "contact" with the dead. These statistics and the widespread reports of those who have had some communication from deceased loved ones suggest strongly that some form of human consciousness does survive bodily death. The next step is to find out if—and, perhaps someday, how—these discarnate beings, or spirits, communicate with the living.

In exploring these questions, we must keep an open mind. Simply asserting that life after death and communications from the dead are not possible or cannot exist because they cannot be proved scientifically is the critics' weakest response to unexplained phenomena. Every day we live with and depend on countless phenomena that scientists freely admit not being able to understand or explain fully—memory, personality factors, how DNA works, the ability to comprehend ideas by looking at black marks on a page. We live in a world of wonder, and it is naïve to conclude that we know or even could comprehend all the mysteries of life, death, and human consciousness.

Contrary to what many believe, the idea that discarnate beings do communicate with the living is not new; it's been around for centuries. The scientific study of spirit communications began in 1882, when the Society for Psychical Research was founded in London. Investigation in the area of psychic phenomena, or parapsychology, continues today around the world in universities and private research facilities, and is conducted by such unlikely organizations as the Soviet government and the Central Intelligence Agency.

Certainly spiritualism, the belief in communication between the living and the so-called dead (we prefer to call them spirits), has suffered from its share of fraudulent practitioners and gullible supporters. During spiritualism's golden age, from approximately 1848 to the mid- to late 1920s, spirit communication—both real and faked—was all the rage in America and Europe. Unfortunately, genuine mediums and serious students were easily eclipsed in the public's imagination by the more spectacular, lurid, and bizarre occurrences attributed to otherworldly entities. Perhaps the age's more vivid and exotic im-

ages persist *because* they glorify those aspects of spiritualism
that were clearly fraudulent, support the status quo, and en-
dorse the prevailing—=and unfounded—belief that genuine
spirit communication is not possible.

We should judge unexplained phenomena using criteria and
seeking results that are fair, reasonable, and appropriate to the
subject and the phenomenon being tested and observed. This
doesn't mean unquestioning acceptance, which in its own way
has proved as detrimental as blind, categorical dismissal. But
we cannot ignore every psychically gifted person just because
some who claim to have psychic abilities are fakes, or are
genuine mediums who may have resorted to trickery at one
time or another.

We must also reexamine what constitutes "proof" of discarnate survival and communications. Like it or not, we live in a
universe we do not yet—and may never—fully understand.
We cannot yet devise a single test to measure or a theory to
explain what is happening when George Anderson and others
like him do what they do. All we have is the evidence, derived
by recording years' worth of readings and tracking their rate of
accuracy.

The term *psychic phenomena* encompasses any occurrence that
cannot be explained by current scientific theory or proven—
and disproven—by orthodox, contemporary scientific means
and includes extrasensory perception (ESP), telekinesis, and
telepathy (mind reading). Certainly thousands of people—
maybe all of us—possess one, several, or every one of these to
some degree. For our purposes, however, we are concerned
only with the abilities through which George receives the spirits' messages—clairvoyance, clairaudience, clairsentience,
sympathetic pain and sensation, and symbolic imagery.
Through these means, George receives information that he
could not possibly have obtained through any of his "normal"
five senses, or, interestingly, through extrasensory perception
or telepathy. These messages consistently contain information
regarding the past, the present, and the future.

We call George a psychic medium, which he is in the most
literal sense of the term. We use the word *psychic* as an adjec-
tive, meaning "lying outside the realm of physical processes
and physical science," for it describes the nature, and perhaps

the source, of George's abilities. We use *medium,* frankly, for want of a more precise word and, because of all of the other terms that have been or are currently in vogue—channel, psychic, clairvoyant—it is the most comprehensive, accurate, and neutral. For George is a medium, a passive conduit through which the spirits communicate.

George is not the only psychic medium in the world, but he is unique among those who possess this gift in several important ways. First, he is deeply religious and insists on being a passive receiver; he will not conjure or call up spirits. He prefers to say that he discerns them. From what George has learned through his readings, we believe that spirits are all around us, existing as some form of energy, perhaps in another dimension. For some reason not all of us can communicate directly with them. Or perhaps we do receive their messages but are not consciously aware of it. (It may be that the conscious mind cannot grasp and retain the messages, just as it cannot recall or make sense of all of our dreams.) To use a crude metaphor, George seems to act as a radio receiver through which the spirits communicate on an energy frequency most of us are not consciously attuned to. In addition, though George is passive in the readings, he does not go into trance (except when he is asked to for scientific tests). He also works in the light, literally and figuratively. He does readings in well-lighted rooms and live on radio and television, and he is known to crack an occasional joke about the spirit in question. Finally, he does not have a spirit guide or any other entity "speaking through" him, such as J. Z. Knight's Ramtha, Arthur Ford's Fletcher, Arigó's Dr. Fritz, or Jane Roberts's Seth. Spirits close to those for whom George is doing a reading (the subject), or close to someone the subject would know, communicate directly to George without a spiritual "middle man." George receives the messages over something like a spiritual party line with an infinite number of connections. He cannot control which spirits come through or how long a communication is sustained.

George's most refreshing and unique difference is his willingness to be tested and his ability to do readings in many different situations. In each he demands only that people respond to his statements in such a way as to give him the minimum amount of information he needs to determine if he is on the right track, or that the messages make sense to the subject. Usually, they are asked to respond with only a yes or a no. Occasionally, however, some elaboration is needed, although subjects are encouraged to keep their responses as brief as possible. In the readings that George has conducted over the telephone and that are broadcast live on radio or on television, the caller is allowed to say only "hello" before George begins to receive communications. This rules out the possibility of George obtaining information or picking up clues about the subject's appearance, gestures, and expressions. George does not know why or from what distance the person is calling.

George also does group readings with strangers. In these, usually held in public, George picks up a spirit's communication without knowing to whom in the group it is directed. Only by asking specific questions ("Did anyone lose a sister at a very young age? Did she go by the name Vicki or Victoria?" and so on) does he narrow down the field of possible subjects to the one person for whom the message is intended. From then on, the subject is asked to acknowledge the information by replying with only a yes or a no. George also does private readings, and as always (except in cases of friends and clients who return to him) he knows his subjects by their first names only.

In each situation, particularly the readings done for radio and television, George and I question the subject after the reading to determine George's rate of accuracy and just what any unfamiliar symbols or confusing, contradictory messages mean. While many readings are quite straightforward and, one might say, filled with meaningful trivia, others are very complex, their content so personal and or so cryptic that only the subject understands. A personal nickname, an allusion to a shared experience mean nothing out of context. The post-reading interviews give us the context and have helped us to understand the sometimes numerous and hidden meanings of the symbols and messages George is given. (How else might George have deduced that a broken washing machine symbolized kidney disease or kidney failure?)

Since George first appeared on my radio program in October of 1980, I have been contacted by many people eager to discredit him. Of those who accepted our invitation to appear publicly with George, none has been able to explain or even hypothesize how George could obtain the content of his messages through any means *but* spirit communication. Those who persist in claiming that George is not in communication with the dead often sum up their "proof" in the following statement: If George were really in communication with the dead, his information would be 100 percent accurate, a statement that presumes that subjects *always* know exactly what the spirit is referring to and that they can and will readily acknowledge every part of the message (not always the case); that human consciousness after death is somehow superior (no doubt an impression derived from watching horror movies), or that we get smarter or more perceptive after death; and that all other areas we regard as "sciences," and therefore correct, true, and real, are 100 percent accurate.

Regarding the first point, many people do not know or recall the names of every deceased relative and acquaintance, or the circumstances of their deaths, or what's going on in a distant cousin's love life. In public readings, which may be witnessed by loved ones and friends, people can be understandably reluctant to acknowledge information concerning such personal matters as an extramarital affair or an abortion. When a subject cannot confirm George's information as correct, we count George's statement as a miss. However, it is quite common for people to record the readings and/or discuss them with friends and family. Often, these people have contacted us several days later with confirmations and corrections. Or, someone may call weeks later to tell us that an incident George alluded to occurred after the reading.

As for the second point, we don't know enough about the nature of human consciousness—"living" or "dead"—to determine how, or if, death affects it. However, many subjects acknowledge that a spirit is using the same verbal expressions or communicating in the same emotional tone that he or she typically used in life.

Finally, there's the matter of accuracy. Consider one familiar example, the National Weather Service, which despite an army of meteorologists and advanced computer technology cannot predict the weather with a rate of accuracy anywhere near George's documented 86 to 95 percent.

How is spirit communication possible? And what is the

purpose of George's gift? There are several theories regarding both of these questions, but no one certain answer. Nevertheless, after many years of knowing George and witnessing his work, I can honestly say that for almost all of those who have had readings with George—be they bereaved loved ones, law-enforcement officials, or the curious—the product of his work is good. As amazed and surprised as one might be to "hear" from those on the other side, rarely is anyone frightened or shocked by what they learn. Most are quite relieved to find that it isn't "spooky" or "creepy." And why should it be? If anything, the majority of subjects find the experience comforting and reassuring. To say that for some a reading with George has changed their lives is hardly an overstatement. The spirits have much to teach us about the nature of the human mind and about the single journey that is both life and death.

Millions of spiritual creatures
Walk the earth
Unseen, both when we wake, and
When we sleep.
What if earth and heaven
Be to each other like
More than on earth is thought?

—MILTON

What if you slept? And what if, in your sleep, you dreamed? And what if, in your dream, you went to heaven and there plucked a beautiful flower? And what if, when you awoke, you had the flower in your hand? Ah, what then?

—SAMUEL TAYLOR COLERIDGE

It is one of the commonest of mistakes to consider that the limit of our power of perception is also the limit of all there is to perceive.

—C. W. LEADBEATER

Why *shouldn't* truth be stranger than fiction? Fiction, after all, has to make sense.

—MARK TWAIN

One

For sixteen-year-old David Licata, the evening of February 20, 1982, was a typical Saturday night. Like his classmates, David was enjoying the ten-day winter recess from school, and he was spending his free time hanging out with friends in his hometown of Commack, New York, a close-knit white-collar suburban community on Long Island's North Shore. David was the second of John and Barbara Licata's three children, and the kind of boy any parent would be proud to have as a son. Popular, easygoing, and responsible, David loved soccer and hoped to play professionally one day. He'd spend afternoons in the yard kicking a soccer ball around, accompanied by the family dog, Muffin. He was large for his age—about 5′ 11″—and good-looking, with longish brown hair and a beautiful smile.

Several weeks earlier, David had made plans to spend the recess in upstate New York with his friend Cory. But when Barbara Licata, a self-confessed overprotective mother, learned that Cory's parents wouldn't be making the trip and the boys would be alone, she insisted that David stay home. Cory traveled upstate alone, and David found plenty of things to do in the neighborhood.

This evening David and a group of friends attended a party. Having promised his mother that he'd be home by 12:30 A.M., David left the party around midnight and started walking home along Commack Road with his friend Bret Coville, also sixteen.

Barbara Licata had gone to bed at 12:30 but lay there wide

awake, then got up when she heard David's older brother, Darrin, come in an hour later. It wasn't like David to be late without at least calling. At around 2:30, Barbara could stand it no longer. She started phoning each of David's friends to ask if they'd seen him; none of them knew where David was. Anxiously looking out the living room window, all Barbara could do was pray. She couldn't shake the frightening feeling that something was very wrong—but what? When two Suffolk County Police detectives knocked at the Licatas' door at 3:15 that morning, she knew: David had been killed.

At approximately 12:05 that Sunday morning, as David and Bret walked along Commack Road, they were struck from behind by a speeding vehicle that immediately fled the scene, leaving Bret critically injured and David dead. But what the Licatas would not know until almost four months later was that even though David had been killed, he did not die.

The coming days were painful for the Licatas. Over one thousand people—family members, friends, classmates, and teachers—came to pay their respects and say good-bye to David. When the coach of the Cosmos, the soccer team David dreamed of playing for after he finished high school, heard of David's accident, he gave David's parents a team shirt, which Barbara placed beside David in his coffin. The coach simply gave the Licatas the last shirt left in the locker room, number 27. He did not know that David had worn number 27 on the Commack High School Varsity Soccer Team.

In their grief, everyone asked the same question over and over: Why? Why David? Why had he been taken from them so quickly and cruelly, at such a young age, when he had so much more to accomplish, when there was so much to live for, when so many others survived? What purpose did his death and their suffering serve? Why would God, if he was just, let something so terrible happen?

Somewhere, closer than any of them could have imagined, the unidentified killer, the hit-and-run driver, was still at large. Barbara Licata was too distraught to be bitter or angry. All she knew was that her son would never wear his new gray suit to the junior prom that spring, for, on February 25, he was buried in it.

No matter how hard the Licatas tried to cope with their devastating loss, the following months brought no answers, and more than once, Barbara found herself thinking about how poorly we are prepared to face death, how little we understand it. In her heart, she had long believed in life after death. Raised in the Roman Catholic Church, she believed in the life of the soul as it travels toward God, perhaps in heaven. She prayed and said the rosary for David daily, always hoping that someday she would see a sign, some evidence that would convince her intellectually of what she was sure of in her heart—that he still existed, someplace, in some form.

Weeks passed. John Licata mourned inwardly, always giving the appearance that he had his emotions in check. For Barbara, grief seemed to permeate every waking moment. She simply could not let David go. Maybe it was no more than a mother's faith, she thought, but she had to hold on to something. Nevertheless, her grief did not ease with time.

Reading as much as she could about the subject of life after death helped Barbara a bit, for it allowed her to lose herself in her thoughts and provided some proof—vague though it was—that David was "living another life" somewhere. She read Adela Rogers St. Johns's *No Good-Byes* and Dr. Raymond Moody's popular *Life after Life*. She took great comfort in the Bible, especially in the Gospel according to John. When Jesus said, "My house is made of many mansions," could He have been talking about an afterlife? she wondered. Could the "house" be God's universe, and the "many mansions" allude to another life after death? She longed for an answer.

Lauren Fremer was a young woman who knew of David through mutual friends. Like everyone else in the community, she knew about the effect of David's death on the Licatas. That May, about three months after David was killed, Lauren telephoned Barbara Licata, whom she had never met, to tell her about a man named George. Lauren described George as "the man with fascinating abilities" and told Barbara he appeared regularly on a local radio program, taking calls from listeners and giving them messages that, he claimed, came through him from their deceased relatives and friends on "the other side." Lauren thought that perhaps Barbara would want to call George—perhaps he could help her communicate with David. She gave Barbara George's phone number, which she'd written down when it was announced on a recent radio show. Though Barbara took the number, she thought little about following up on it. She had some idea of what she was searching for, but this didn't sound like it. She put the paper with the phone number in a dresser drawer.

Three days later, Barbara's longtime friend Rhoda came over for a visit. As Barbara talked to her friend about what a hard time she was having coping with David's death, Lauren's call came to mind. She was recounting what Lauren had told her about the man on the radio, when Rhoda interrupted to say, "That's funny. I've been meaning to tell you that one night my daughter Arlene wanted to use the phone to call a local radio station. When I asked her why, she said, 'Because I want to get through to talk with George.' Then she told me that George said that a young boy was killed in a tragic accident, that he played the drums, and that he was very, very restless from the tremendous sorrow and anguish that people were feeling. It sounded so much like David, it was chilling. Of course, I thought it was just coincidental."

Suddenly it struck Barbara that this seeming "coincidence" held a special meaning for her. As she listened to Rhoda and thought about it, she felt compelled to reach George. That his name had come up twice in just a few days was uncanny. Perhaps this was the sign. She dialed George's number.

Whoever answered George's phone asked Barbara no questions about who she was or why she was calling; all she told him was her first name and that she wanted to see George. The person politely explained to her that so many people wanted to see George privately that he had no open dates until nearly a year from then. Having come this far in her search for David, she was reluctant to give up, but she couldn't wait so long. Barbara took the possible delay as an indication that her sign from David was fading.

Less than a month later, in early June, yet another friend of Barbara's mentioned George to her. This time Barbara was not surprised to hear his name, and she listened eagerly as the neighbor told her that George would be on the radio on Sunday night of the upcoming July 4 holiday weekend and would be taking phone calls from listeners. That evening Barbara telephoned the radio station, Long Island's WBAB, an FM rock station with the unique distinction of carrying a nightly talk show. Her call was forwarded to my wife, Chris, the producer of *The Joel Martin Show*.

From her many years' experience as a talk prog...
Chris was used to handling such calls. Frequently the ...
very strongly that he or she needed to speak with George. ...
asked for special consideration so that their calls could be put
through on the radio program without their having to spend up to
an hour redialing the busy number. Others called to get George's
home number so that they could arrange for a private reading.
Barbara was willing to be in the first category, but Chris, sensitive to something in Barbara's voice, knew that she needed to
speak with George immediately. It would be impossible for Chris
to give each caller such personal attention, but every so often
someone like Barbara called, and Chris knew intuitively that the
situation called for special efforts. She asked Barbara only one
question, "Are the police involved?"

"Yes," Barbara replied.

"Then I think we should try to arrange for you to see George
privately as soon as possible."

Chris promised to try to make the appointment for Barbara
and asked her to call back the next day at about the same time.
Then she added, "Please remember when you call me back
tomorrow, don't tell me anything about yourself. I don't need
to know, and George absolutely must *not* know anything in
advance about your circumstances. That's his rule. Don't even
tell him your last name when you identify yourself."

"I understand," Barbara replied.

The next evening Barbara called Chris as planned and was
told that George would see her on Tuesday evening, June 8,
and was given his address. After being assured by Chris that it
was all right for John to go with her, Barbara thanked Chris
and said good-bye.

When Barbara told John about her past few days' experiences and the upcoming appointment with George, he stared
silently at her. John was skeptical, but he knew this was not the
time to argue with his wife about charlatans and séances. She
seemed somewhat consoled by the prospect of visiting this
stranger. And, in truth, his cynicism and disbelief about
George didn't upset him as much as his fear that his wife was
looking for something that she might never find. Though he
suffered from David's death, he felt that Barbara was more
vulnerable. The last thing she needed, John thought, was another disappointment. Yet he could see that she needed to visit

⹁his man. Vaguely recalling something he'd heard about George, John had to admit he was at least curious about meeting him. He was confident that he'd be able to spot any "tricks" George might use, and in that way he could protect his wife. If nothing else, this could comfort her—and him, he had to admit—and that would be welcome relief. He agreed to go.

The Licatas told no one of their plans to see George. One reason for the secrecy was to ensure the integrity of the reading. If no one who knew anything about them was aware of their visit, no one could give George advance information. But there was also the matter of their feeling self-conscious, even a little embarrassed that they were seeking the help of a psychic medium. As the date of their meeting neared, Barbara's enthusiasm grew. But when June 8 dawned, she also felt fear—but of what? She didn't know. She kept repeating to herself, "I have had absolutely no contact with anything on a psychic level."

That Tuesday evening, the Licatas made the short drive from their home to George's apartment in nearby Babylon. Barbara nervously folded and refolded the slip of paper bearing George's address. When they pulled up in front of the garden apartment complex, they were surprised. It all looked so . . . normal, nothing like the stereotypical weathered old Victorian house they'd learned to expect from watching horror movies. Barbara was trembling as they climbed the eight steps to George's door. There was no name on the bell, but according to the directions, number 97 was the right apartment. John rang the bell.

He stared straight ahead, expressionless. Barbara muttered, "God, I'm frightened." Then, seconds later, a casually dressed young man with penetrating brown eyes opened the door.

"We're here to see George," Barbara offered.

"I am George," the man replied.

"Oh. I'm Barbara. This is John."

They said nothing else as George smiled warmly and showed them inside. Barbara was still nervous as she looked around. It seemed like a typical well-kept apartment. Just inside the door was a contemporary dining room table and several chairs, to the right a comfortable sofa faced a large television. There was a highly polished wooden coffee table in front of the sofa and, near one wall, a Victorian-style wooden rack filled with knick-knacks. In one corner was a grandfather clock and near it an easy chair. A glass-enclosed hutch with china and a small music stand holding a large dictionary completed the furnishings of the living-dining area. On the walls hung several religious paintings. A small, meticulously clean kitchenette could be seen behind the dining room, and a partially closed door faced Barbara; she could see that it was the bedroom.

She turned her attention to George. As he invited them to sit at the dining table, she realized that though she really didn't know what a psychic was supposed to look like, George wasn't what she was expecting. He was slightly built, with curly black hair and a neatly trimmed beard. Surely, he wasn't much older than thirty, if that. He seemed very relaxed as he sat down across the table from them. He held a legal-size pad and a pen, for what purpose Barbara did not know.

She asked if she might tape-record the session on her cassette recorder, and George said, "I don't mind. It's up to you." George said a prayer, asking God for protection and crossed himself. Every now and then during the session, he glanced up at Barbara and John, and once he squinted at them, as if to focus his vision.

Barbara was praying silently to herself that the visit would be fruitful, when she gave a start. George had begun to scribble rapidly across his pad. Neither Barbara nor John had any idea what George was writing—or why—but their reading had begun. After several moments, George spoke.

"I see you surrounded in black. A death—" George began, but caught his own words and corrected himself—"a transition, so to speak, a going to the other side."

The Licatas nodded.

"A young person."

"Yes," Barbara confirmed.

"A very unpleasant sort of passing. A sudden form of passing."

"Yes."

George put his hands to his temples, and moved his fingers toward the back of his head, finally pushing his palms against the base of his skull.

"Does it have to do with the head at all? My head is pounding. It started to pound the minute you came into the room."

"Yes."

"This person is related to you."

"Yes."

"The person is very, very restless. I feel the person in the room. Just say 'yes' or 'no.' Don't elaborate. Was it some sort of accident?"

"Yes."

"But there is something strange about it."

"Yes."

"Because I'm getting question marks after the word 'accident.'"

Barbara interrupted as George was explaining his confusion about injuries to the face and the head. "May I elaborate?"

"I'd prefer if you didn't. If they want to, they'll come back or will use another approach to clear it for me."

As George spoke, he continued writing. Although some psychic mediums receive their communications through this so-called automatic writing, George uses it primarily as a means of concentration.[1] He filled page after page with words, names, and abstract images that flashed before him from what he called "the other side."

"Is this person a child to you?"

"Yes."

"Is there any other physical injury besides the head? Anything in the back at all?"

"I don't know."

George persisted with this point. "I'm getting pain in the back as well. Just listen to what I'm saying. Was there a vehicle involved?"

"Yes."

"Okay, I just see a vehicle in front of me. There's a vehicle involved. Is this a son?"

"Yes."

"Okay, then it's him I'm speaking with. Was someone with him when this occurred?"

"Yes."

"Was a girl with him?"

"No."

"Did you ever lose any other children?"

1. Interestingly, George is in control of the writing, but two handwriting experts who compared samples of the automatic writing and George's normal script concluded that the two "types" of writing had nothing in common and could not have come from the same person.

"No."

"Do you know somebody in the family that lost a young girl?"

"No."

"Do you know a young girl that passed on?"

"Yes."

"Because she's with him."

"Yes."

"Okay. Because that's what's confusing me."

"Yes."

"Okay. Did this girl pass on before him?"

"Yes."

"Because she was the one who met him when he came over to the other side, and she's standing there with him and that's why I was thrown off for a second. . . . She passed on young as well."

"Yes."

Suddenly John Licata, who sat silently and who had so far let his wife respond to George's queries, shuddered. He had been watching and listening but neither fully believed nor comprehended what was taking place. However, when George described a young girl greeting his son, John's skepticism began to waver. There was absolutely no way that George could have known that a young female friend of David's from their neighborhood had been strangled about four months before David was killed.

George continued writing rapidly, tearing off each completed sheet and setting it near him on the table. Then he said, "He's very, very restless. Let's hope he can get it off his chest now, whatever he has to say, so he can be at better rest. Was he very sensitive, very emotional?"

"Yes."

"Because that's how he's coming through. Just bear with me. He has to calm down. He's speaking so fast, I can't understand what he's saying. Would you say there's something strange about his case?"

"Yes."

"He's trying to explain something to me. I can't get it out of him. Late teens, early twenties."

"No."

"Just teens."

"Yes."

"Okay. Was he tall?"[2]

"Yes."

"That's what it is. He just appeared to me for a second. He looked pretty tall. I don't know if this is his age or a specific number, but does sixteen mean anything?"

"Yes."

"That's his age," George said, nodding confidently.

"Yes."

"Okay. He says, 'Thank you.' When he crossed over, he said he was sixteen, but he's a big kid. . . . He said he wasn't alone when this accident occurred. Someone else played a role in it."

"Yes," Barbara acknowledged.

"That's what he tells me. Someone else was involved."

"Yes."

"Another male."

"Yes."

"Because he says it was a male. . . . Was your son struck on the head?"

"Yes."

"Was he severely cut by this blow?"

"Yes."

George suddenly stopped writing and looked into Barbara's eyes. "I'm afraid to say it. Was he murdered?"

"Yes."

"That's what he says. Just bear with me for a second. I'm getting so much emotion [that] I keep getting knocked to the edge. It keeps going down because of what he's trying to get across. Does broken glass have anything to do with this?"

"Yes."

"Because I keep seeing glass smashed in front of me."

"Yes."

"Was he hit with anything like a bottle?"

"Not a bottle."

George paused to explain. "Sometimes I try to interpret what I see. . . . I see broken glass shattered in front of me. Was someplace being broken into? Besides his being murdered, was there any other crime around?"

2. George could not have assumed that David was tall by looking at John and Barbara, since each stands at 5'4".

"I don't know how to answer that."

"I keep praying for him that he take it easy and calm down and get off what he has to say. Is it possible that his murder was an accident?"

"Yes."

George looked up from his writing again and shook his head sympathetically. "Do you feel it was deliberate?"

"No."

George nodded. "I have to say it wasn't. He says to me it was an accidental murder. It wasn't deliberate."

"Right."

George began writing again. "Without telling me anything but 'yes' or 'no,' do you have any suspicions as to who it could have been? Because he says it's somebody he knows."

"Yes."

"It definitely is. It's a male."

"Yes."

"Did your son have any trouble with his chest?"

"Yes."

"No wonder I can't catch my breath. . . . Was your son very athletic?"

"Yes."

"Because I'm seeing that symbol as well." George then shifted in his seat as he raised his arms and brought his hands to the back of his head, as he had done earlier in the reading. Again he asked, "Was he struck in the back of the head?" When Barbara replied affirmatively, George repeated, "Was he struck in the *back* of his head? Because he was hit from behind, he tells me. That's for a fact."

"Yes."

"I keep feeling as if someone is hitting me on the back of the head." George shook his head from side to side as if to shake out the sympathetic pain that surged through his head. Though George had grown accustomed to the sensations of sympathetic pain, he was still a bit uncomfortable with it. Fortunately, the pain usually lasted only a few moments, or until George acknowledged what the spirit was trying to communicate about pains, injuries, or other physical sensations it had endured before passing on. "Was he out socially? He says, 'I was out socially.' I see him . . . he's off . . . this might be a symbol, as I say, a dance place there. And I'm off, I'm outside of it, around it. Was he near a place of social gathering?''

"Yes."

To the Licatas, George seemed to be talking to himself. In fact, he was "speaking" to the spirit of their son. Though he usually could "ask" questions or request clarification through his thoughts, sometimes he found himself speaking aloud. "All right," George was saying to what the Licatas were by now certain was the spirit of David, "calm down. Just tell me everything exactly as you want to."

John and Barbara watched and listened. After a few moments George resumed the writing. "Was he found near a car? Why do I keep seeing a car?"

"Yes."

"Was he in a car?"

"No."

"Near a car?"

"Yes."

"He keeps showing me himself near a car—"

"Yes."

George turned to the Licatas and explained, "He's going right to his face. There's something about the face he wants to tell me. I don't know what."

George again turned his attention to the spirit. "What do you want me to see?" he appeared to be asking the air. "I don't understand what you mean."

George was both frustrated and apologetic about his inability to comprehend the spirit's message. "Maybe he means that I'm not seeing something right," he offered, then warned the Licatas again not to divulge anything more than simple acknowledgments about the messages. "Did he have very dark eyes?"

"Yes."

"Very dark hair?"

"Yes."

"Tall, good-looking."

"Oh yes," Barbara said, beaming. Her husband nodded in agreement.

Looking up at the Licatas, George said, "He appears next to you. He shows me what he looks like. Was he near any place where there would have been alcoholic beverages when it happened?"

"Yes."

"They weren't in the right frame of mind. Nobody's been nailed yet, though."

"Right."

George returned to the young girl who had passed over before David. "He keeps saying, 'She met me when I came over.'"

"Yes."

"'She brought me into the light,' he says."

"Yes."

"You know her also."

"Yes."

"'Cause she says hello to you. She says, 'You remember me. You know who I am.'"

"Yes."

George's focus returned to David. "See, this is very strange because it seems he was not a troublesome young man."

"No."

"It seems that he was at the wrong place at the wrong time."

"Right."

"Did he go out alone?"

"No."

"Because I see friends. He went out with friends. A group of people."

Barbara interrupted, "George, can you send a message to him or do you just receive?"

"I can send back, but he can hear you also. He's standing next to you, so undoubtedly he's perceiving anything you're thinking or feeling or whatever." After a moment, the reading continued. "Any other bodily injury at all besides the head?"

"No."[3]

"Was he big on track or something?"

"Not track."

"Some type of sport where you're using your legs."

---

3. At the time of this reading, Barbara knew that David had suffered fatal head injuries. She would not learn until some three months after this reading that David's pelvis had also been broken. Earlier in the reading, George stated that he felt David had suffered back injuries. Now he was referring to it again. Although Barbara was unable to acknowledge it at this time, George was in fact correct.

"Yes."[4]

"Do you know John?"

"Yes."

"Living or deceased?"

"Living."

"You don't know a John that crossed over, do you? Think for a second."

"My grandfather," Barbara said, after a moment's thought.

"Okay. That's what I wanted to hear because he says, 'John is over here.' When you didn't seem to recognize him, your son said to ask your husband and he would know who it is. 'I've seen John over here,' he says. He says, 'John is over here with me.'"

George repeated what he had stated earlier: "It was an accidental murder, he keeps saying."

"Right."

"But he's not holding any hostilities toward the person. He's being very forgiving. He understands. But in any case, do you know Rose?"

"Yes."

"Deceased?"

"Yes."

"Because he says, 'Rose is here with me.'"

"My grandmother," Barbara explained.

"He says, 'John is here with me. Rose is here with me also.' . . . As soon as Rose is over close to him, he calms down. It becomes easier. Why does he keep showing me a car?"

"Whose car?" Barbara asked.

"I don't know. He keeps saying to me, 'Near the car, near the car.' . . . He keeps showing me cars—"

"Yes."

"Was there water nearby?"

"No."

"Was he found near water?"

"No."

"Was there a river, a brook nearby?"

"No."

"It must mean something. He keeps insisting, 'Yes, yes, yes.' He keeps saying 'yes.'"

---

4. David was a soccer star at his high school.

"I don't know," was all Barbara could say.[5]

For several minutes George gave out a series of names that Barbara and John acknowledged.

"Is it possible that the person who did this to him is older then he?"

"Yes."

George then spoke of something metallic, which he saw symbolically as a weapon. Barbara was not clear about the meaning of this message. George may have been referring to the vehicle that struck and killed David or some other weapon at the scene of the crime, which could not be fully explained because of lack of information.

"Okay. Your son shows me this vision in points. The only reason I pay attention to it is that I don't know what's going on here, and you confirm it as accurate. . . . This person is not emotionally stable, not balanced mentally. The reason I say this is that anybody who does this isn't. Did your son know this person?"

"I don't know."[6]

Then George asked Barbara questions about the person's employment, which she could not answer. "This man that the police picked up, did they question him or whatever?"

"Yes."

"Your son says you know who it is. The suspect's not related to you."

"No."

"Did he live near you?"

"Yes."

George said to the spirit, "Keep it coming," then turned to the Licatas and asked several more questions about the suspect, which they could not confirm. "Would you say that your son was a little naïve?"

"Yes."

"There is something specific about this man, the suspect, that makes me feel extremely uncomfortable. I haven't pinpointed it yet. Let's just say I wouldn't want him around me."

5. Months later Barbara discovered that directly behind the location where David's body was found lies a sump where the neighborhood youngsters went fishing. George was correct, then, about there being "water nearby" the scene of David's accident.
6. The suspect lived in the same neighborhood as the Licatas. It is possible that David may have known him by sight.

"Right."

After a second's pause, George continued. "Is this man bald?"

"I don't know."[7]

"Is he married, or was he?"

"He's married."

"Is his family around? Do you know him personally?"

"I did."[8]

"Does the name Robert mean anything to you?"

"Yes."

"Living, he says living. Somebody your son would have known. Anyone close to him?"

"Yes."

"He gives the name Robert. He says, 'How is Robert?'"

"Fine."

"'Tell him you have heard from me,' your son says. Your son is the type to let bygones be bygones."

"Yes."

"Definitely, because he's not vindictive in this case. He's very . . . like 'I'm sorry it happened but I forgive him for it.' Very forgiving."

Barbara nodded.

George went on. "The person they suspect . . . there had to be some sort of contact. They knew each other, though—"

"It's possible."

George interrupted. "Let it go until it's clearer. What does the rosary mean?"[9]

"Rosary?" Barbara asked.

George nodded. "I just see a rosary being held up in front of me."

"I say a rosary every day for David."

7. When the Licatas saw the suspect at his trial months later, they noticed that he was balding.
8. In 1963 Barbara shared a hospital room with the suspect's wife. Both women had just given birth. They socialized briefly after that, but the relationship cooled. Barbara saw the suspect only when he had come to visit his wife in the hospital nineteen years earlier.
9. An interesting question, especially in view of the fact that, not knowing John's and Barbara's last names, he had no reason to believe they were Catholic.

"Okay, because he held it up. He just went like this in front of me. He held up a white rosary."

"That's my rosary," Barbara answered.

"'Tell my mother what you see and that it's very significant.'"

Barbara indicated that she understood.

"Do you have a daughter?"

"Yes."

George had some difficulty in interpreting the girl's age. "She's also tall. That's why I'm getting thrown off, because of her size. He calls out to her: 'Please tell her that you have heard from me. Tell her I send my love. I'm fine. I'm at peace. Please continue to pray for me.'"

Barbara nodded.

"I know his name now. I heard you say it—David. So he was called Davey, I suppose. Why does he keep saying 'Davey Crockett,' kidding around? Was he the type who joked around?"

"Oh yes."

"He seems to be even joking with me, saying, 'Ha, ha, Davey Crockett.'"

George then returned to the subject of David's accused killer.

"The man . . . he shows me again. I'll see if I can . . . He gives me that description he gave me before." George then described details of the suspect's clothing, health habits, hairstyle, and temperament.

"I don't know."[10]

"Well, the first thing he asks both of you to do is forgive. That's the first thing he asks. I have to be honest with you. He's not coming through vindictively."

"I'm glad," Barbara replied.

"When you first came in, he was so excited about this that I couldn't keep up with him, but now he's calm. As soon as the other relatives . . . seem to draw near him, especially that girl—he seemed to ease."

"Can you give me her name?"

10. Though Barbara was unable during the reading to recall details of the suspect's appearance, George's physical description of him was essentially correct. George also correctly provided a portion of the suspect's last name.

"Not as of yet." George paused and looked up from his writing and continued. "He's in good hands. He keeps assuring you that. And the prayers that you've been sending help tremendously. He says, 'I'm in the light, I'm in the light.'"

Barbara and John seemed comforted by George's—or rather, David's—words as they listened.

"It was not done intentionally. I'm sure the man just didn't want to go out and harm the boy. It was an accidental murder, he says. Something was done to provoke it." Pointing to John, George then said, "The name Theresa. It goes to you."

"His grandmother," Barbara said.

"He went like this," George said, gesturing toward John. "Your son said, 'It goes to my father.' He pointed to his father. He said, 'She's here with me also.'"

"Who's Sal?"

"Grandfather."

"Because he says, 'Sal is here also. Sal is with me. Theresa is with me and the other people identified.' . . . Do you have a pet dog?"

"Yes."

"Because he's asking for the pet dog."

"Yes."

"Would you say that he was a very spiritual young man?"

"Yes."

"You know, this is the impression I get. I'm a little taken aback for a youngster of sixteen. He seems to be very spiritual, sharp up there, not vindictive. He's . . . it's the type of young man you hate to see this happen to."

"Yes," Barbara said. "When can I ask a question?"

"You can ask one now, but whatever you do, try to ask it so that you are not giving me any feed at all."

"Will you ask him if he's happy? Does he feel our love for him?"

George assured her, "Oh, he definitely does. That's why he came in before and said about being at peace and held up a rosary to you. A white rosary. He said, 'I receive this. Keep it coming.'"

"Yes."

"Do you know Joseph?"

"Yes."

"Living."

"Yes."

"Does David know him?"

"Yes."

"Were they close?"

"Yes."

"Cousins."

"Yes, yes."

"He just said, 'Joseph, how is Joseph? My cousin Joey.' Were they good companions? He's just asking. He said, 'Say hello to my cousin Joey. I know what happened. Send him my congratulations.'"

Barbara promised she would. Joey and his wife became parents in May 1982, three months after David's passing.

"He has a brother who is very hostile. David is saying he shouldn't be hostile. 'I forgive, so should he.'"

Barbara listened without saying a word. She nodded affirmatively. She knew this message went to Darrin, who was still very bitter and angry about his younger brother's killing.

"Did David play an instrument?"

"Yes."

There was some confusion in the symbols George received as to what instrument David played.

"Has he passed on within the year?"

"Yes."

"It's unbelievable. He says, 'I've only been over here within the past year.' And he's incredibly attuned over there. 'Don't think of me with the so-called dead. It's the best thing you could do.' He keeps saying that again and again; that the constant prayer, the flow of prayers, especially the rosary, brings you right into the light. So definitely keep it coming."

Barbara appeared comforted by George's elaboration of David's message for her and John.

"Has someone been to his grave recently?"

"I don't know."

"Do you feel him around you?"

"No," Barbara answered.

"Because he says, 'I am near. But don't believe that I am dead, because I am not.'"

"Can you ask him a question?"

"Sure."

"Ask him if he was able to see his funeral."

"He was saying about flowers at the grave. He said something about a very nice funeral . . . My fault. I ignored [it], I figured maybe I shouldn't bring that up. . . . All the grandparents crossed over?"

"No."

At this moment George was experiencing a common problem, determining from the spirit's message whether the person he or she referred to was dead or alive. "Is there a grandmother here? Because he calls out to her. I think she's devastated. I think this is her pride and joy we're speaking of, and he said to me there are three grandparents over here with me.[11] There's one grandmother still on the earth. 'Please, I won't forget her. Please send her my love.' He had a beautiful smile, beautiful teeth and smile. He says, 'I know I'm her pride and joy and she would be heartbroken if I didn't single her out.'"

"Yes."

"Your mother."

"Yes."

"Does she speak Italian?"

"Yes."

"I hear Italian being spoken. He says, 'She'd know what I was saying right now.' She must be taking this badly. Please tell her he says, 'I am at peace. Please pray . . .' Who is devout to the Blessed Mother?"

"My husband's mother, I think," Barbara said, as John nodded in agreement.

"Again, there's a woman who came into the room with your son and she immediately went over here and pointed. She looked around and said, 'I'm devout to what you have displayed here.'" By way of explanation, George told the Licatas, "People who are really strong in their faith here adjust beautifully over there."

Barbara had more questions. "Ask him if he knows what his mission was in life? Why he died so young?"

"Just the answer I get. Soul growth for you, your husband, your family, himself. He says it's an accidental form of passing. Yes, it's something. It's a grace. It's a lesson to be learned by everybody, including himself."

11. In fact, there are only two. Both of Barbara Licata's parents, Lucie and Joseph are alive.

"Does he know how many people were touched by his passing?"

"Oh yes, he knows. That's what he says."

"Does he miss us?" Barbara asked softly.

"He says yes he does, but you'll be there someday with him. It's when your mission is fulfilled here. You'll be there also. Was he into this sort of thing? . . . Was he very religious, within himself maybe?"

"Yes."

"That's what it is. He's very, very sharp for the other side, especially considering the circumstances."

"Can our prayers make him go to different planes, or does he have to do that?"

"Oh definitely—"

"Even masses that are said for him?"

"Oh definitely. Without a question of a doubt. It's like receiving telegrams to them. You keep going in a positive way continually. Because when John Lennon passed on, and we made a contact from him, he said that the vigil—that outburst of prayer—immediately brought him up another level over there because it was so powerful. They were sincere, loving thoughts. That's why I try to encourage people, whether Catholic or not, that it's very important that they pray for the so-called dead. That they are alive."

"Did he suffer when he died? I hope he didn't suffer."

"No, he said to me he didn't. It was pretty quick. He says that he was frightened at first when he got over there because he didn't know what happened, which is natural. But then that girl came up to him."

"Does he mention her name?"

"He doesn't. He just gives me that feeling again. He says, 'She immediately came over to me,' and then he said, 'Rose came over to me next. I knew who they were.' The ones he would vaguely remember came over to him first. The ones that he did not remember came next, he says. He knows who they are now. . . . I know your name is Barbara. But is there another Barbara?"

"Yes."

"Because he just asks for her. I don't know why, but he asks for her."

"Does he know that his friends have come to visit?"

"Definitely. He asked that before, for all his friends. Seems like he was very popular with everybody. He keeps saying, 'Soul growth for everybody. Tell everybody you have heard from me. I send my love.' Of course there are certain people he wanted to single out. Was he very active? Because he speaks so fast sometimes. He's so excited because he hasn't seen you in a while.''

"Yes.''

"Now that he's aware that he can do this, he's so excited that I can't keep up with him sometimes. He's going ahead of my mind. That's why I'm missing out on certain things and then recalling them again . . .''

John glanced at his wife. She nodded. She understood.

George continued. "I see the tunnel in front of me and I see them filing into it again. It's like that movie *Resurrection*. They go into the tunnel with a light at the end, that's what it looks like. That's what I'm seeing now. That's my clue that they have to go, because your son has gone back in again. What's this about the hair? He smiles and goes like this to me.'' George moved his fingers through his own hair as if he were alternately combing and smoothing it. "Was his hair long or very thick?''

"Yes,'' Barbara confirmed.

"Was he always being complimented on it?''

"Yes.''

George stopped writing now. "He says keep the prayers coming very quick. He says, 'Don't worry about me. All is well with me. I'm in good hands.' Undoubtedly, you've been praying for your son. He says please not to stop. Keep it coming. He's in the light because of it. It means he's with God, so to speak.'' George paused for several seconds. To Barbara it seemed like an eternity. Finally, he said, "I'm losing the energy.''

"Tell David we love him,'' Barbara said, hopefully.

Forty-five minutes had passed, the reading was over. Barbara Licata was deeply moved and comforted by what had happened. Both she and John would meet George again to receive many more communications from David in the years ahead. In the brief time they had spent with George, their perceptions of death and their attitudes toward it were profoundly changed. But the Licatas were just two of hundreds of people who had had similar experiences with George.

As they left George's apartment, neither said a word. Deep inside, Barbara knew that this was the sign from David she had sought. As we'll see, it was only the beginning.

Two

George Anderson, Jr., was born on August 17, 1952, to Eleanor and George Anderson of Lindenhurst, New York, a typical postwar suburban Long Island community. The Andersons were a hardworking, middle-class family; George's father was employed by the Pennsylvania Railroad and his mother was a housewife. The Andersons had three older children—Janice, eighteen (from Mr. Anderson's previous marriage), Donna, fifteen, and Al, two—each of whom was, like baby George, a normal kid. The Andersons remember George's early childhood as unremarkable. He was a happy child, quiet and gentle, with curly black hair and large brown eyes.

The Andersons were a very religious family. George Anderson, Sr., a first-generation American of English-Scotch ancestry, was Episcopalian, but he agreed with his wife that their children would be raised in the Roman Catholic Church. Eleanor, a devout Catholic of Irish extraction, saw to it that the family followed all of the Church's teachings and practices, including attending Mass and observing meatless Fridays. Although Mr. Anderson never converted to Catholicism, he worshiped with his family.

In October of 1958, six-year-old George contracted chicken pox. The disease followed its familiar course—itchy rash and fever—until one day between two and three weeks after he first fell ill, when his body temperature rose precipitously. The virus attacked his central nervous system, resulting in an in-

flammation of the brain and spinal cord known as encepha-
lomyelitis, a rare complication. George was almost totally
paralyzed, unable even to lift his head to drink from the cup his
mother held to his lips. Over the next several days, not even
the doctors could predict with any certainty what course
George's illness and paralysis would take or what their lasting
effects might be. It wasn't until weeks later that the virus had
run its course, but though George had recovered from the
disease itself, he still could not walk. He had to be carried from
place to place, his mobility limited to crawling very slowly, a
process he found quite painful. His parents feared the worst—
that their son might never walk again—but a family physician
assured them that in time George would make a full recovery.

Then one morning in January, approximately two months
after the paralysis set in, George got out of bed and walked. He
neither knew nor cared what made him better. He was just
overjoyed to be darting from room to room, from house to
yard, up and down the stairs, like any other normal child. He
said a special prayer to God in thanks for being able to walk
again.

With George walking again and apparently free from any
other physical problems resulting from the disease, all seemed
well. If George felt in any way different from before he fell ill,
he said nothing. He went about the business of being a healthy,
normal, active six-year-old.

But unbeknown to either George or his family, something in
him had changed. It would be many years before anyone would
attempt to theorize how the disease might have affected him
and enhanced, or revealed, his ability to communicate with
discarnate beings—the dead. And although the final answer to
this puzzle is not—and may never be—known, we do know
that it was only after the paralysis occurred and subsided that
George began to hear the voices and see the visions that would
have a profound influence on his life.

Suddenly, seemingly out of the blue, George could tell the
people around him what had happened to them and those
around them in the past, sometimes referring to events that
took place years before he was born. Sometimes he spoke of
things that were occurring in the present that he could not
possibly have known about. But most startling of all was his
foretelling of events that had not yet come to pass.

That George was somehow different now became clear when he did what any six-year-old would do with such wonderful knowledge: share it with a friend. In one of his visions George saw "someone" telling him that his six-year-old playmate Tommy's grandmother would soon be going to "the next world." At the time, George neither understood nor questioned what he was seeing or hearing. He just took it in, and then reported it to Tommy. "Your grandma has black around her," little George offered nonchalantly. "She's going to the other side."

"What do you mean?" Tommy asked.

"Oh, don't worry, because people on the other side are waiting for her to come over so she won't be alone. She won't be there by herself."

"What do you mean? What do you mean?" Tommy asked, panicking.

"Well, your grandpa is there. Your grandpa came to me and said that he's waiting for her to come over and be with him, and soon she will, too."

"Do you mean my grandma is going to die?"

"Oh, no," George replied. He explained to Tommy that she would not die, so there was really nothing to be afraid of. Then, thinking that Tommy would want to know more about the visions, George tried to comfort him. George could not understand why his friend was crying at this news; he hadn't intended to upset him.

Understandably frightened and confused, Tommy ran home and told his parents what George had said. His mother and father assured their son that his playmate had an overactive imagination. When Tommy's grandmother did die unexpectedly a week later, everyone who knew of George's "prediction" dismissed it as mere coincidence.

But George sensed that it was more than that. He had experienced similar visions, or visitations, from what he would later come to call the other side between the chicken pox episode and his "reading" for Tommy. The negative reaction to his prediction of Tommy's grandmother's death surprised George. No one believed or understood him, and the reactions would range from disbelief to ridicule. He developed a shrewd defensive coping mechanism. Rather than expose himself to the predictably confused and frightened reactions, George became very private and somewhat withdrawn, discussing or revealing his experiences only when he felt compelled to or believed that he might be in the company of someone who could help him understand them.

That his special secret provoked negative reactions perplexed George, who had no way of knowing that not everyone saw and heard the same things he did. In addition to perceiving the spirits of deceased people close to those he knew in this life, George also had other spirit companions. One, a woman in lilac robes and bathed in purple light, would appear to George in his room, particularly when he was despondent. The Lilac Lady, as George would think of her, was the most common vision, the most familiar spirit. Occasionally, he also saw the spirit of an older man materialize. This unknown man wore a tweed suit and tie, muttonchop sideburns, and always carried a cane. As a child, George thought it was just another vision of someone he did not know. As a young adult, many years later, he was researching his family's genealogy when he learned from relatives what his great-grandfather looked like. He recognized the spirit as his paternal great-grandfather, James Jones, who had died in 1926. Although the two spirits frequently materialized, George never feared them. Rather, he was intrigued by and drawn to them, particularly the Lilac Lady.

In the five years since Tommy's grandmother's death, George had kept all of his unusual experiences to himself. Unsure of how to express what was happening, he didn't even dare broach the subject with his own family. One day, however, when he was eleven and attending Our Lady of Perpetual Help Roman Catholic School in Lindenhurst, he told another student about a vision he had had. Someone reported it to George's teacher, a nun, who ridiculed him in front of his classmates. The humiliation hurt him deeply.

In spite of embarrassment, George continued to speak occasionally about other visions. When word of them got back to his teacher, she called George's parents and without saying why, told them to "keep an eye on him." Though she never explained to Mr. and Mrs. Anderson that George claimed to have seen visions, what she did say would plague George throughout his childhood: She stated quite bluntly that she believed their son was becoming "mentally unhinged." This was the first of a series of unscientific, subjective "diagnoses" George's teachers and other school authorities would make, in different terms, throughout his school years. Still, George's visions grew stronger.

One day during class, George experienced a vision of such power that he could not keep himself from blurting out to the entire class what he was witnessing. He saw a spirit form clothed in clerical garb, which he described to the class in detail. A nun, finding the whole incident intolerable, picked up a thick geography book, cracked George over the head with it, and screamed that before the end of the school year, if she had to, she would "beat him sane."

Eleanor Anderson was sympathetic to her youngest son's problems and supported him as much as she could. But she was not totally certain about what to do. Raised in the traditional Roman Catholic faith, she believed that the school authorities knew best and that good parents followed the school's suggestions. As George once recalled on my radio program, his parents' attitude toward school was typical of the time: "If we find out you've been bad at school, you'll catch it at home, too." No wonder, then, that whenever Eleanor approached George about what might be troubling him, he declined to discuss it. She and her husband did not know then that George was afraid to confide in them about the visions and voices because he feared receiving the same punishment from them he'd been suffering at the hands of his teachers. (Although he wasn't a bad or troublesome child, George did commit the usual childhood infractions. But after seeing the nuns' reactions to his visions, he became deathly afraid of being caught at something minor, like talking in class.)

On the rare occasions when George tried to tell his mother that he was seeing "visions of ladies in lilac or white," Eleanor didn't know what to make of it. To her, George was still a sweet, sensitive child and deep in her heart, despite the school authorities' warnings, she could not believe that anything serious was wrong with him. George's father, however, disciplined his son in the hopes that it would motivate him to do better in school. Every once in a while, George got a spanking, or would lose certain television privileges; he was once warned that if he did not shape up, he couldn't go trick-or-treating at Halloween.

Seventh grade proved to be relatively pleasant. There were no major confrontations with teachers or other students. Twelve-year-old George had learned to keep his secret. Of all those who knew of George and his "ability," there was one person who sought to understand him, a teacher named Sister Bartholomew. George remembers her as a woman of patience, the only person he knew then who seemed to be open to the subject of what he called his "unusual experiences."

One day she and George were discussing spirits, ghosts, and related phenomena. As George spoke, the nun listened intently, and he came away with the impression that she understood the subject better than anyone else he had confronted. One morning, the class was told that Sister Bartholomew would be away for a short while and that a substitute teacher would be taking her place. Sister Bartholomew's father was ill. As George listened to the announcement, he psychically received the impression that her father was going to die. When he later learned that his "impression" was correct—in fact Sister Bartholomew's father did die—he was compelled to say something to her.

The first day she returned to school, George waited until the end of classes to offer his condolences. For some reason he felt safe enough to say, "You don't have to worry about your father. He only crossed over to the other side. The voice told me, 'He is at peace.'"

The nun smiled gently as she answered, "Yes, George, I know. I agree with you. It's just hard to accept the adjustment."

George nodded. He understood. Then he took a tremendous risk and continued. "I feel your father around you, Sister Bartholomew." Much to George's surprise and relief, the nun did not appear upset by his statements. In fact, she seemed comforted by George's message.

But aside from Sister Bartholomew, George did not dare to offer his readings or predictions for classmates, teachers, or friends. Usually his visions were of spirit entities. Occasionally, they would be of events, such as a nun or another student falling ill. In these instances, George kept quiet, though deep inside he knew that his information might help them. Years later he explained: "I thought I would be burned at the stake." The fear of what retribution awaited him if he revealed his knowledge was so great a strain on the boy that he left home each weekday morning "white as a sheet," with a look of terror on his face.

The haven of acceptance George found in Sister Bartholomew was short-lived. In eighth grade George encountered the personification of intolerance, Sister Vincent de Paul. Although she never struck George, she humiliated him mercilessly in front of the class. She criticized and derided him, and despite his good grades, she would complain that George daydreamed too much. Her frequent screaming—"George Anderson, get your head out of the clouds!"—had no effect. The "daydreaming" was out of George's control. This strange, unexplained energy within him was becoming so intense he had no idea how to contain it. As a result, George's parents were often called to school.

During one visit with a teacher, the Andersons witnessed her giving George a loud scolding. George was deeply embarrassed, as any child would be, but the sister had much more to say. For one thing, George would not be allowed to participate in the graduation ceremony in the local church. This was the final humiliation, although it proved to be an empty threat. It was no wonder that George was becoming a self-described "emotional wreck." His parents still had not the slightest inkling of what their son's problem might be; he wasn't talking and the school authorities' advice was never specific. All they ever said was that George should "be watched." No one ever told his parents why.

George began the ninth grade at St. John the Baptist High School, also on Long Island. With the passage of time, he was perceiving the visions and the voices with greater intensity and frequency. And whereas his reports of these incidents would be dismissed during his younger years as the products of "imagination," the older he got, the more threatened and frightened others became of them. Not surprisingly, his classmates often harassed him about his abilities. Several students once tried to cram him into a small locker, but generally just calling him "weirdo" or otherwise insulting him would satisfy them.

One day, while another kid was taunting him cruelly, George blurted out, "Oh, you've got some nerve talking to me like that after I see your father's a drunk and beats on you and your mother every night. Just because you come to school in a bad mood, don't take it out on me!'' The startled youth quickly withdrew from his victim in fear. How did George "see" the boy's father beating the family? How could he possibly know what no one outside his home knew? After word of the exchange got around, many of George's peers, fearful of his ability to "see" into their private thoughts and lives, stopped bothering him altogether. Others simply acted as if George did not exist. Gaining even a modicum of acceptance from others his age seemed out of the question. George was a loner, an outcast.

Probably because of the rejection from his peers, George continued to seek out adults who might be able to help him. As confused as those who knew about George's visions were, few—except perhaps George's parents, who by then regarded them as fantasies—seemed to have much sympathy for what the visions meant to George. During his freshman year, George met a priest with whom he felt comfortable. Certain that the priest would understand his experiences, George ventured to confide in him. The priest listened attentively, but then he too suggested that George imagined things.

Having these psychic powers wasn't always a problem, however. Besides keeping bullies at bay, George's abilities served him in other unusual ways. One day during his sophomore year, he sat quietly listening to Sister Aquinas lecture on the French Revolution and the fate of the royal family.

"Louis XVI was executed," she stated, to which George nodded in agreement, "and Marie Antoinette followed soon after." George nodded again.

"The princess, little daughter Maria Theresa, was executed."

"Wrong," George said quietly.

The nun, who didn't hear him, continued, "The dauphin was executed next. The dauphin is the prince who is heir to the throne."

At that, George could no longer keep quiet. "Wrong! I know what happened to the royal children."

"George, I'll put you through a wall if—" the nun began before composing herself. "All right, George, what do *you* think happened?"

Suddenly, George, who had never read or heard a word about the children's fates, found himself standing before the class and saying, "First of all, the girl was never executed. She lived in the tower until she was taken to Austria by sympathetic aristocrats. The people more or less just sympathized with her in the tower, and they let her go."

Sister Aquinas lost her temper, telling George that she had never read any such thing. (If only she'd known that George hadn't either!) "What do you think happened to the dauphin?"

"He was in prison, but he was smuggled out of the country and taken to England."

The nun stared at George until he sat back down. But when she later researched the subject, she discovered that what he said about the princess was correct. She was not, however, able to corroborate his version of what had happened to the dauphin. But how did George know?

All George knew was the information was "just there." He later reasoned that it either was given to him by spirits or might have resulted from the recall of a personal past-life experience.

How George did learn what he knew was as amazing as how he knew what he had *not* "learned." His older brother Al would devote many hours to his studies, while, unbeknown to him, George would literally sleep on a book or look at the information once. From then on, he had the book's contents in his mind. During a test, George would place his hand on the examination paper, read the questions, then close his eyes. The correct answer would then often flash in front of him. Sometimes George would place his fingers directly on a letter of a multiple-choice test, and a vision or form would appear and indicate whether or not the answer was correct. Despite the obvious benefits of this "psychic cheating," George occasionally wondered if this was ethical.

Increasingly, the burden of his experiences forced George to seek out someone who might understand him. For a young person like George, who knew little about psychic phenomena, visions, and voices except what he'd learned from the Church, the question was not so much why he was having the experiences, but why he was obviously so different from everyone else. He dared to think that Sister Perpetua would have the answer. Though he had no classes with her, from what he knew of her, he sensed that she might be sympathetic to his plight.

One day George told her what was happening and became very emotional as he tried to explain. He started crying, "I'm seeing these visions at home. Sometimes even in the cellar. I see this beautiful lady in my room all the time. I sense things and I hear voices. I see things taking place before they happen. With other kids, I know what's going on in their lives. I see visions in chapel. I'm drawn there in the afternoon, and I feel presences there. I don't know what's happening, Sister."

"Why are you crying about all this?"

"Well, it's starting to get frightening. I'm the only one who can do it. Nobody else can, and everyone's calling me names and putting me down for it."

"Okay, let me see. Are there any problems at home?"

"No, Sister."

"Are your parents abusive to you?"

"No."

"Are your parents drunk?"

"Absolutely not."

"Are you going to church regularly?"

"Yes, Sister."

"Do you go to confessions and sacraments?"

"Yes."

"Are your parents bringing you up to be Catholic?"

"Definitely. Especially my mother."

"All right. Look, I think we're going to have to call your parents down and find out what this is."

When George's parents came to the school, Sister Perpetua told them that George's visions were the result of "extreme loneliness." In her opinion, George was creating the visions to fill a void in his life, to compensate for having no friends. She suggested to George's parents that they "keep an eye" on him. It was the same well-meaning but vague and ultimately dangerous pronouncement they'd heard before.

A few months later the visions became so intense that they began to affect George's schoolwork. At various times during the day, he'd feel himself being drawn to the chapel. Each time, he'd be overcome with a need to cry but never could until he was inside the chapel and praying. Then, the tears would roll down his face and he'd feel better. For all George knew, he was experiencing a spiritual initiation, a rapture state. Perhaps, he thought, he was being called to the priesthood, and the visions and voices were "a sign." Right after the prayers, George felt an immense surge of energy. In desperation and confusion, he told several nuns at school about this. They in turn contacted his parents and referred him to the school nurse. By now the school authorities were convinced that, at age fifteen, George was on the verge of a nervous collapse. They insisted that he be taken immediately to a local mental-health center supported by the Church.

At the center, George was put through the "usual battery of tests." He looked at abstract images and described what he saw. He answered a series of—to him—inane questions: How many days are there in the week? What's the capital of France? What do you do at home? Do you have any friends? How many times a day do you masturbate? Do you like boys better than girls? Do you like girls better than boys? Though his parents were told that he had passed the tests "with flying colors," they were also encouraged to put him under the care of a staff psychiatrist.

George obediently agreed to go, hoping perhaps that the psychiatrist might help him learn to deal with or banish the visions and cope with his problems at school. However, the visions increased, and his weekly sessions with the doctor were not helping him overcome his daily problems. Having diagnosed George as a passive schizophrenic, the psychiatrist prescribed Librium, a sedative. Later, George was switched to Valium, another sedative that would years later be shown to be highly addictive. For a while, the situation seemed under control. Eventually, the frequency of George's sessions with the doctor dropped to every several weeks, then to every two or three months.

But the visions didn't stop. For several days in late May of 1968 George was overwhelmed by a sense that some tragedy was about to befall Democratic presidential candidate Senator Robert Kennedy. He recalled having the same feeling when he was eleven, just before John F. Kennedy was assassinated, and again immediately preceding the death of Martin Luther King, Jr. George felt compelled to unburden himself. He confided in one teacher, saying that he'd seen a vision of the senator draped in black, and that he knew he would not live and was going to make "the transition to the other side."

"George, are you at it again with those weird visions?" she admonished him. "Stop talking like that!"

In early June after Senator Kennedy died in Los Angeles, the day after he was shot the teacher recalled George's words. Had it been a prophecy? Nothing more was said about the subject, but from then on, George would catch her staring at him, a look of terror on her face, as if to say, "How could he know?"

Years later, the memories of these days are still too painful for George to recount at any length. Over the years of knowing George and working with him, I have heard the stories emerge in bits and pieces. Today, when telling them for listeners and viewers, George often uses a tongue-in-cheek, at times even sarcastic tone that is both humorous and poignant. Clearly, he's learned from his boyhood experiences and has put them into perspective, viewing them as something he was destined to endure. At the time, however, the pain was nearly unbearable.

The early need to keep his experiences secret worked with the mind-numbing prescription drugs to almost totally repress the visions and voices. On what George would call "the freakin' blue bombers" (10-milligram doses of Valium), he slept up to twenty hours a day, which definitely distorted and weakened the visions and voices. Though George could still see, hear, and sense them, he felt as if the "channel" for these communications was "clogged." No doubt countless psychic visions, dreams, and experiences were lost, partially because, as George explained it, "most of the time I was too busy keeping my backside protected to be thinking about anything psychic. Other kids and teachers were trying to beat it out of me."

One student in particular was exceedingly cruel to him. His taunts and physical abuse would often reduce George to tears, but, knowing that his opponent was larger and stronger, George decided fighting back was futile. His frustration and anger built until one day he could hold them in no longer. In the course of a session with his psychiatrist, George said, "That kid wouldn't stop hitting me and putting me down for having these visions and seeing a psychiatrist. So I knocked him right on his ass, plain as day. I should have killed him!"

From this simple statement—the kind of remark "normal" kids make every day—she concluded that her patient's condition was deteriorating. She called in his parents and said, "George is apparently becoming violent. These mental delusions he is having are making him a violent person—a paranoid. He must be committed now. Because the private psychiatric hospitals are beyond your means financially, he should be sent to a state psychiatric facility. He's sixteen, so he can't be put in with young children; he'll have to go in with adults."

Mr. and Mrs. Anderson were badly shaken by the psychiatrist's recommendation. George's father continued to hold to his strong faith in authority, however. To his way of thinking, the teachers and psychiatrists had to be correct about his son. After all, people were authorities because they knew best, or at least better than the rest of us. They had only George's best interests at heart. Despite her feeling that further investigation was needed, George's mother went along with the suggestion. After years of trying to understand her son, she was at a loss to comprehend what really was going on. Obviously, there *was* something different about her son—though she never believed he was mentally ill—but at this moment she and her husband felt powerless to do anything but go along with the doctor's suggestion. After all, what if the doctor was right?

For his part, George had trouble comprehending what the commotion was all about. He had responded to a bully in a manner most adults would applaud. He had stood up for himself; his anger was justified. And then there was the matter of the visions and voices. He'd learned during years of study that others had had experiences that sounded similar to his: St. Joan of Arc and St. Anthony of Padua were both clairvoyant and clairaudient, while St. Gerard Majella discerned spirits; the Church authorities *believed* them. But, as George would later surmise, modern man, and modern organized religion in particular, relegated miracles and belief in God to the past, or to a neat corner of one's life: Friday night Sabbath, Sunday Mass. Visions and voices just did not occur to ordinary, "normal" people in this day and age.

Back at home, George was told that he was going to be sent to a "hospital" for "a rest," and if he followed instructions he'd be fine and people would be nice to him. George understood the real message behind the euphemisms. As he later quipped, "Basket weaving is good therapy."

One day soon after the episode in the psychiatrist's office, George and his parents made the short drive from their home to the psychiatric center, a state-run institution that houses patients ranging from alcoholics and sexual deviants to the criminally insane. The large, bleak concrete building, one of several on the grounds, was identifiable only by its number. The family was directed to a reception area, where they waited for a staff psychiatrist to see them.

As George sat in silence, a nurse walked up to him and said casually, "Gee, you're kind of young. What are you doing here?" George fought back his tears as he shrugged. The expression on her face said more than her words dared: This is no place for someone like you. As she walked away, George thought, What if they leave me here? I'll go nuts with all these kooks running around; I know what this place is. His head began pounding. A nurse gave him an aspirin and a cup of water, and he sat, waiting, while his parents spoke to the psychiatrist.

Suddenly George was overcome by a sense of calm, and he saw the Lilac Lady standing before him, bathed in purple light. "George," she said, "you are going through a 'soul growth,' an initiation. There is nothing to worry about. You are not going to stay here. I am with you, and I am not going to abandon you."

But once the spirit disappeared, George could not help but think to himself, How could I not worry? Nobody is going to listen to me about her and what she just told me—this is the stuff I'm being told I'm nuts about. He was shaken from his thoughts by the psychiatrist's voice.

"How do you feel, son?"

"Not too good right now."

After about fifteen minutes of asking George what seemed to be innocuous general questions, the psychiatrist said to a nurse, "I don't know if they should leave him here." It was then decided that a second psychiatrist would evaluate George.

The second doctor, who appeared to be in his mid- to late thirties, was leaning back in a large swivel chair with his feet propped up on his desk. He was confident, almost cocky. He looked at George, chain-smoked cigarettes, then asked, "What's your problem?"

"I don't know," George replied. "Everyone's telling me I'm schizophrenic because I'm having visions, and I beat up this kid in school the other day, and now they're telling me I'm violent. But there's nothing wrong."

"What are these visions you're having?"

George explained the visions and voices to the doctor, who listened attentively then said, "Very interesting. What kind of sex drive do you have?"

"Not much of anything right now. Actually none at all."

"Okay, tell me more about your visions."

George complied, adding more details to what he'd said earlier.

"Are they harmful to you?"

"No. If anything, they're very comforting and reassuring." And then George told him all about the Lilac Lady.

The doctor smiled. "We don't put people away for seeing visions of beautiful ladies. Do you have any sexual problems?"

"No."

"Do you feel you're under a lot of pressure at school, George?"

"Not from schoolwork, but I get roughed up from other students, emotionally."

"All right. Go wait outside, please."

The psychiatrist followed George out of his office and while George and his parents waited outside, he confronted the first doctor. The door was accidentally left ajar, so George overheard their entire conversation.

"I recommend shock treatments," the first psychiatrist said.

"Are you out of your mind?" the second replied loudly. "Get him the hell out of here. There's absolutely nothing wrong with that boy. Call the mental-health center and tell them they—or the school, or somebody—should be put away. Not him. He's your average sixteen-year-old boy. Maybe he's having fantasy trips, visual and auditory hallucinations, but they're harmless. If you leave him here with grown men who are pedophiles, he'll be raped, sodomized. Tell his parents to take him home."

For George's father the relief at hearing the good news soon turned to anger. When he realized what might have happened to his son had he been committed, and when he thought of the emotional hell the family had already gone through—all because of their blind faith in the "authorities"—he vowed it would never happen again.

George was relieved to go home. George's school, having deemed him "uneducable," suggested that he be enrolled in the local public high school. George's mother, however, felt very strongly that he should receive the best education available, and so she made arrangements for him to be privately tutored at home. Now that mental illness had been ruled out, the reasonable explanation for George's experiences was given as the stress of attending school. George was still taking tranquilizers, but in greatly reduced dosages (he finally stopped altogether on his own). His parents believed that George had been on the brink of a nervous breakdown and that it had been averted just in time. If he stayed home and "took it easy," he would be fine.

The presences, however, became stronger. One day George asked his home study teacher if a friend could sit in on the lesson. When she looked up and saw no one in the room but the two of them, she was puzzled. George then told her that a boy named Perry wanted to stay for the lesson. It was only when the teacher said, "Sure, George, whatever you say," that George realized only he could see Perry, a boy about sixteen who appeared to him dressed in the style of the twenties or thirties.

After receiving his high school diploma, George enrolled in Suffolk Community College on Long Island, where he earned a two-year degree in liberal arts. He also spent some time in Dublin, where relatives of his mother lived. At this point, George had no specific career goals, and he made a decided effort to block the voices—an impossible task—and not to speak of them to anyone. The only clue that might have explained one aspect of his abilities came after a standard audiometer test revealed that his hearing range was abnormal: He could hear sounds at both the lower and higher ends of the frequency scale, sounds very few human beings could hear.

His first job after finishing school was working as an operator for the New York Telephone Company. Now and then, when he felt bored or mischievous, he'd play a little game. After he answered a caller's request for operator assistance, he'd get an impression and somehow "know" something about the circumstances, events, and names of people the caller might have known who were deceased. Eventually George was moved to a clerical position.

With the passage of time, George, now in his early twenties, found his childhood resentments were fading. He and his mother would talk about spiritual and psychic matters from time to time, and sometimes they'd even discuss his ability. They both began to take an interest in psychic phenomena, and this led her to more easily accept George's ability. As an adult, he could finally share things with his mother that he could never even mention when he was younger. Looking back on her son's childhood, Eleanor Anderson regretted that she and her husband had been unable to understand and help him more.

One evening in 1973, Eleanor suggested to George that they attend a meeting of a local psychic group she'd heard about through friends. She thought it might be interesting and instructional. At first he resisted, protesting that he didn't want to be part of a group of "psychic old ladies," but they went anyway.

George would come to regard this evening as "an initiation." In this supportive environment, he slowly allowed his ability to reemerge. But now, ironically, he was as skeptical about his psychic abilities as people had been about his experiences when he was a boy. Slowly, he allowed himself to do readings for close friends, and then small groups in his neighborhood. In 1975 a locally known psychic named Kathleen predicted that his ability would bring him success.

George was becoming an object not so much of ridicule as of curiosity. Times had changed; suddenly books on all manner of psychic phenomena were being read by millions. Dr. Elisabeth Kübler-Ross's work with the dying and with near-death experiences was known to many, and its gradual acceptance, at least as theory, made it possible for people to discuss the subject now without being classified as kooks. Gradually, people in Babylon, where George had moved after college, came to know of him. One of those people was a young blind woman named Madeline.

Three

The chain of events that led to my meeting George seems so unlikely and random that I can never think about it without believing that it was predestined.

It all started when a young woman called in to my live radio program to speak with that evening's guest, the popular and accomplished psychic-clairvoyant Robert Petro. In a gentle, frightened voice, she told us that she was losing her sight, the result of a complication of juvenile diabetes.

"Will I ever see again?" she asked, hastening to add that she doubted she could cope with being completely blind.

Petro spent the next several minutes reassuring her. The girl seemed to calm down as she listened to his words of encouragement, urging her to remain optimistic. His psychic prognostication was that she would find the strength to rebuild her life. He concluded their conversation by suggesting that she come to see him the following week when he would be speaking at a university on Long Island. He said he would like to meet her personally.

Schedule limitations usually precluded my attending public appearances made by guests on the program. However, Petro was a fascinating man, and when he personally invited me to attend his forthcoming lecture—on psychic development—I readily accepted.

When I arrived on campus, I found an audience of about one hundred people. I worked my way through the crowd so that

Petro would see me. He did, and kindly introduced me to the audience. Soon after, as I listened to him speak, I felt someone take hold of my arm. I turned abruptly.

"Mr. Martin? You're Joel Martin. Nice to meet you. I'm a longtime listener of yours. My name is Peter."

"Nice to meet you," I replied.

He smiled and nodded. Peter was a physically imposing figure in his early thirties, well over six feet tall and powerfully built. His chiseled features were framed by long brown hair and a beard, more typical of the sixties than of the late seventies. He was dressed in a loose-fitting shirt, jeans, and sandals. Despite his otherwise rough appearance, he had gentle blue eyes. He told me that he was a long-distance trucker and that he listened to my talk program as often as he could. He was particularly drawn to the shows devoted to psychic phenomena. He remarked that he had a strong interest in the teachings of the late psychic seer Edgar Cayce, and that, coincidentally, his truck route took him between the New York–Long Island area and Virginia, where Cayce's research center still operates. He said that he knew why I was attending the lecture—"to meet the blind girl who called in to your show last week. It was a very moving call." Before I could dispute his contention, Peter told me to follow him to another part of the lecture hall where, he said, the blind girl was sitting. I felt compelled to go.

"Excuse me, miss. You're the girl who called into *The Joel Martin Show* last week to speak to Robert Petro," Peter said.

"Yes," she answered.

"This is Joel Martin."

She seemed as surprised and self-conscious to meet me as I was to be introduced to her. "I'm Madeline," she said.

I turned toward Peter, the stranger who had brought us together. As he smiled at me, he started for the exit. I managed to say in a loud voice that I hoped we would meet again. "Perhaps someday," Peter answered. "Keep up the good work on the air, especially the programs about psychic phenomena." Then he was gone.

Madeline and I had a friendly conversation and agreed to meet again in several weeks. Within a few months of that second meeting, she and I had arranged for her to begin training for the job of production assistant on my program. Because of her vision problems, she was forced to abandon her plans to become an artist. Though eventually totally sightless, she was to work on my program for the next two years. With the aid of braille materials, which we largely improvised, she adjusted to a myriad of clerical and technical tasks necessary to the preparation of my nightly radio show.

Was Peter's only purpose in my life to bring Madeline and me together? I would ponder that frequently. During the time that we worked together, I'd noticed that her sense of the psychic was uncanny. She was a very determined person. One day in the spring of 1980, she launched her campaign to get me to meet a psychic named George.

"He was so accurate at telling me details about my life—relationships, health, and the names and descriptions of relatives and friends who died. I asked him where the information came from. He told me he was receiving it from those who had passed on to 'the other side,'" Madeline said. "It was incredible!"

"Madeline, if what you're telling me is true, then George—whoever he is—somehow is communicating with the deceased, the afterlife," I said.

"That's right," she replied without hesitation.

"Well, that would make him a medium. You don't believe in that, do you?" I retorted.

"Why not?"

"I'd expose him on the air as a phony in a minute," I threatened.

"Just see him once," she pleaded. "Big deal. One time. Make up your own mind."

I had to admit I was fascinated by the idea that someone could communicate with the dead. I'd been covering various aspects of psychic phenomena on my show for years. My general attitude toward the subject was one of open-minded skepticism. I conceded that there were things for which we have no true explanation. Ultimately, though, I had to admit that—possible or not—the idea of communicating with the dead struck me as somewhat morbid.

"Madeline, isn't that in bad taste or depressing to some people? That is, *if* this guy really can do what you claim."

"He knew things about me he couldn't know. Even names."

"Maybe he's a secret admirer," I offered, half-kidding.

"Don't be funny. I never even met him before."

"Madeline—" I protested.

"Listen, he did it for me, and it's not depressing. Just the opposite. If this man is communicating with the dead, then they're not dead. They are still alive. Who doesn't want to know what happens when they die? If this guy George is real, then we don't die! That's not depressing or in bad taste, is it? It's great!"

"Let me think about it, Madeline. Besides, we held a séance on the air last Halloween."

"That's not what George does," she replied impatiently before landing the final blow. "You're supposed to be so open-minded."

"I am," I protested, "but this just doesn't seem possible."

I thought about it. What did I have to fear? If this guy George turned out to be a fraud, I was confident that I'd be able to detect it, and certainly expose him publicly. Though psychics and other guests interested in what can most fairly be described as unexplained phenomena often appeared on my show, I had also exposed several hoaxes, among them, on radio, the so-called Amityville Horror. In another instance we exposed an alleged psychic medium named Connie who claimed that, while in a trance state, the spirit of a man named Thomas, who had been her instructor in college, was speaking through her. (In fact, her explanation for her control was in many ways similar to that expressed by J. Z. Knight, a woman who purports to be the instrument, or channel, through which Ramtha, a long-dead former resident of Atlantis, brings his message to the world.) Connie had thoroughly convinced an acquaintance, a researcher in parapsychology, of the authenticity of her claims. I agreed to have her on the show.

Once the show began, she went into a self-induced trance. Her eyes rolled back, her head rotated on her neck, and she began to speak in a voice about two octaves lower than her usual voice. I questioned and probed "Thomas's spirit," and at the end of the program pronounced myself skeptical of the whole business.

The next day I got a phone call from a woman named Myra, inquiring about that show.

"How exactly did you know Thomas?" I asked.

"I'm his widow," she replied without hesitation.

She agreed to participate in a second show with Connie/Thomas. I invited Connie to return, and several minutes after she went into trance, I asked "Thomas" if I could introduce him to someone.

"Yes," the low-pitched voice of Connie's alter ego replied.

At a prearranged signal, Myra slipped into the studio and sat down across a table from Connie.

"Hello, Thomas, do you know who I am?" Myra asked softly.

"No," the alleged spirit answered.

"This is Myra. Do you remember me now?"

"No."

"Thomas, I was your wife."

At that, Connie's eyes popped open and she blushed a crimson red before returning to her trance state. We never heard from—or of—Connie again.

For the next several months Madeline continued talking about George. She insisted that he was the best psychic she had ever met and that he deserved to appear on my show. I withheld the right to decide on the latter claim, but having never seen her so excited, I agreed to meet the mysterious George.

In anticipation of my introduction to George, I joked that perhaps he would float in on a mist, or perhaps I should be ready for someone in a turban and long-flowing robes. Madeline did not find this amusing. It was early evening when George arrived, on time, at my office. Although polite, he seemed indifferent to me. He had come over straight from his job at the phone company, and was dressed in a sports jacket and slacks. Except for his eyes, he looked younger than twenty-seven. Unlike so many alleged psychics I'd met, he expressed no interest in media or publicity. Nor did he try to persuade me of his abilities. He was actually rather shy and soft-spoken. I might never had met him were it not for Madeline's persistence and pleadings. Had I known what lay ahead, I would have greeted this occasion with much more enthusiasm, for what happened next literally stunned me.

I felt sufficiently comfortable with and curious about George to invite him to join me in an empty studio. There was no conversation between us except an exchange of brief, polite greetings. In the studio we sat across from each other at a long white table. Madeline stayed in the studio with us, while Chris, my wife, observed the proceedings through the window of an adjacent control room.

"Madeline tells me that you receive messages from the dead," I said.

"From those on the other side," he answered, almost as if to apologize for correcting me.

"Do you know how or why it's happening?"

"No."

"Don't they call people like you mediums?"

"Well, some people do. Actually, I think I'm more a small than a medium," he quipped, smiling.

Frankly, I was taken aback by his self-deprecating sense of humor. I was so used to seeing people claiming to have psychic abilities or knowledge coming on with a portentously solemn, pseudo-religious air that his remark took me by surprise. Over the years, George's sense of humor would prove invaluable in helping to get people to understand and accept his gift.

"George, I understand from Madeline that your ability as a medium is considerable. That is, if you can do what she claims. Can you do it for me?"

"I don't know. I can try. But I might not be able to demonstrate anything. It's up to the other side."

"The other side?"

"Yes, from the spirits of those who've passed on."

My curiosity was aroused, but I refrained from asking any more questions. Years of experience with people working in the field of parapsychology had taught me that charlatans can pick up a wealth of personal information from the most subtle, unconscious visual and verbal clues.

"Just one warning, George. If you're a phony, I'm going to tell you so."

"I know all about your reputation," he answered softly.

"Does that frighten you, George? The thought that your supposed ability might be exposed?"

"I don't really care at this point," George replied calmly. "I'd like to know what's going on also. I want to know what I'm doing as much as anyone else. I'd like to understand my ability better. I might as well find out now—one way or the other."

George then said that he was ready to start. He had asked for several blank sheets of paper and a pen. These, he explained, were for the automatic writing. He warned me to answer his questions only by indicating "yes" or "no," and not to offer any information beyond that: "Let the spirits do the work." He prayed ("Let the Lord bless and keep me. May he show his face to shine upon me and give me peace and accuracy"), crossed himself, and began.

George looked at me and began writing rapidly. From where I sat I could not easily make out what he was writing. Before I could inquire, he asked, "Do you take the name Solomon?"

"Solomon," I returned rhetorically, neither affirming nor denying.

"Yes, Solomon," George answered.

"Do you mean Sol?" I deliberately offered another version of the name as a test for George, knowing that in the majority of cases, the supposed psychic will pick up on the subject's "clarification" and follow it. What I would try to find out was how firmly George held to his interpretation of the reading and how confident he was in his "source."

"No, actually, he's saying 'Solomon' to me."

"Yes, yes, I do."

"Father vibration," George continued.

"What does that mean, George?"

"It's a father figure to you," he replied.

"No." Again, though I could guess that we were talking about my grandfather Solomon, a learned man and devout Orthodox Jew, I tried to throw George off his track by denying him.

"You're saying no. He's saying yes," George insisted.

"You hear him?"

"Yes."

"A father figure?" George repeated.

"Yes." After a brief pause, during which George continued his writing, he looked up and said, "Wait, I hear him clearer now. It's definitely a father figure. But he's saying 'grandfather.' Solomon was your grandfather?"

"Yes," I answered in surprise, amazed that George wasn't really asking me a question but asking me to confirm the information he was receiving from the other side.

"There's a Jewish star—you know, the Star of David—over your head."

Before I could think, I glanced up but of course saw nothing. I could see him drawing the star over and over. I meant to nod in the affirmative, but all I could do was shake my head in disbelief. Without my confirmation, George continued, "The Star of David. Was your grandfather Solomon a very traditional Jew? Because that's what he's saying. He's saying he was a traditional Jew."

"Yes," I answered.

"Your grandfather Solomon is saying he was very proud of you when you were confirmed. That was the high point for him, so to speak, where you were concerned. But after your confirmation, things changed. Your grandfather says you left the faith, so to speak. At the time, that was a disappointment to him."

I nodded yes, for everything George was saying was true.

"There's a young woman with short blond hair standing behind you."

I spun around in my chair and again saw nothing.

"I see her spirit!" George exclaimed.

"You do?"

"Yes. She's saying you know who she is."

"Yes," I acknowledged.

"She passed suddenly."

"Yes."

"She's pointing to her head and face."

"Why?"

"She's trying to show me where she was hurt or injured. Was she killed quickly or instantly?"

"Yes."

"I can feel the pain in my head and face," George explained.

"You can?" I asked, incredulous.

"She says it was an accident. It was an accidental form of passing."

"Yes."

"Do you take the name Shirley?"

"Yes."

"That's her. She says you need to be stricter with your

daughter. She's moving her hand very quickly. Pointing her finger and waving it at you very quickly—"

"Stop!" I shouted, before realizing what I'd said and apologizing. George ceased writing. I would not let him go further. This stranger had pried far enough into my personal life.

"I've heard enough, George. Very impressive demonstration. You were very accurate." Looking down I could see that my knuckles had gone white from clutching the edge of the table.

"I was correct?" George asked, surprised.

I did not elaborate on anything George had said. Nor did George make any inquiry. I asked if I could see the automatic writing he had produced and he said yes. I thanked him for his time.

I was impressed and now more curious than ever. Though I was not ready to admit it fully to Madeline, I wanted to observe George more closely. I asked him if we could meet again. I explained that his demonstration was sufficiently impressive, but I wanted to study it more, if he would permit me. At first he seemed reluctant, explaining to me that he could not always be accurate. I assured him that I had no preconceived notions or expectations, only questions. I suggested that together we might discover how and why he was a conduit for messages from the dead, and, perhaps one day, he might consider demonstrating his ability on the radio. Finally, George agreed. We made an appointment to meet the following Monday evening, same time, same place.

As I watched George walk to his car, I felt both comforted and bewildered. I'd never experienced anything like this. All during the next week I'd replay the reading in my mind over and over. When Madeline asked how accurate George had been, I replied that he was correct about "some things." But I'd lied. George had been accurate about *everything*. He had not generalized, there was no ambiguity. He knew things— names, details, events, opinions, even gestures—that no one else could have known. How did he do it?

I recalled everything I'd ever told Madeline about myself and pondered the possibilities. Madeline swore that she'd told George nothing about me, and even assuming that George had heard each of my radio programs since I'd come to Long Island

radio in 1972, he could never have obtained all of this information. George's reading was an incredibly accurate report on
significant events in my life. For example, my grandfather
Solomon, who, by the way, never allowed anyone to refer to
him as Sol, officiated at my bar mitzvah. It was the proudest
day of his life. Shortly thereafter, I began questioning my
faith, and when I married my first wife, a Catholic, he and my
grandmother were shattered.

The woman who came through was my late former wife
Shirley, the mother of my daughter. She had been killed instantly just a year before when a car struck her as she crossed a
Brooklyn street. George's physical description of her was accurate, as were the details of the location and type of injuries
she sustained. But the most astounding revelation was the hand
gesture he described. Whenever Shirley became annoyed with
me, she would rapidly move her hand, pointing her finger at
me. Even the message George gave me regarding our daughter
was exactly what Shirley would have said; she was much
stricter with our daughter than I was. These were things only I
knew about, things I'd shared with no one. In fact, the only
thing a radio listener would know of Shirley was the fact that
she had passed. Further, before my daughter moved out to
Long Island to live with me after her mother's death, no one in
the neighborhood really knew us intimately. For the first time I
asked the question I'd repeat a hundred times in the coming
years: How was this possible? Had my grandfather and daughter's mother communicated to me through George? Why they,
and not anyone else I had known who had passed on?

I relived the reading time and again, searching my memory
for evidence of tricks. George had worked in a fully lighted
room, did not go into a trance state, and seemed so matter-of-
fact about it all. I reexamined the sheets he'd written on. I saw
the words "Solomon," "confirmation," "Shirley," "marriage," "accident," "head," and the Star of David drawn
about a half dozen times. Although I refrained from jumping to
conclusions, I had to admit that there was something going on.
It flew in the face of everything I'd learned and believed about
science and religion, the nature of life itself.

During the week between that first reading and my second
scheduled meeting with George, I telephoned my friend and
longtime colleague Stephen Kaplan for advice and assistance.

Kaplan enjoys an international reputation as a parapsychologist and teacher, though he approaches the subject with more skepticism than just about anyone I've ever met. He took special pleasure in publicly exposing hoaxes—in fact, it was he who encouraged me to go public with the Amityville Horror story.

After I described my experience with George to him, I asked, "What strange unexplained energy or force could be responsible?"

Kaplan told me in some detail that he believed, unquestionably, that mediumship was genuine but that the majority of those claiming to have the ability were frauds or magicians. Only a handful of people in the twentieth century—Edgar Cayce, Arthur Ford, and the Brazilian peasant Arigó—had received even grudging widespread acknowledgment of their mediumistic or clairvoyant abilities. And very few were able to present evidence in public tests with any record of success.

I then told Kaplan that, while sitting with George, I felt what I could only describe as a sort of curtain between this dimension and the other parting wider than I'd ever believed possible. He understood the analogy and agreed to assist me in investigating the mystery. He would be the first test subject for George, whom he'd neither met nor heard of before. They would talk over the telephone, with George knowing nothing about the man he was speaking to. If George was indeed some sort of instrument of communication, we could expect him to reveal things about Kaplan that I myself did not know and would have no way of passing on to George prior to the reading. Kaplan issued one warning, though. If George turned out to be a fake, he would expose him.

That Monday night George arrived at the studio and we greeted each other cordially. I explained to him that I wanted him to do a reading for an anonymous subject over the telephone. Despite the few experiments he'd conducted while he was working as an operator, George shook his head and said, "I don't think I can do it."

"Why not?"

"'Cause I've never tried it over the telephone, this way."

"Well, what is there to lose? You said you wanted to find out if you could demonstrate your ability publicly. If you can't do it over the telephone, we'll find out. Obviously, we found out last week that you can do it in person. You did it for me."

"I don't know."

"George, I really feel that you can do this on the telephone. And, if you can, it will help you better prove that your ability is genuine. And we'll be able to present it on the radio in the future."

"I'm definitely not ready to go on the radio," he protested.

"Well, maybe not yet. But you'll never satisfy your own curiosity about whatever your capabilities as a medium are if you don't at least make the effort. I can't say more than that."

"Well, it's up to the other side to tell me, and they don't tell me everything. But, if you think I can . . ." he said, hesitating.

"Yes, I think you can. Let's try."

George sat down at the table and put on earphones so that he could hear the anonymous caller. He would speak into a microphone, and the session would be tape-recorded. Chris sat in the soundproof control room and placed the call to Kaplan in New York City. When the phone console at the table lit up, it was my signal that Kaplan was on the line. I pressed the button and said, "Hello, caller."

"Hello," Kaplan responded.

"George can hear you," I said. "Please don't say anything about yourself. And absolutely do not give your name. This is a closed-circuit demonstration of his skills. Just say 'hello' so George can hear your voice quality."

"I understand," Kaplan replied. "Hello, George."

Suddenly George looked very intense as he began writing rapidly across a sheet of paper. "I know this may sound strange," he began, "but someone asks me to ask you this. Are you a mature man?"

"Yes."

"Is there a woman close to you that has passed on?"

"Depends on who you mean."

"She says you're over thirty."

"Yes."

"Was there a woman in your household who had a great influence?"

"I had an aunt who passed on."

"Was she in your household a great deal when you were growing up?"

"Yes."

"Is this on your mother's side?"

"Oh yes."

"Was your aunt married?"

"Yes."

"Has her husband passed on also?"

"Yes."

"Okay. I feel him around also. Your aunt is around you because of great movement."

"I'm always in a state of flux," Kaplan replied.

"Do you take the name Elizabeth, living or deceased?"

"Yes, I know a woman who calls herself Elizabeth."

"She's not family. Are you in contact with her? Or were you recently?"

"Recently."

"Is there a business connection?"

"She's a client."

"Is she very emotional?"

"Yes."

"Does she have suicidal tendencies?"

"It wouldn't surprise me."

"If she contacts you, please give her time. She needs someone to talk to."

"Okay."

"Is there an illness in your family?"

"Yes."

"A male."

"Yes. Is it physical or mental?" Kaplan asked.

"Physical, I'll say," George answered.

"Yes, there is."

"Physical illness. A condition in the chest."

"Absolutely."

"Would your aunt who passed on know this man also?"

"Oh yes."

"Is there a possibility—I'm not predicting death—but is there a possibility that he could pass on?"

"Absolutely."

"Because the aunt is waiting for him. Is he your brother?"

"No."

"Is he close like that?"

"The person who is ill—yes."

"Okay, because the brother vibration is very strong. Does this person who is ill have a blood relation to you?"

"Absolutely."

"That's what it is, very close."

"Yes."

"Is this someone you've shared many experiences with?"

"All the time."

"That's where I'm getting the brother. It's someone who is very close. Is this person very, very weak?"

"Physically, yes."

"Are you on good terms with this person?"

"Yes."

"That's the thing. There are very close ties there. Has your father passed on?"

"Oh yes."

"Would your father know this person?"

"Absolutely."

"Yeah, that's the thing. Now I'm getting that it's a father-son vibration."

"It certainly is."

"That's what he says. 'It's my son.'"

I interrupted. "Why don't you tell George who he's talking about, caller?"

Kaplan replied, "George is talking about me!"

I confirmed what Kaplan said. "That's right, George. You're talking about the caller."

"This gentleman is the one who is very seriously ill?" George asked in total surprise.

"Yes," Kaplan acknowledged.

George was stunned. He waited for a moment and then returned to the reading.

"Your father is very much around you. Was he a harsh man?"

"Yes."

"Do you take the name Jack?"

"Yes."

"Was he close to you?"

"He was my uncle. He was married to the aunt who I told you before lived next door to us when I was growing up."

"Do you take the name Harry?"

"Harry was my grandfather."

"He's passed on also."

"Oh yes."

"Do you recall him very well?"

"Sure."

"Well, I don't know if I should tell you this. He's waiting for you also. They're around you because they're aware of your condition," George explained.

Kaplan quipped, "Tell them they can wait. I'm traveling soon—but physically, not astrally."

George spent the next several minutes apologizing profusely for what he considered an intrusion into the caller's personal life. But he had no explanation for his obvious confusion in not recognizing, psychically, or interpreting the message, that the person to whom he was speaking was the same person the spirits were referring to.

As it turned out, George's description of Kaplan's health problems was correct. Four years earlier, at the age of thirty-five, Kaplan had suffered a severe heart attack and had recently been diagnosed as having arteriosclerosis as well. Though I knew of his heart attack, I had no idea that his state of health was as precarious as George described. The accuracy of the description did little to alleviate George's unhappiness about not being able to identify the subject of the spirit's message. But, on the whole, I felt that it was a remarkable reading, especially considering the fact that it had been done over the telephone.

After George left the studio, I phoned Kaplan to get his impressions of the reading. He was confident that there was no way either George or I could have known all of the details revealed in the reading. We exchanged ideas about mediumship and the possibility of survival after bodily death and communication between the "deceased" and the "living."

Kaplan said, "I would say that he is genuine. We still need more examination. Now the job will be to get the evidence." He also cautioned, "Right now there is no other way to test George. No technology exists yet to test a medium or to communicate with an afterlife."

George and I continued to meet regularly over the summer for readings. In one case, he spoke over the phone with a couple. He did not know that they were my parents, who were living in another state. In fact, even if George had known their names, which he did not, he wouldn't have had a clue that we were related, since I changed my last name many years ago. In this reading, George gave them details of the passing of an aunt, messages from her spirit to her former husband and son, and he spoke of another uncle who was going to die soon— something my parents knew of but I did not.

When I later spoke privately with my father, I was amazed to find that he felt comforted by the reading. My parents, both then past seventy, found in the reading answers to several questions about life after death. Clearly, George's abilities served a greater purpose than simply being used for parlor tricks.

One evening, as we were preparing for another test reading at the studio, Chris was standing near George, arranging the sound equipment. Suddenly George began writing on a blank piece of paper.

"Do you take the name Joseph?" he asked.

"Yes."

"Father vibration."

"Yes."

"He's passed over."

"Yes."

"He's calling out to your mother. He's saying hello. A greeting."

Obviously moved and surprised by the message, Chris just nodded. George then went on to give details of her father's life, health, personality, and appearance. He also described her father's death.

"He passed from something with the heart or the blood. It seems to be both, but it's hard to make out what he's saying."

"Yes," Chris replied. "He was forty-six when he died of a cerebral hemorrhage. He suffered for years from a heart condition and hypertension."

Then George repeated for Chris what seemed to him to be a cryptic message exactly as he "heard" it: "'I wasn't going to do with it what you thought I was.'"

Although George was puzzled, Chris immediately understood the statement. She then told us that her father had kept a handgun, which no one else in the family knew about until it was discovered after his death. Finding it brought to mind all the times when he'd had financial difficulties and joked that he would go out and shoot himself. While he was living, of course, those comments went practically unnoticed, for, as far as any of them knew, their father did not own a gun. After they discovered the gun, her father's remarks took on a whole new meaning. And here he was, in some way communicating to Chris about something that had occurred *after* his death, in a statement that revealed he was aware of the discovery of the gun and the family's reaction to it.

Eager to learn more about George, I enlisted many people in my investigations. A longtime professional acquaintance agreed to be an anonymous subject for a telephone reading. During the reading George told him details about his father's abandoning him.

"Would there be a reason why he apologizes to you?" George asked.

"Oh yes."

"Was he very irresponsible?"

"Yes."

"You haven't heard from him since God knows how long."

"Fifteen or twenty years."

"Has he—your father—passed on?"

"I don't know."

"That seems to be who's giving me the message. Let me see if I can get him in. Were you named after him?"

"Yes."

"Your mother comes in very understanding. She gives me the impression that she's seen him on the other side. It's a strong possibility that your father has passed on."

"Do you take the name Daniel, living or deceased?"

"That's close enough," the caller replied.

"Someone held up, psychically," George explained, "the book *Robinson Crusoe* in front of me and said, 'Look at the first name of the author.' Does your father have anything to do with Daniel?"

"Yes."

"Because he's the one who gave me the message. He seems to play games."

"That was him," the caller acknowledged.

"He seems not to have lost that on the other side. He keeps clowning with me." George then offered a message that the caller acknowledged as correct about a specific legal situation. "Your father's going into the future."

Several days later, the caller approached me and said, sarcastically, "Good trick the other night. You told that psychic George enough about my life to convince me he was real."

After several minutes wasted arguing with him, I realized it was no use. How could I have told George anything about the caller, that I did not know? Further, if there were collusion, why wouldn't George have brought up those things that I did know—the caller's profession or the general area he lived in, for example? Those things had not come up. Although the caller never admitted it, I can only guess that, after spending several hours rehashing the reading and reexamining all the details, he came to the conclusion that the reading was in fact genuine. The next day he apologized to me.

One thing that emerged in this reading, which we would continue to see over the years, was the unorthodox means by which George receives messages. In this reading the name Daniel came through to him in what would strike most of us as a roundabout, imprecise manner. Instead of the presence actually saying the name, he pointed to an image of the book *Robinson Crusoe* and instructed George to take the first name of the author (Daniel Defoe). As we'll see in later readings, this was only one of many means of communication for George, but a crucial one.

By keeping and studying records of hundreds of readings, we've noticed certain patterns, and George has become more adept at picking up on these "clues." Very often, the communications come to George in what can best be described as "his terms," through images from operas, films, television programs, books, personalities, and Catholic figures and imagery George is familiar with. How do the spirits know, for example, that his favorite opera is *Aïda*, or that he will deduce that the spirit means to communicate something about high finance when he perceives, or is given, the image of the New York Stock Exchange floor?

The first, most obvious explanation for what George was doing would be telepathy—mind reading. As we learned several years later in tests, however, George is not particularly skilled in telepathy. If he were, we might expect most of the readings to focus on whomever the person being read had in mind or most wanted to hear from. In fact, however, we've found just the opposite is true: Often at the end of their readings, subjects will express surprise or disappointment that someone they were thinking of or were expecting to hear from never came through, while someone they might have forgotten, never known, or known only casually would communicate through George. For example, at a recent group reading for a room full of strangers, George gave one young woman a very long reading, which included messages from two friends and several relatives, all of which she acknowledged as correct. Then, at the end, a detailed message which could have come only from an ex-neighbor who had killed himself several years before, came through. The young woman acknowledged the message, but asked, "Why him?" We do not know.

Another aspect of George's ability that cannot possibly be attributed to telepathy is revealed in the messages that come from the other side that concern the future, such as his early reading for his little friend Tommy.

In the middle of a reading for a friend of mine named Jim, George suddenly asked him if he had taken a trip recently. Jim replied that he had not, but George insisted that he psychically saw Jim driving on a steep mountain road, then negotiating a sharp, treacherous curve as a speeding car came around the bend and threatened to hit Jim's car head-on. The best Jim could do with the information was to relate it to a trip he was going to take along the winding mountain roads of New England, but that was in the future. George explained that the message came from the spirit of a friend of Jim's who had been shot to death years earlier.

Two weeks later, a badly shaken Jim called me to tell me that, while driving on a mountain road in Vermont, he turned a corner to find a speeding, oncoming car in his lane. He swerved and just barely avoided a serious accident. The scene was just as George had described it. But how could it be? If the explanation were telepathy, then it would require that Jim—and the hundreds of other people George has given future messages to—have foreknowledge of events, a possibility that is extremely unlikely. (And that raises the question of why these people wouldn't know these things themselves, without having to be told about them from the other side speaking through a channel like George.)

This was a question that would arise countless times. How could spirits know what was going to happen in the future? And if they did, why weren't they communicating through George to send their loved ones warnings of *all* forthcoming accidents, illnesses, and tragedies, or, better yet, tips on the stock market and the winning lottery numbers? George has surmised that on the other side there is no concept of linear time as we know it, no designations of past, present, or future events. Further, those on the other side have impressed on George that we all live—both here and there—by the moral and physical laws of cause and effect: karma, if you will. Assuming that is the case, the spirits are really not so much "predicting" the future as they are deducing it, as we would make deductions and assumptions based on our knowledge of cause and effect and the probability of certain events given specific circumstances and conditions. We take for granted that if it's dark outside, it must be night. And after a period of darkness passes, the sun will rise and it will be light again. If we see dark clouds during the daytime, we guess that perhaps it will rain, but we know that if it's January and we live in New York and the temperature is below freezing, it may snow.

From what we can gather, the spirits can see, understand, and perceive the course of our lives in a way that's similar to the admittedly simplistic example above. For the spirits to see into the future, for them requires no greater effort than "turning the corner," as George would say. Somehow, the ability of the living here on earth to "predict" events—much as "If I scream at the cat, she'll hide under the sofa, but if I turn on the can opener, she'll come running out"—is heightened, expanded, virtually unlimited on the other side. Events that would seem to us to lack meaning, relevance, or connection to one another perhaps are related but in ways that we cannot comprehend. (Consider, for example, events that we usually attribute to coincidence, sheer luck, being at the right—or wrong—place at a certain time.) But for those on the other side, watching over a loved one here in the physical world might be like watching one of Rube Goldberg's inventions in action. The information George has gathered through hundreds of readings suggests that what we here regard as the inexplicable, complex, and sometimes irrational unfolding of events seems to appear to the spirits as no more complex, unpredictable, or difficult to understand than what would happen when the mouse jumps from the platform to the seesaw and the ball on the other end flies into the air, landing at the top of the ramp. It then—*of course,* we would say—trips the wire that opens the chute, and the egg drops a few inches down and breaks in the bowl.

As the summer drew to a close, it was clear that, despite our dozens of hours of tests, there was still much more to learn. The factual details about subjects and their lives was nothing short of astounding, and that alone would grip anyone interested in the field. But what was more astounding—and crucial—was the information George gleaned through these readings on the very meaning of life and death. In order for us to do more tests, we needed to find a wide range of anonymous subjects and to spark the interest of specialists in all disciplines who would be willing to challenge, test, and discuss George's abilities. The perfect forum for us to achieve both of these goals was for George to demonstrate his ability on radio, to go public.

Four

As of late September 1980, George still had not agreed to do readings for anonymous callers on live radio. Over the preceding few months, I'd witnessed and collected notes on several dozen private test readings. I had also invited observers to the readings—a wide range of interested parties, such as radio station employees, personal friends, and anyone else I could persuade to come see George in action. Without exception, all were impressed. But now what?

Paradoxically, George seemed terrified at the prospect of doing readings over the air, yet he took his psychic experiences in stride. That he almost constantly received messages from the deceased—sometimes those who had been viciously murdered or had died violent, excruciating deaths—or saw spirits materialize (even in his home) wasn't nearly as frightening to him as the idea of dealing with those of us on the physical plane.

Shortly before fall our assistant, Madeline, left. She had grown increasingly independent, and, while we were all very happy for her, we knew that we would miss her. Although she and George were not close personal friends, Madeline has a special place in this story. Had it not been for her persistence, he and I might never have met. And her belief that George would successfully display his mediumistic ability on the air never wavered.

However, George's continued resistance placed me in a difficult position. We'd gone as far as we could go privately.

Results from the test readings we had conducted were quite remarkable. His rate of accuracy was consistently in the 85 to 90 percent range, but each reading raised more questions than it satisfied. What were the meanings of certain symbols and visions? Was there any significance to the patterns some of the readings followed? Why would a spirit bring up topics that seemed quite trivial yet never mention those of profound importance to the subject? How did George know that a subject had a deceased pet? Or that a subject had recently visited a communicating spirit's grave? If these questions could not be explored, we could go no further. I had no choice but to confront George.

When he arrived for our next weekly session, I said, "George, either you want to go on the radio or you don't. I simply do not have the time to pursue this any further, no matter how much I wish to. You obviously have an ability. I'm convinced there is something there. But now it's up to you. What do you want to do?"

"I'm not trying to be difficult," George replied apologetically. "I am grateful for all your time and attention. I just don't know if I'm ready."

"I feel you are ready, George. God gave you this ability or gift, and you're ignoring it. That's a shame."

George appeared hurt as he silently stared down at the floor. He wasn't trying to be difficult; he was just confused as to which way to go. Nonetheless, I continued, "I have to insist that you decide now."

"But I thought we were making progress together."

"Yes, but now what?"

"I don't know. More time?"

"No, George!"

"No?"

"George, I have to do this. Either you have to demonstrate—in public, on the radio—or we've completed our tests. You said that you wanted to understand more about the origin and nature of your ability. This is your chance. I can't force you; it's up to you now. Go on the air. Trust me. Now or never again—at least not with me. I'll give you one minute to think it over. You say yes or no. That's it."

I was sorry to upset George with my ultimatum, but nothing

I had said before made any impact. George just kept staring at the floor.

"I'm scared," he admitted. "When would I have to go on the radio?"

"Next week."

"Next week? To take calls?"

"No, I just want to introduce you to the audience. Then, two or three weeks after that, you'll come back to take calls from listeners."

"Okay, you win. Yes."

We scheduled George's radio debut for midnight, October 6, 1980. For this first show, we would simply discuss George's experiences and abilities.

George sat across the studio table from me. I tried to ignore his obvious fear as I made the standard nightly introduction to my show. Then I presented George.

"Of all the things that we have done on the Joel Martin program over the years, among the most interesting are the psychic expeditions, those adventures that take us into the psychic realm with many distinguished psychics from around the nation and the world. One of the areas, however, that we haven't really dealt with in detail is an area that I am finding increasingly fascinating. This is the subject of mediumship and automatic writing.

"My guest tonight," I continued, "whom I discovered only recently right here on Long Island, I believe someday—if he is not already—will be in the league with some of the great psychics of the world. He is truly one of the most incredible people I have ever met in this field, and he will, at a future time, be taking telephone calls and speaking to listeners. But I wanted to introduce him tonight, briefly, as a way of acquainting this show's audience with a gentleman I will introduce only as George, as a way of protecting his privacy.

"George's unique gift is mediumship. He has the ability to receive communications from the spirits of the deceased, believe it or not. He utilizes a technique called automatic writing to facilitate the messages he is receiving from the spirits of those who have passed on. I welcome you, George."

George replied with a silent nod—not great radio technique.

I plunged ahead. "George, would you agree with the brief definition of mediumship I just gave the audience?"

"Yes," he responded.

"George, this process of automatic writing. What exactly is it?"

"Well, it's a form of—I guess you could call it communication with the hereafter. Entities from beyond the veil—from the world hereafter—send messages through your mind, which transmit into your hand and are written out. Also, sometimes I can hear the entities speak to me. They ask me to write out the messages for my own personal reference, so I won't forget them and I can recall them later on. It's basically a form of transmitting messages or contact with the hereafter for purposes of helping us on this side of the veil."

"George, when you say 'this side of the veil,' you mean on this earthly plane?"

"The earth. Yes," he answered.

"And so, basically, what's happening is that spirits really are communicating with you? I don't know if 'people' is the right description once somebody has left this earthly plane."

"Yes, spirits are communicating with or through me. I would call them entities or, even better, spirits. People who have shed the flesh of the body, and have gone back into the spiritual form of life."

"And the spirits are communicating through you to those people around you on earth?"

"Yes. The spirits use me as a channel for the purpose of communicating with someone here that they want to speak to."

"Are you familiar with the author Ruth Montgomery?"

"Most definitely."

"What do you know about her familiarity with and relationship to mediumship and the technique of automatic writing?"

"I'm familiar with the fact that she was a very good friend of the late Arthur Ford, who was a renowned medium. And who I feel, even if someone disagrees, did bring in the authentic message from the spirit of Harry Houdini. Any of the books she has written are excellent in this field, and I've read every one of them. They most definitely give a legitimate contact with the hereafter, and I also find them very reasonable to believe."

"So," I said, "you would believe Ruth Montgomery when she says that the late medium Arthur Ford communicates to her through this technique of automatic writing?"

"Oh, definitely, yes," George replied.

"Why would mediums have the ability to communicate with deceased loved ones, friends, acquaintances through various techniques? For example, some engage in automatic writing, such as you. Others, I have heard, claim mediumistic abilities while in trance states."

"Well, it's different stages of spiritual contact. Some entities would communicate by a form of trance. That has happened to me, also. Although I shun it."

"Why?"

"Personally, I'm a little nervous about it. But I am intrigued watching someone else do it. Trance is one form. Perhaps when an entity feels you are a medium or a channel between the two worlds, and they discover that you cannot or are not comfortable communicating by form of trance, they would come through automatic writing. There is also—which I have done—just sitting with a person, and communicating with the spirit by personal contact or by voice. But I've gone to automatic writing, because I don't feel as drained during a reading with that method."

"Let's talk about how you chose automatic writing as a technique. Or was it something that kind of just happened to you?" I asked.

"No."

"George, were you sitting around one day when all of a sudden you picked up a pen and it started to write, virtually by itself?"

"No, because I was always prejudiced against automatic writing with myself, because I would feel that it was my imagination writing out the words and messages. But I have discovered now from my readings that when I began to become very tired, I was impressed to hold a pen. And, as I continued, the writing would begin, and it would also give me a form of concentration."

For the next several minutes, we discussed the origin of

George's ability. He described the visions and voices that began in his childhood, and how he could sense or foresee events around people that no one else could. He hastened to add that he kept all of this very much to himself then and candidly admitted that those in authority thought he "might have some mental problems." Especially moving was George's description of his childhood loneliness. Although there were spirit entities who comforted him when he became despondent, few others could—or would—help him.

I asked George for more clarification about the childhood visions and voices and how he could be certain that they weren't hallucinations or figments of his imagination.

"At the time," George began, "I would see visions away from me. I would also see visions in my mind, which would be a form of seeing with what I understand to be the psychic eye. I saw into the past, the present, and the future. How could I know the names of people who have passed on, or give messages that someone on the other side was concerned about someone here—and I'd be accurate—if I was imagining or hallucinating?"

His answer surprised me, for it had an assuredness I had not seen in him before.

"George, you're a strict Roman Catholic?"

"Yes."

"Very devout, from what little contact I've had with you."

"Yes."

"And you don't see any conflict between Catholicism and your psychic skills?"

"I don't. But apparently the Church does. With all due respect to the Catholic Church, they don't seem to understand my ability. Yet it's a religion that has such a great deal of psychic phenomena in it."

"Well, in this country—no disrespect intended against anyone's personal beliefs—some of those who are religious tend to shun or criticize this subject," I said. "However, that's not always true in other countries, even some Catholic countries, such as several in South America."

"Exactly."

"George, how would you answer someone who suggests, right now, that your ability is the work of the devil or demonic in nature?"

"It's a shame that what the Church does not understand, they consider to be the work of the devil. Recall back, the apparitions at Lourdes, France, in the last century. It is considered, to this day, an outstanding psychic apparition, and a very high, spiritual one. The Church authorities, then, were about to have Bernadette Soubirous put away for mental incompetence, and also because they could not understand why the Blessed Mother would appear to this ignorant peasant girl, Bernadette. I think it was because the Blessed Mother was trying to tell us something. Just because those higher authorities in the Church didn't know it all as well as they thought they did, they tried to mislabel it. My ability is not demonic. I avoid any use of it for evil purposes. I use my gift only to help people," George replied. "The devil doesn't do that."

"Now, you eventually discovered that this was a psychic gift. Despite the misunderstanding by the adults around you, were you able to somehow gather your own strength to realize there was nothing abnormal, and to talk about your gift and actually put it into practice?" I asked.

"No. What happened was that when there was talk that I could be mentally incompetent, it frightened me, and I tried to block it out of my mind and completely forget it, which I did for numerous years. So it lay dormant. Then, after I was out of school, I began again to become interested in such subjects as astrology and Chinese philosophy. I also attended my first spiritualist séance, which I went to as a skeptic and, to be honest, also just for fun. One of the women there was a medium who told me, 'You're a medium also.' Unfortunately, I didn't know what she was talking about, so I told her, 'No, I'm a small.'

"She began by saying not to reveal anything about myself, family, my circumstances. She said, 'Keep the conversation general.' We entered to have the séance, and she and some of the other ladies there brought in messages and distinct evidence from members of my family that there is no possible way they could have known," George explained.

"That brings us to today."

"Yes."

"After years of interviewing a great many psychics on this program, I would have to rank you as among the best. Although, I admit, at first I was skeptical. It is really quite fantastic to hear names of loved ones come back, names that you don't even consciously recall. And it's fascinating to hear George speak to people and often tell them details about events yet to happen.''

"Thank you.''

"Are you finally comfortable about your ability?''

"To a certain degree I'm still a little uneasy. I do find it intriguing. I sometimes still try to put it off as possibly my imagination, but I've had enough proof for myself that there is some unusual contact made where I cannot refute it any longer as being the work of my imagination.''

"George, you did a number of test demonstrations during the past weeks for me and others. You brought forth names and circumstances of deceased loved ones. Could it be that you were picking up on me or others? Picking up what each of us was thinking, if not consciously, then subconsciously?''

"In other words, you mean telepathy. Was I reading your mind.''

"Yes.''

"It's possible some people could think that it's that,'' George replied. "But it seems that when people come to me for private readings, sometimes they come specifically with someone on their mind that they want to hear from. Yet I will not be able to get them a message from that person, because they are thinking so intently about that person, they are holding the thoughts to themselves. I'll bring them everyone else, and at the conclusion of the reading, they'll say, 'You did not bring in the person I wish to hear from.' And I'll say, 'Well, then, if you decide to come back to me again, you must keep your mind blank.' If I were mind reading, why wouldn't I pick up on what the person who comes to me is thinking? So while there obviously is such a thing as mind reading, or telepathy, that's not what I'm doing.''

"George, for some people, your accuracy is somewhere between 85 and 90 percent?''

"It's possible. It depends a great deal on the person I'm doing the reading for. Usually by the person's voice, or the minute they come to me, I know I can or can't read them. I usually attempt anyway for at least five to ten minutes. If I find out that nothing seems to click, then I just give up and tell them that if they would like to come back some other time, I would be willing to try again. But I don't usually waste their time. With other people, the spirits seem to be able to communicate loud and clear and with great accuracy.''

"George, is it you who is doing the automatic writing, or is it the spirit who is doing the writing through you?"

"It's the entity or spirit writing through me. The spirits are using my physical being for a moment, just to write out their name or situation."

"Would it be possible, perhaps, to do this without automatic writing?" I asked.

"Yes, in the beginning when I first started readings, I did them by just sitting with the person. But I've found that the automatic writing seems to ease the strain upon my energy to make the contacts."

"George, do we all go to what you've called the other side when we die?"

"Yes, we do," he answered, "but I prefer to say that we make the transition."

"So we don't die?"

"No. We shed our physical bodies, and the soul then goes on to the other side in a spiritual form. So death is a transition to another dimension, but it is not a termination."

"Then there is no reason to fear death?"

"No, there is no reason to."

"George, I assume that you believe that the soul can return in a new body?"

"You mean reincarnation? Yes, I believe in that."

"And the messages you have given sometimes include warnings of death, and warnings of ways to avoid accidents. Therefore, you're able to get these messages from the other side and talk about the future?"

"Yes. If there is someone on the other side who is concerned about a person. There is no conception of time there, from what I've been told. They, the spirits, can see into the future, and if they foresee a dangerous situation happening, they're just as concerned there as they would be about you here. So they would try to forewarn you, *if* they could or are meant to. If, more than likely, the tragedy cannot be prevented, I do not see it and I do not get the message. Usually, if it is told to me, it's because there is still time to call attention to it, so the situation can be prevented."

"George, do you know how this is happening?"

"I really don't know, but I would like to find out."

"But, you see a picture, I assume? That is, a vision or a voice comes to you?"

"I receive both visions and voices. I call it 'clairsenses.' It's a sensation that comes over me. I feel it. I sense it. I've been told there are different forms of receiving messages, psychically. Clairvoyance is psychic seeing. Clairaudience is psychic hearing. I would have to say that at times I do have clairvoyance, because I see the person in spirit appear in front of me, and I can describe what they look like. I have clairaudience, too, at times, because I hear the voice; I hear the name. And this gives even greater belief to the person coming to me that their loved one really is there with him, and is trying to help, if this be so, or is greeting him."

"George, if somebody introduces you, is it appropriate if they call you a psychic? Are you comfortable with that designation?"

"I would say I'm more a medium. I've been told I'm a medium, because I work as a channel for spirits that have passed on. But I'm psychic."

"Okay, George, let's call you a psychic medium. Would that be agreeable to you?"

"Yes."

"Would you be willing to submit yourself to my callers, and have people from the listening audience speak to you over the telephone?"

Things had gone smoothly so far, but I wondered how he would answer. I sat glowering at George.

"Yes, I would," he answered.

Those were the words I wanted to hear, although, as he said them, George looked and sounded like a groom at a shotgun wedding.

"Have you ever been tested by anyone from the scientific realm?"

"No, sir."

"Would you allow that?"

"Yes."

"All right, we will do that at some future time. Meanwhile, George, let's look forward to returning in the next few weeks to talk to callers and communicating to them messages from deceased loved ones and others they might know from past experiences in their lives."

"Yes."

"You'll bring people messages and tell them what is happening on the other side of the veil?"

"Exactly."

Our interview concluded. When we broke for several recorded commercials, George exhaled an audible sigh of relief but said nothing.

"George, you were great!" I exclaimed. "Well, are you less scared now?"

"No."

"Why not? You were excellent. I thought you couldn't speak."

"I really can't—that well."

"But George, you just did."

"Thanks, but that wasn't really me."

"It wasn't you? Who was it?"

George silently pointed above him. I looked up at the fluorescent lights on the ceiling, and then, puzzled, I stared at George. "I don't understand."

He cast his eyes downward as if he were confessing a sin. "Well, to tell you the truth," he said softly, "*they* were giving me the answers."

"*They?*"

"The spirits, from the other side. They always help me when there is a crisis."

"Well, I guess I have a lot to learn."

Suddenly it struck me that perhaps George was not one person, but two different people. One, confident and articulate, had been demonstrating his remarkable gift. The other was gentle, insecure, and frightened at the prospect of public attention. Could spirits have been providing George with answers to my questions, just as they had helped him on tests in school and now used him as a communications channel? Could mediumship fall within the realm of positive possession?

Within several days we scheduled the promised call-in show for three weeks hence and began announcing the forthcoming date on the air. Everything was set, or so I thought, until one day when George asked, "Do I really have to go on the radio to take calls next week?"

"Yes."

"What if I'm not ready?"

"You were weeks ago, George."

"What if I'm still scared?"

"Too bad. Don't be!"

"I don't know if I can do it yet," George protested.

"George—"

"Okay, okay."

"You're doing it. The spirits will help you."

"I hope so."

"George! Conversation closed!"

By finally agreeing to do cold readings live over the radio, George was not only making possible more extensive testing than we could ever do by depending on acquaintances for subjects; he was also going to be demonstrating his abilities for thousands, and by taking calls he would be giving countless people the opportunity to learn firsthand what mediumship and spirit communications were all about. Having not fully researched the history of parapsychology, I honestly did not appreciate just how extraordinary a feat that was. It seemed to me that if one had such a tremendous ability, one would be only too happy to share it with the public, to prove that it is for real, to silence the critics once and for all. Despite having interviewed dozens of people who claimed to be psychically gifted, I had never been offered cooperation in any test or demonstration in which the person being tested could not set at least some of the rules and dictate a few of the conditions. George's response—hesitation and all—was unusually open. As George later confessed, though, he wasn't as anxious to prove himself to the world as he was to prove to himself that his rate of accuracy wasn't just the product of some kind of unconscious trick he had learned to pull off.

Subjects that are generally lumped together under the heading "paranormal" have always been popular with the public, and the seventies brought forth a wave of books and magazine articles on such topics. In that time several other types of paranormal phenomena came to the fore, joining UFOs, haunted houses, ghost stories, and all manner of bizarre occurrences. Again, it's important to bear in mind that the only thing George has in common with someone like, say, the psychokinetic Uri Geller is that current knowledge and scientific theory cannot account for their abilities. That the public was willing to consider and discuss such controversial topics as the Bermuda Triangle, pyramid power, the ancient astronauts, and life after death did not mean that those were all aspects of the same phenomenon but that people's minds were now a little more open. Even people who didn't necessarily believe in them were curious. In the years I'd been broadcasting and presenting guests who spoke on a wide range of such topics, I found that good open-minded skepticism often brought us a lot closer to understanding than blind acceptance.

By the time I met George in 1980 not only had the public's attitude toward psychic phenomena changed, but our ability to design and conduct tests of psychic ability had been greatly enhanced by a new generation of machines. It may seem like a small point, but simply by having access to personal computers to help work out statistics on probability, or videotapes of readings to study and compare—things we couldn't have obtained easily five years earlier—we could now build upon our information. And then there were the products of medical technology, such as thermography, brain mapping, and other methods of tracking the physical products—or, as one doctor calls them, the footprints—of psychic events.

Just the fact that George could perform a reading over the radio or on television, live, before tens of thousands of people made him different. Today, on a single local broadcast, more people can see George than were able to witness all the private individual readings the great twentieth-century seer Edgar Cayce gave in his lifetime. And because of this, the public need not rely on a journalist's or a subject's account of what he or she witnessed. Anyone who wants a personal confirmation of George's abilities needs only to pick up the phone.

Of course, much of this would come later. All I knew was that if George was a genuine psychic medium who received messages from the deceased, the most thorough way of testing him was to expose him to tens of thousands of strangers and let the results of these cold readings speak for themselves.

October 26, 1980: George and I spoke briefly prior to the program. I heard him mumble something about being nervous. Then he spent several minutes alone in the studio before we went on the air. I remember thinking that anyone glancing into the studio and seeing George pray would probably assume that he was a condemned man about to be executed.

At eleven P.M. I introduced the show and my guest. This was live radio and an experiment in the paranormal, I explained. "Tonight, communication with the afterlife. Is it possible? We will attempt to communicate with the spirit world through George."

We reiterated highlights of our first conversation, and again George explained the definition of mediumship, the mediumistic process, and our summer of testing. Once again he admitted that he did not know how or why spirits were communicating through him. We also decided that, for legal and moral reasons, George would not give out any tragic news or forewarnings.

I implored my listeners to keep their minds open, then invited them to call. Within seconds of my announcing of the phone numbers, all ten lines were lit.

"George, are there instructions for the people who will be calling in?" I asked.

"The best thing is to keep your mind blank. Don't think of anything important that may be on your mind, because if you do, you could be holding the thoughts to you. If that happens, I may not be able to pick up on the spirit communication."

"Anything else, George?"

"I would prefer also if the callers just say 'yes' or 'no.' Please don't provide me with any details or elaborations. Don't even give your own name. Because if you say something, and I get a message afterward that's the same or similar, I'm not confident enough in myself, and I'll say, 'You just told me that.' I'll think it's my imagination and I'll block the message out. . . . Of course, there's the possibility that a person cannot be read. I should be able to know that in the first few minutes. If I bat zero on everything, I'll just have to say, 'Sorry.'"

"Also," I added, "think carefully before you say yes or no."

"Most spirits, if they are aware enough, will try their best to communicate with a name you will know."

"Okay, let's take our first call," I said.

"Good evening, Joel. Good evening, George," the woman caller said.

I reminded her of the rules, and asked her to say something general about the weather.

"The weather today is windy and cold," she replied.

I explained to the audience that what probably sounded to them like mice scurrying in the background was George writing. I mentioned that the words and symbols were usually illegible but could be made out sometimes. "Caller, do you take the name Frank, either living or deceased?" George asked.

"I can't think of anyone right now."

"Anybody in any connection with yourself at all? A friend of yours, possibly. I keep writing the name Frank out. Usually if it writes out continually, somebody from the other side feels they are in the right place."

"I did have a friend I worked with once by the name of Frank."

"Passed on? Just say yes or no."

"I really don't know. No. I haven't seen him recently."

"When you did know him, was there any situation around him that you were aware of that would prominently stand out?"

"Yes."

"Was he an older person?"

"No. He was young, in his twenties."

"Was he very confused? He seems to have a great deal on his mind. I don't know. The thing is that, even though you're not that friendly with him, someone on the other side knows that you know him."

I interrupted to ask, "Why would this person who is only a friend come through to this particular individual?"

"Well, they see the opportunity to reach Frank, using me as a channel. Also, they know this caller is in contact with him. Whoever it is, they are insistent. They keep writing his name out."

I looked at George's pad and then verified this for the audience. George had written the name Frank at least a dozen times.

"George, you say Frank is still alive. He is not coming from the spirit world. Where is Frank coming from?" I asked.

"There is somebody in the spirit world that would know Frank and feel they have to reach out to him at this time."

"With a communication from the spirit world to this lady, through you?"

"That's it. Because she knows who he is. I'm trying to establish who Frank is."

"What if you can't?" I asked.

"Well, then, I'm going to try to cut the communication from him, and get someone else from the other side in. The thing is that if I can't get verification for certain, then the spirit cannot break through from the other side," George explained calmly. I had never before seen a medium who would stop in the middle of a reading to answer questions about the process without becoming confused. Despite my interruptions, George continued, unfazed.

In the next several minutes he provided the woman caller with another name of someone in her life. This time she recognized and acknowledged a shortened form of the name but was unclear about the person's current circumstances, although she suggested that George might be correct in the detail he had given.

I thanked her and moved on to the next anonymous caller, a man. George seemed undisturbed by his failure to resolve the issue of Frank with the first caller. I wondered if the reason was nervousness, or if George wasn't really psychic after all. Or, perhaps, if his ability was weaker over the telephone than in person.

George was writing as he spoke to the second caller, and he correctly identified the caller's specific career concerns, and went on to tell him that a spirit from the other side, acting as a guardian angel, was encouraging him to continue his creative pursuits. George gave the message from the other side, "Move forward with the creative field you are already in." George had written the word "creative" repeatedly.

I asked the caller if it applied.

"Yes," he replied, "I was painting today."

George also gave the caller the name of one relative who passed on, and provided a message from that relative to his widow still on earth.

I wondered aloud if this reading was accurate.

George replied, "As soon as I start to get my positive verification, the entity will build with further information. But until then, they just hang in there, and if they feel that they're not getting the response, they just leave.''

Of the third caller, George asked, ''Do you know Charles, living or deceased?''

''Yes.''

''Living or deceased?''

''Living.''

''Family?''

''Yes.''

''Close to you by blood?''

''Yes.''

''Your father is deceased.''

''Yes.''

''Did your father know Charles?''

''Yes.''

''Okay. That's who's giving me the message.''

''Yes.''

''Your father is calling out to him, 'Charlie.'''

''Yes.''

''Is he an older person?''

''Yes.''

''Around your father's age?''

''Yes.''

''Were they brothers?''

''No.''

''Close like that?''

''No, not that close.''

''Do you take the name Michael?''

''Yes, living.''

''Family?''

''Yes.''

''Was your father a very family-oriented man?''

''Yes, he was.''

''That's why I'm getting all the family names. Did he know Michael?''

''Yes.''

''Did your father speak another language?''

''Yes.''

''Was he born in a foreign country?''

''Yes, he was.''

"Do you take the name Joseph?"

"Yes."

"One who is deceased."

"Yes."

"Uncle?"

"Yes."

"I've got the Uncle Joseph deceased. Did your father have a condition that affected the blood?"

"I don't think so."

"Did he pass from something that would spread through the body?"

"Yes."

"That's why I saw the blood. I have to interpret symbols, and there's a million ways of interpreting them," George explained. "Uncle Joe passed before your father."

"Yes."

"He says, 'I've seen your dad here on the other side.'"

"Were they very close?"

"Yes, pretty close."

"Okay."

"Did your father have a condition in the chest?"

"Yes."

"Did he have cancer?"

"Yes."

"He liked music. Opera."

"Yes."

George told us, "I psychically hear operatic music. Do you take the name Tony, caller?"

"Yes, deceased."

"Relative also."

"Yes."

"Is there a joyous occasion coming up?"

"Yes."

"The spirits, the family, are gathering, and I see white, symbolically. . . . Will you be affected?"

"Yes."

"Every time I ask your father his name, he smiles at me and says it was a common name. But I can't make out what he's saying. Did he have a dry sense of humor?"

"Yes."

"Do you recognize a short, heavyset, balding man?"

"Yes."

"An uncle?"

"Yes."

George concluded the reading, and I asked the caller what the upcoming occasion he'd be celebrating was.

"I recently became a grandfather. It's a christening."

On the fourth and fifth calls George was similarly accurate, describing specific situations and giving out correct names of deceased loved ones. We paused for several commercials, and during the break George stared blankly at me. When I complimented him on his performance, he smiled and nodded. As we opened the second hour, George was once again engaged in automatic writing as he greeted a male caller. Within seconds, he was writing the word "mother" over and over.

"Someone on the other side is calling out to your mother, from the other side. A child's voice is calling out to your mother. It's calling out 'Mother, Mother.' They say it's your mother."

The caller paused and then answered, "My mother had two miscarriages."

I interrupted to ask George if a child not carried to term could communicate from the other side.

"Yes," George answered, "it could, because the spirit, supposedly, enters the body at the time of birth."

George moved on to tell another caller, a man, about a "strong vibration" he felt around a specific forthcoming career change, and to advise him about it. The caller accepted the message as accurate.

"Do you take the name Thomas, living or deceased?"

"Living."

"Family."

"Yes."

"Someone close to him on the other side passed on?"

"Yes."

"Has this person been passed on a very long time?"

"Yeah."

"Someone is calling out to him. Any particular reason?"

"No."

"Has Thomas's father passed on?"

"Yes."

"Thomas's father is here. Is there any situation around Thomas?"

"Yes."

Another caller asked George why the spirits do not communicate directly, and why George frequently had to translate symbols. George explained that doing a reading is like "putting together the pieces of a puzzle." It requires "decoding and interpreting" words, sounds, pictures, physical sensations, and feelings, some of them very personal and understood in their pure form only by the subject. The process was similar to putting together a giant jigsaw puzzle without knowing what the finished picture should be. In addition, several spirits can compete on a "psychic line" from the other side at the same time. He referred to them as "crossed signals from competing spirits."

George next told a man that someone on the other side was calling out to a daughter and apologizing for the "troubles" they had when he was on the earth. George explained that the man who had passed on slowly deteriorated, and that those around him "went through a difficult time emotionally before he passed." The caller said this was correct. George described the man as coming through weakly and speaking very slowly. "He doesn't rush, even on the other side."

The caller acknowledged, "That's exactly how he was in life."

"Any trouble with a daughter? He speaks out; it's cleared."

"It's my grandfather."

"He's apologizing to his daughter again."

"She's right here. It's my mom," the caller said.

In the last half hour of the show, the volume of calls had increased. George immediately greeted a male caller, "As soon as I heard your voice, someone on the other side said, 'A break in a relationship.'"

"Yes," the caller acknowledged.

"Have you had a break in a relationship recently?"

"Yes."

"Was it your doing?"

"Yes."

"You were recently close to marriage?"

"Yes, about two years ago and again, about five months ago."

"Someone on the other side is saying, 'No. You're not ready for it yet.'"

"You're correct, George."

"I see a symbol of a wedding band, but I'm being told you're married to your career."

"Yes."

The messages were coming from a spirit George correctly identified as the caller's late grandfather.

After several more calls, I paused to ask George more about the psychic symbols. He explained that he actually senses or sees them and then begins the process of interpreting what they mean.

"It's a matter of symbols and verifications," he replied.

Following a few more readings—each highly accurate—the program ended. There was no question that George was a hit, yet he seemed troubled by the first call and his inability to correctly interpret the information about Frank.

The next day I received a telephone call from a woman who introduced herself as Vivian. She explained that she had been last night's first caller, the one who couldn't acknowledge Frank. During the few moments she was on the air with George, she told me, she was so nervous that she blanked, but within minutes of hanging up, it struck her. She knew who Frank was and why he was calling out to her.

Vivian said that she had once worked with a young man named Frank Davis Jr. and had been friendly with his parents up until the time Frank senior passed away from cancer. She was certain that Frank Jr.'s father was calling out to him through her. As I spoke to Vivian I realized that I too had known Frank Davis and his son. Frank Sr. was a neighbor whom I'd come to know quite well during the year before his death. Though he suffered a great deal, he was sustained by a deep religious faith and a sincere belief in an afterlife. I had helped him untangle some bureaucratic snafus and had grown very fond of him. George had said during Vivian's reading that someone in the spirit world who knew Frank was reaching out to him. Vivian believed that the spirit of Frank Sr. was calling out to her because she knew both his son and his widow. Now she seemed annoyed with herself for failing to make the connection. But I was also upset: Could Frank Sr. have been calling out to me? By not acknowledging, had I deprived the caller or Frank's family of an important message? Unless Frank Sr. returned at another time, I would never know.

Five

After only a few appearances on the show, George was so popular that the station's lines were jammed two hours before airtime. More than once we received so many calls that local phone lines were overloaded and service disrupted. Of course, we at the station were thrilled by the response, but we got many complaints from George's employer, New York Telephone. They asked us to try to "control" the calls. All we could do was to stop giving out the phone number once the lines were loaded—but it was futile.

George's reputation spread quickly by word of mouth. Even diehard skeptics felt compelled to call in or write. One man, who identified himself as a born-again Christian, informed us that George's gift was genuine but of diabolic origin. He went on to say that he would be praying to God to "block" George's ability to receive the messages within twenty-four hours. Of course, his prayers proved to be in vain. At least he believed that George was for real. From what we could determine, the source of George's appeal and perhaps the purpose of his gift was to give comfort and reassurance to the survivors of the deceased. While all of the readings were highly accurate, several were so dramatic and touching that even George and I would be taken aback.

One such reading took place on Thanksgiving Eve, 1981. The caller was a man who, judging by his voice, could have been anywhere between twenty to fifty. He said hello, and then he and I chatted briefly about one of my favorite film stars, Mickey Rooney.

"As you spoke, sir, I kept getting music around you," George said, opening the reading.

"Yes," the man replied.

"Is it part of your life?"

"It was."

"It should be. Did you play an instrument? Write music? Anything on that scale?"

"I was a disc jockey."

"That solves it. The minute I heard your voice, I kept hearing music around me, and I just kept writing it out over and over again."

"Understandable."

"And it will become a part of your life again in the future," George predicted. "Has there been a recent passing around you?"

"Very recent."

"A male?"

"Yes."

"Your father."

"Yes."

"That hit me like a bullet. Did he pass on from a sudden heart attack?"

"Yes, he did. God, Jesus Christ." The caller was obviously very moved by what he was hearing.

"I'm a little shook up at this end," George admitted. "Do you know Edward living or deceased?"

"I am Edward."

"I would say he passed on within the month."

"Two weeks ago. This is why I'm calling."

"He says there was bitterness when he passed on."

"No," the caller replied, hesitating, as if confused by what the message alluded to.

"No," George said, insisting, "he says there is bitterness from someone who couldn't understand why he had passed on."

"Yes."

"Why there was no warning. And he says, 'It was my time to go.'"

"Oh God, oh Jesus." By now the caller was so overcome by

emotion that I wondered how much longer he would stay on the line.

"So it had to be."

"George, this is incredible!"

Even I had trouble believing my ears. "Sir," I asked, "do you know George?"

"I have sat for George in the past, but this is an incredible reading."

"There is no way he could know who he's speaking to?"

"Absolutely not. This is my father talking through George to me."

"You haven't seen George since your father passed?"

"No."

"Then there's no way he could have known about it?"

"No."

"Then let me keep going," George said. "Do you have a sister?"

"Yes."

"Your father was extremely close to her?"

"Oh God, yes."

"Because he calls out to her. Was she near him when he passed on?"

"He died in her arms."

"Well—"

"We're talking almost two weeks ago," the caller repeated.

"He says to me, 'Tell her that I am very close, all is well.' I'm getting wishes for a good holiday season. He's sending out the greetings. I get two names in front of me. Either the name Allison or Alice."

"Alice. Oh, that's incredible."

"Is this the sister that's close to your father?"

"He died in her arms."

Again I questioned the caller. This reading was stunning. He denied that George knew who he was or the circumstances of his father's death. George continued.

"Well, he calls out to you, he calls out to your sister. He says, 'Please tell everyone I'm at peace, I'm fine, I send my love.' There's also a woman passed on with the same name as your sister."

"Yes. That's my grandmother."

"And she says she was there to meet him when he came over."

"Oh Jesus Christ."

"I'm getting a strong pain in the heart, so apparently he went from a very swift massive heart attack. Before I left the house—"

The caller interrupted George. "I'm just looking for something else."

"He asks for your mother. I assume that you're getting together for the holiday, and he will be there with you in spirit. You can rest assured of that."

"I'm a believer, but this is incredible. My sister Alice is listening to this right now. It has a calming effect on me. Does my dad say anything else?"

"He's very close to all of you. I think he's made it obvious in those messages."

We had compiled notes and tape recordings on hundreds of readings, and after receiving dozens of phone calls and letters from callers who were kind enough to contact us and correct information they'd given out erroneously or add information they'd failed to acknowledge in the reading, it was becoming clear that George was probably far more accurate than we believed originally. While each reading was a test that confirmed George's ability, the tests as a whole raised even more questions about its nature, sources, and limitations. Besides the readings George did on the radio and privately, he made himself available to selected individuals and groups, all of whom were encouraged to bring forth whatever evidence they might find that George's abilities were not genuine. These situations were intended to expose George to skeptics, for while the listening audience provided us with a vast pool of potential subjects for readings, it's safe to assume that the majority of listeners and callers already believed in at least the possibility of discarnate communications. The most closed-minded skeptics probably did not even listen to the show, at least not in the beginning.

We scheduled the first gathering for January of 1981. Approximately twenty people, some friends, others professional acquaintances, were invited. Among those attending were Stephen Kaplan and his wife, at least three writers, an archeologist, a man with a doctorate in physics, several teachers, a commercial artist known for his study of UFOs, a photographer, several college students, and some people who worked at the radio station. The group was made up of an equal number of men and women, with people of various ages, racial and ethnic backgrounds, and religious persuasions included. The gathering took place in an empty studio at the station, and, without exception, everyone was very curious about George, though few had reached a definite conclusion about him.

Kaplan got the evening rolling by proclaiming himself the expert on debunking psychic frauds and then searching the room for electronic listening devices. Kaplan theorized that a cleverly concealed "bug" would allow George, or me, to eavesdrop on our guests' conversations and then use whatever information we obtained in the readings. After a thorough search, Kaplan pronounced himself satisfied that the premises were electronically "clean."

Kaplan then announced that he had brought along an uninvited person who was sequestered in a separate room and asked if George could demonstrate his ability by reading that subject. George agreed, and Kaplan returned moments later with a young woman.

The woman and George took seats on opposite sides of a table, and, as expected, George began his automatic writing. From where I stood, I could see over George's shoulder. The word "blood" was written repeatedly on the sheet.

"Ma'am, please don't tell me anything about yourself. Not even your name. Just answer yes or no."

She nodded.

"Is there some reason why I would see blood around you? In the psychic sense, that is."

Kaplan interrupted and asked George to repeat his strange question.

"Well, to tell you the truth," George explained, "I psychically see blood bursting all around her. But it doesn't seem to be in the sense of danger or violence."

"Yes," she acknowledged.

George continued to pour out details of the woman's life, including specifics about her marriage, which clearly made her uncomfortable. He gave her several names of persons and their relationships to her, which she confirmed as correct. George explained that the messages were being received from the woman's late mother. Then George returned to the blood that he was seeing again in psychic symbols.

"I still see blood bursting. I also see blood in vials or containers, almost the way you would in a blood bank."

"Yes."

"George," Kaplan said, "would you like some clarification?"

"Well," George replied, "I could continue and probably interpret what I'm seeing, because I feel that the blood signifies something about someone in her life."

"Yes," she said.

Kaplan then said, "This woman's name is Ann Hughes. She's a writer and currently she's working on a book about vampires."

"Oh, that must have been why I saw the blood," said George, surprised at the unlikely connection.

"But, there's more," Kaplan added. "She's married to a hematologist."

Following this successful reading, George spent time talking to everyone there, answering questions and discussing the reading. People wanted to know how George could be certain that his abilities were not the product of something demonic, how he received and interpreted the symbols. He spoke about precognition and why he believed that it did not negate free will, about his childhood, and about what he had learned through his readings concerning life after death. The last topic was by far the most popular. After all, what did it really matter if George could deliver a message from someone else's deceased loved ones? Certainly the message would be meaningful to that individual, but the real significance of George's gift was what the existence of the messages meant for *all* of us. If the deceased were communicating, then they were *not* dead.

It was time for another demonstration. We'll call the man who volunteered to be a subject Barry Hollander, a salesman. I had met him a few months earlier through a mutual friend and was fascinated by his obdurate skepticism about all psychic phenomena. There was simply no talking to this guy. Throughout the evening, Barry had been loud and argumentative, and, despite what had transpired with Ann Hughes, he wasn't changing his mind one bit. He announced loudly that the entire evening was a setup and that George was a fraud. Alternately laughing and taunting, he then demanded that George read him, claiming that he could not be read.

George shrugged his shoulders and acquiesced. He invited Barry to sit down, then began writing very quickly. Barry sat with his arms folded tightly across his chest, his face set in a smug grin. His verbal assault didn't appear to have bothered George, who was engrossed in the communication. Then George remarked to no one in particular, "Emotions during a reading can build or deter the communication."

"Why?" I asked.

"Because the spirits start to get upset on the other side and it wobbles their vibration." Then, turning to Barry, he said, "Do you take the name Sophie?"

"What?" Barry asked, obviously surprised.

"Sophie," George repeated.

"Yes."

"Living or deceased? I feel she's passed on."

"Yes."

"Mother or mother figure?"

"No, not my mother."

"Well, then like a mother. She's saying, 'I was like a mother to you.'"

"Yes."

"Not a grandmother?"

"No."

"Was she an aunt?"

"Yes, yes." At this last fact, Barry's grin faded, his face paled.

"Why does she keep saying she was like a mother to you?"

"She was," Barry replied quietly. "She practically raised me. I was very close to Aunt Sophie. She was like a mother to me."

"This is silly," George said. "Forgive me. I'll tell you what I'm seeing, but it doesn't make any sense. She's pinching your cheeks. Is there any reason why she would do that?"

"Yes," Barry replied, now obviously frightened. "She always did that to me when I was a child. It was a sign of affection."

Some of the others, who had found Barry's earlier tirades embarrassing and obnoxious, burst out laughing. Barry, back

to his old, belligerent self, regained his composure and stated
that this was all a clever trick. He dared George to tell him
something very personal—even intimate—about himself.

"No," George protested.

"I dare you."

"No."

"See," Barry said, quite pleased with himself, "you
can't."

"Please don't ask. I don't want to pry."

"Why not? What can you tell me?"

"Okay, if you insist," George answered reluctantly.

Barry, thinking he had George beat, looked up and smiled
broadly at everyone in the room.

"Are you having marital discord? Because your aunt is saying there's a serious lack of harmony on the homefront."

Barry stiffened. His wife stood in one corner, visibly upset
but silent.

"Your aunt is saying that there is too much anger at home.
Marital tension. It's bordering on violence."

Barry stared at George, nodding slightly, but did nothing to
indicate that he wanted George to stop. George went on to
describe a terrible marriage, with details he could not possibly
have known except through Aunt Sophie. When Barry had
heard enough, he rose quickly from the chair and tried in vain
to dismiss George's reading. Mrs. Hollander demanded to be
taken home.

"How could you do that?" she screamed at Barry. "How
could you tell that man about us?"

"But I didn't!" Barry protested.

"Then who did? Not me! You know that. How could you?"

"But—"

Then they were gone.

For most of 1981 we were frequently joined on the air by a man
we'll refer to as Dr. David Gold, a physicist on the faculties of
two local universities. He was the first scientist to come forward and speak publicly about his observations of and findings
on George. He once stated, "Since matter can be neither created nor destroyed, it is reasonable that when we die, an energy
in some form survives and moves onto another dimension,

where it communicates or transmits back through George, who is essentially a receiver, a human receiver."

In July of 1981, Gold participated in a program with George and Father Tom Hartman, a Roman Catholic priest. During the discussion, Father Hartman spoke of the soul; Gold spoke of an energy that survives human bodily death; and George spoke of spirits. Each was talking about the same thing. Of course, this is not an original revelation—Lawrence LeShan's excellent book on the paranormal is even called *The Medium, the Mystic, and the Physicist*—but it demonstrated clearly that we all think about something, regardless of what we call it, to which we ascribe certain qualities, primarily its ability to survive our deaths, its indestructibility. The idea that perhaps, deep inside, we all have this knowledge seemed to be reinforced with each reading and each person we talked to.

At this point, there was virtually no doubt in my mind that George was anything but genuine. However, I knew that if my contention could be publicly substantiated, we would attract other researchers. Even if none of them could tell us exactly what George's ability was, at least we might determine what George's gift was not. And that information would prove quite effective against stubborn and unreasonable skeptics. We also sought well-grounded answers for those who refused to accept not only George's but anyone's claim of psychic ability or experience because of the ignorance, confusion, and doubt cast upon the entire subject by both the charlatans and the psychic debunkers.

In an interview, one debunker summed up his proof that such things were impossible: "Psychic phenomena are anti-scientific." I replied that for science to ignore psychic phenomena was what was unscientific. My staff was once contacted by one of the nation's most famous debunkers, who happens also to be a magician. We were only too happy to have him on the show with George, but for some reason he never came on. On the one hand, there were fanatics—on both sides—whose mottoes may well have been "My mind's made up, don't confuse me with the facts." On the other, there were the interested scientists and other intelligent people who would affirm George's abilities, but only off the record.

One day I received a phone call at the station. "Mr. Martin, my name is Dr. Abrams. I am a psychiatrist with a state agency that deals with mental health. I heard your radio program last night as I was driving home. Your guest was a man you identified as Psychic Medium George.''

"How can I help you?" I asked.

"The man on your program, George, claimed he was in communication with the deceased,'' he answered in a stiffly polite tone.

"Yes.''

"He claimed to be giving callers messages from those who have passed on. George claims he is receiving these communications from those now in spirit form in another dimension. He -is purporting to be a medium. Is that all correct?''

"Yes.''

"Mr. Martin, I am a thirty-year veteran of the psychiatric profession, and I hold a deep interest and belief in parapsychology and survival research. I have my own very definite theories. George gave quite an impressive demonstration—''

"Thank you, doctor.''

"*Or* he was the greatest psychic hoax I have ever heard perpetrated publicly, and I will spare no effort to expose both you and George as frauds!''

We had come to expect and even accept a degree of public skepticism as understandable, but this man's intimidating tone and his charges challenged our integrity. I controlled my temper as I replied, "Dr. Abrams, I assure you that what you heard was no hoax or fraud. It was genuine. There was no collusion. Those who phone George are random and anonymous to him.''

"Very well, Mr. Martin,'' Abrams replied, sounding as if he didn't really believe me. "I'm in no position to refute or support you at present. I must find out for myself, however, if George is a genuine breakthrough in mediumistic communications, or—''

"Or what?''

"Or.'' He paused for a moment, then took a different tack. "I have a responsibility to protect the public from deception in the field of parapsychological research. You see, I take the subject very seriously.''

"So do I, doctor.''

"Well, then you understand that I must find out for myself.

I'll perform my own test of his ability, and then I will report my findings to you.''

"And will you admit it, if George is genuine?" I asked.

"Yes," he promised.

"Will you appear on the air, if he proves he's genuine?"

"Yes. But first let me determine that. We'll be speaking again, Mr. Martin. Thank you for your time. Good-bye."

Dr. Abrams's call was both annoying and flattering. From the moment George had consented to do public readings, we'd been trying to interest scientists, doctors, psychologists, writers—basically anyone with extensive knowledge in an area that might be relevant to our understanding of George. One respected molecular biologist posited that the answer would be found in not one particular field of science but several, specifically physics (to explain the energy), neurosciences (to explain George's brain function), biology (to explain other physical functions), and genetics (to explain why George is not the only member of his extended family with psychic abilities; several members of his family have had premonitory experiences repeatedly).

Years later another doctor articulated our problem beautifully, saying, "How can we find the answers if we don't know which questions to ask?" But even with those limitations in mind, we still thought it better that people ask questions. All we asked of those who sought to investigate George was that they bring to their task a sense of open-minded skepticism and that they come on the show and discuss their findings—pro or con—in public.

At least Dr. Abrams had taken an interest in George. Whatever the doctor had planned, I soon put the conversation out of my mind, certain that I would find out eventually.

Several months after his call, George phoned me to tell me about a very unusual reading. Earlier that day a man wearing soiled clothing, unshaven, and reeking of alcohol came to him. George assumed he was a derelict but reluctantly invited him to take a seat. As the man staggered to the chair, George wondered how he'd even found his way there. Once slumped in the chair, the stranger sat with his eyes partially closed.

The writing began. George glanced up and saw the face of Sigmund Freud over the man's head. What could it mean?

"Sir, are you a professional?" George asked.

"Am I?" The man slurred his belligerent reply.

"Well, I'm impressed to say that you are. Is it the medical profession?"

"Why do you say that?"

"To tell you the truth, I see the symbol of Sigmund Freud's face over you," George explained.

"You do?"

"I'm being told that you are not what you appear to be. Are you a psychiatrist?"

"Yes, I am," the man answered, suddenly sober. He then congratulated George on his accuracy and explained his purpose. "It was a masquerade. You see, George, I heard you on the radio several months ago and I had to find out if what I heard was true. I doused myself with alcohol because I thought that appearing to be a drunken bum would be a good way to test your ability as a psychic medium. But it didn't work. I'm happy to say that the trick is on me!"

It was Abrams, and several days later he phoned to tell me what had occurred.

"I appreciate your calling back to let me know that you found George to be genuine," I said. "Now, will you go on the air to speak about the experience and about your theories on parapsychology and the mind?"

"Well," he replied, hesitating, "that poses a problem. I don't know if I can keep that part of my promise to you, although I do believe that George's ability is authentic."

"Why not?"

"To be candid, Mr. Martin, I fear my colleagues would never understand or accept if I spoke publicly. I am truly sorry."

As I hung up, I wondered if Abrams knew that Sigmund Freud was once a member of both the English Society for Psychical Research and the American Society for Psychical Research, or of Carl Jung's extensive writings on the paranormal. Sadly, while his reluctance was understandable, I knew that Abrams would have been only too happy to come on my show if he'd found George to be a fake. His colleagues would have understood—and probably applauded—that.

Not all of George's surprise visits were as pleasant. Less than a year had passed since he had first appeared on radio, and the demand for private readings had increased so dramatically that he was booked up months in advance. With those readings, the radio shows, and the time he spent working with law-enforcement officials on special cases, he had almost no free time, yet he was still holding down his full-time job at New York Telephone. Even though most people had to have an appointment for a private reading, now and then George would see someone who seemed to need him.

One night George phoned me at the station, frantic. He explained that he had just hung up from the latest of a series of anonymous threatening phone calls he'd had in the last few weeks. He was certain that the caller was a man for whom he'd done a strange reading just weeks before.

George was living alone in a rented house at the time. It was a Friday night, and the last scheduled reading for the evening had just ended. The two elderly women he had read for were walking out the front door when a tall, slender man appeared. He was plain-looking, with long dark brown hair and wire-rimmed glasses. George guessed that he was around thirty. He wore an ordinary sports shirt, sweater, slacks, and tan trench coat, yet there was something suspicious about him. As the two women passed him on the sidewalk, he covered his face with both hands. George immediately felt what he described as "uncomfortable vibrations," and he noticed his cats and dog retreating as if they too sensed danger. Initially he was reluctant even to speak with the man, but he claimed to have come on a friend's recommendation and so George relented.

George showed the man in. The stranger sat down, took off his glasses, and asked, "Do you want me to concentrate?"

"No," George answered. The question struck him as peculiar. Sitting across from the stranger, George began automatic writing and immediately saw two psychic symbols: a triangle and the scales of justice, which seemed to grow larger.

"Are you involved in some kind of legal situation?"

"Yes," the man replied.

"A severe situation, because the scales of justice—the symbol I see—are large."

"Yes," the man answered nervously.

Then George saw the triangle overshadow the scales. "Are you involved in a love triangle?"

"Yes."

"Does the love triangle relate somehow to the legal situation?"

"Yes."

"Are you married?"

"No."

"Is this your wife?"

"No, no, no!" the man snapped angrily.

George changed the subject when he saw psychic symbols of musical instruments, which the man acknowledged were related to his career. Suddenly George saw a clear vision of a woman standing near the man. When George described the vision, the man froze and asked, "What does she look like?"

"Oh, I'd say she's about twenty-five to thirty with long blond hair. She's very attractive and well-dressed."

The man sat expressionless. George saw symbols of musical instruments around the woman's spirit also, and she indicated to him that she played the piano. Then the woman's spirit accused the man of murdering her. Before he thought about what he was doing, George blurted out, "Are you being accused of murder?"

"How did you know?" the man screamed, jumping to his feet. He quickly regained his composure and sat down again. "How did you know that?"

By now George was frightened. Was the man sitting just a few feet away from him really a murderer? He swallowed hard, took a deep breath, and answered, "Because she's saying that you murdered her."

"Where is she?" he demanded, his eyes darting around the room.

"She's standing next to you," George said softly. "Is what I see true?"

The man ignored George's question and asked, "What's her name?"

"Do you take the name Jean?"

"Oh, my God! That's incredible!" The man's eyes met George's, but all George could see was the woman's spirit showing him a murder scene. Psychically George saw the woman being stabbed repeatedly, beaten, and falling down on what looked like a living room floor. Her hands were raised in front of her body in a futile effort to protect herself. Eyes wide with terror, she fell, one arm outstretched, the other in a clenched fist. George didn't dare offer aloud what he was seeing. He heard the spirit say over and over, "I'm Jean. That son of a bitch murdered me! When is someone going to do something about it? He murdered me! He murdered me!"

It was unusual for a spirit to come through so angrily. From past experiences, George knew that sometimes the spirits of the recently deceased harbor "normal" human emotions. Jean's spirit wanted revenge, a feeling she would undoubtedly hold until she adjusted to the other side and to the fact that she was no longer in her physical body.

The man ordered George to stop. Had he virtually confessed to having killed the woman? He had stopped just short of saying anything that could be used against him legally. Besides, despite the fact that law-enforcement agencies do call on people with psychic abilities to help them solve cases, information obtained psychically is inadmissible in a court of law. A moment later, the man was gone.

Shaken, George couldn't stop thinking about what had just occurred. Why had the man been so bold? Had he come for the reading out of guilt, or because he wanted to know if a psychic or a medium could "tell" that he had committed a crime? Was the woman's spirit haunting him? Or was he seeking further information to help him elude arrest? Had the man even known that she was dead?

Several days later George received the first threatening call, followed by another two. The caller told George that he would be killed, and George asked me for advice. The police would have to be notified, I said. George phoned, and minutes later a policeman arrived, but not the officer usually assigned to George's neighborhood. George prefaced his account with his standard self-deprecating disclaimer, "I know you'll think I'm crazy, but . . ." Luckily, the policeman knew something about parapsychology and believed that George's concern was warranted. The police department provided extra patrols around George's house for several days as a precaution.

Over the next several months George and I became friendly with the officer, and he kept us posted on what was happening with the case, one of the most highly publicized murders in the tristate area. Despite the great amount of detail George's reading had revealed, following it up was frustrating. George and the policeman even traveled out of state to give another police department a detailed description of the stranger, the woman, and the vision. (George has worked with the police at other times, but only at their request. These readings are always free and kept in the strictest confidence.) Although the case was never solved, the phone calls ceased, and George never saw the stranger again.

At one point George was being questioned by a skeptical assistant district attorney. Not content simply to state that he didn't believe in discarnate communications, the ADA continued insulting George. When George felt that he'd had more than enough, he said, in a very polite voice, "You know, your mother is telling me that your wife would be very unhappy to learn about Wendy." The man looked as if he'd seen a ghost. We later learned from some of his colleagues that he was involved in a secret extramarital affair with a woman named Wendy.

As always, we welcomed anyone with something to offer—pro or con—regarding George and his ability. One of our first guest experts was Max Toth, the author of *Pyramid Power* and *Pyramid Prophecies,* two highly successful books, and a lecturer, researcher, parapsychologist, hypnotist, and authority on electroencephalography. We met in the mid–1970s when he came on the show to discuss *Pyramid Power,* a controversial work on the energy inherent in pyramid-shaped objects. Years before, Toth had attended a magicians' school, where he had learned the real tricks of the trade, and he enthusiastically accepted my invitation to examine George live on radio. He promised to tell me—and the audience—if he detected any sign of fraud or collusion.

Was there more to George than we could see? Toth was encouraged to spare no effort in revealing anything about George or his readings that could be duplicated by a magician. I neither knew nor cared how he would go about testing George; my only condition was that the test be appropriate, that it be designed to investigate only those phenomena George experiences.

This would seem obvious. However, too often investigators design and administer tests that reveal something about a person's psychic abilities without any regard to what specific psychic ability that person claims. This error stems from the widespread public perception that anything that is mysterious, unexplained, bizarre, or abnormal falls under the heading psychic phenomena, and that all are, in some way, essentially the same, when in truth these subjects have in common only that they concern occurrences or phenomena that are assumed to operate outside the usual laws of nature as we know them.

Surprisingly, even many "expert" researchers fail to make these crucial distinctions. As an acquaintance once said, this approach is analogous to viewing all of science as one subject, even though we know that every field of scientific study—from astrophysics to zoology—contains many areas of further specialization. One physician said many of the tests people like George endure were "about as relevant as checking your eyes with a stethoscope." Not only has George been tested for psychic abilities other than those he claims to possess, but the fact that he "failed" an ESP test was construed to mean that he has no psychic abilities whatsoever.

Sometimes the validity of a test would be judged not by its relevance or quality but by its results: Several times during 1981, George did readings while experts monitored his physical responses with an electrocardiograph to measure his heart rate and an electroencephalograph to measure his brain-wave activity. One physician who participated in these tests theorized that if George was working in a self-induced trance state, where the spirits communicate through direct voice, his heart rate would be lower than normal (i.e., in the nontrance, nonpsychic state). Results of an electroencephalogram indicated that during a reading his brain-wave activity alternates between the alpha (deep relaxation, "passive awareness") and the beta (alert, physically active) states. (The other two types of brain-wave activity the electroencephalograph measures are theta [deep tranquillity, sometimes unconscious] and delta [deep sleep, total unawareness] states.) Given this information on George's brain-wave activity, the doctor assumed that his heart rate would be slower as well. This struck all of us as logical, and we expected the findings to concur. However, when the electrocardiogram showed George's heart rate increasing from his normal 70 beats per minute to 113 or 114 while in a trance state, the doctor simply refused to accept it. Rather than view this unanticipated result as a phenomenon worthy of further investigation, he became furious with

George, going so far as to denounce and insult him. As always, George politely endured the abuse; later at the pair's request, he revealed to both the doctor and his wife a fact that each had kept secret from the other.

Max Toth understood the problem of establishing George's credibility and agreed with our premise. He would scrutinize George by whatever means he deemed appropriate but would be searching specifically for evidence of genuine mediumship and psychic fraud. On the night he was to appear on the program, Max Toth arrived at the studio shortly before air time. With him was a young woman to whom I was not introduced and with whom I was allowed no conversation. When George arrived, he was asked to remain in a separate room while Toth, the woman, and I sat in the broadcast studio. I explained to our listening audience what was going to happen and introduced Toth and George to each other. At Toth's request, I referred to the young woman as Miss X. She appeared to be about thirty, petite, with short light-brown hair wearing glasses, a high-necked long-sleeved blouse and slacks.

Toth reiterated the purpose of the demonstration, asked George several general questions, and then instructed George to begin Miss X's reading. George's pen glided over the sheets of paper as usual, yet he seemed uncomfortable. Whenever he looked up at her, he shook his head and then blinked before glancing at the words on the sheet and then back at Miss X. It was as if he couldn't believe what he was receiving.

Finally George exclaimed, "My God, there are flames all around her!"

"What?" Toth asked in a flat, emotionless tone.

"She's surrounded by flames—you know, fire. Psychically there are flames all around her."

George continued the reading for several minutes and then repeated his description of the disturbing scene that flashed before him. He said that Miss X appeared to be in an office or some other place of business, and that she was engulfed by flames. Until this point, neither the woman nor Toth had confirmed or denied George's statements. Toth then requested that George clarify or elaborate on his vision.

Without hesitation, George repeated, "Flames are surrounding her. She must have been in a pretty bad fire from the way it looks."

I asked George if the psychic symbolism or vision could mean that she had been just burned by a fire rather than actually in a fire, as he described.

"I would say no. From those flames, they're telling me she was burned as a result. It was an accident, but it was serious. She suffered greatly," George answered.

Both George and I winced at this description, but Toth and the woman remained expressionless.

"George," Toth said, "you said, 'They're telling me.' What do you mean by that? Who are 'they,' specifically?"

George appeared relieved to change the subject. "I feel it's on the father vibration. Has your father passed on, Miss X?"

"Yes," she replied.

"The 'they' I refer to are the spirits. It's the spirit of her father who is telling me about the fire—the accident."

"Anything else about her father, George?" Toth inquired.

"Did he have a condition in the chest?"

"Yes," the woman answered.

"Well, I keep writing out the word 'pulmonary.' I'm no doctor, but I know that's the chest. I'm feeling some sort of condition in the chest. It's something pulmonary. That's the best I can decipher what your father is saying. He just keeps saying 'pulmonary.'"

After George provided several more messages, Toth ended the demonstration.

George stared sympathetically at the young woman. I asked Toth to clarify and evaluate the reading. How accurate was it? Was George a genuine psychic medium or not?

Toth began by introducing Miss X. "This is my fiancée, Ellen."

"Ellen, can you tell us how accurate George was?" I asked.

She explained that several years earlier she had worked in the second-floor office of a limousine rental company. Downstairs was the garage, which housed vehicles and gasoline pumps. The second-floor rest room was under construction, and because the electricity had not yet been installed, illumination was provided by candlelight. Apparently gasoline fumes had wafted up from the garage and filled the rest room, so that when Ellen struck the match to light a candle, the room exploded in flames. Ellen was engulfed in them and badly burned. She confirmed that the scene of her accident was exactly as George had described.

Toth then told us that Ellen had dressed in such a way as to cover the scars on her badly burned arm. He explained that it was impossible for George to detect any clues from her physical appearance, and that even if George had seen the scars and knew they were the result of burns, he might have started with a more general question such as "Did you ever suffer a burn?" to try and fish for an answer. But without any response from Miss X, George *saw* a specific moment of her accident. Another point was that George did not initially refer to burns in general. He described psychically seeing the fire engulf her, and repeated his vision emphatically, despite the lack of response from either Toth or Ellen.

Ellen also explained that George's description of her late father's health was accurate. Toth found the fact that George had scribbled the word "pulmonary" several times fascinating, for it had a double meaning. As a young man, Ellen's father had suffered from tuberculosis, and years later he died of cardiac arrest following a pulmonary embolism, a blood clot in the major artery between the heart and the lungs. This was certainly a "condition of the chest," as George had described it.

For the benefit of the listening audience, Toth reiterated that Ellen was absolutely unknown to George and me. The information George had ascertained was known only to Toth, Ellen, and perhaps some family members and close friends. As far as Toth was concerned, the specificity of the details ruled out collusion.

To help us better understand what Toth had been looking for, he then spoke about how he had carefully observed George's body language, comparing it to how a charlatan might have behaved in these circumstances. Before a cold reading, in which the alleged psychic or medium is meeting the subject for the first time, the medium makes a statement to the subject. For example, he or she might open the session with a general, provocative statement such as "There's some problem in the home" or "There's a new love interest in your life." The phony medium then closely observes the subject's reaction—the facial expression and body language, as well as any verbal response—for clues about the subject's thoughts or general frame of mind. Some alleged psychics might make a series of such statements until one prompts a meaningful reaction. From there, it's basically a matter of narrowing down the subject's range or concerns and interests and then providing "messages" that seem likely to address those concerns.

In contrast, Toth declared, George did not engage in any conversation with Ellen prior to the reading; his first words to her were "There are flames." Also, George was definite about the spirit communication he received, even though he had no "clues" and not even Ellen's or Toth's acknowledgments or denials. "George hits immediately," Toth remarked. "He does not hesitate. He sticks to his guns. He repeats exact conversations. He describes situations and events in the lives of the subjects—past, present, and future. He also frequently provides the names of the living and deceased in the lives of the subjects. That is definitely rare, and it is a sign of a genuine medium. There are no clues, visually or verbally, for him to work from."

Toth suggested that when George said he received messages from Ellen's father's spirit, George had "locked into a psychic connection through which he read or interpreted the major points about her."

I asked, "Why only those two points: the fire and her father's health?"

Toth replied that in his opinion this was caused by either the subject's frame of mind or that of the spirits. Those two key elements in her life could have been in Ellen's conscious mind or her subconscious. Another possible explanation was that the spirit of her father, perhaps knowing how important these two events were in Ellen's life, wanted them conveyed to comfort her. By sending these two particular messages, he also proved to her that he was the source of the communication and that it was genuine. Toth was interested too that George "was getting his information through many different channels." He continued, "George doesn't have a spirit guide. He has *all* the spirits. Others have a modicum of psychic ability, but theatrics have taken over in many of them. They need gimmicks."

"What do you think of George?" I asked.

"I didn't witness any gimmicks. He's a damn good psychic medium. He definitely has a mediumistic ability. . . . The spirit communication is an acceptable explanation.

"George does not necessarily tell people what they want to or come to hear," Toth observed. "And he will not back down from a spirit communication even if the subject disagrees or cannot acknowledge. He's obviously unperturbed by skeptics or those who claim they are negative, even hostile to the subject. He is not frightened by being publicly tested under controlled conditions.

"And, of course, his accuracy is impressive. The statistical probabilities of his guessing have to be ruled out. On a percentage basis, George has a very high accuracy rate."

"George is not 100 percent accurate," I remarked. "Of course, no one is. But in your professional opinion, what accounts for those elements in his readings that are in error, even though they may be a small percentage?"

"Well, as I said earlier, a phony would not go into specifics as George does and certainly would not offer names, accurately, of the deceased or living in the subject's life. George knows when he is right. When is he wrong?" Toth asked rhetorically, "I would say 90 percent of his supposed inaccuracies are due to the subjects' inability to correctly acknowledge, associate, or remember what George is reporting as he hears it from spirits. It is a very human problem."

"I wondered," I said, "if some people are so stunned by hearing a name or incident that they were certain no one else could know that they cannot bring themselves to immediately recognize or accept the fact. I know that was the case with me when I first met George. Of course, sometimes there is confusion or misunderstanding about what George is attempting to interpret from the often cryptic symbols he receives, psychically. Also, people won't admit some things aloud. And there are times when George's communications from spirits are for events that apply to the future. Obviously these cannot be confirmed at the time they are given since they have not yet taken place."

After a few more minutes of discussion, the show ended. We were all impressed with George's reading. But George himself seemed absolutely amazed when, as we closed the show, Toth referred to him as "the psychic's psychic." No one could ask for more than that.

Six

In the fall of 1981 Viacom, one of Long Island's largest cable television systems, offered George and me our own weekly program. In addition to George's regular radio appearances on _The Joel Martin Show,_ we were now cohosting _Psychic Channels,_ a weekly talk show presenting a wide range of guests—physicians, clergymen, scientists, psychologists, authors, and other experts—discussing various aspects of psychic phenomena and the unexplained.

Although the cable facility's management and crew were friendly and cooperative, some on the staff were skeptical. Even a few who'd heard George on the radio still doubted that he could successfully demonstrate his gift on television. It was a valid concern. Our radio broadcasts were done in a very quiet, peaceful environment with few distractions. The show aired at midnight, so there was rarely anyone in the building besides George and me, sometimes joined by guests, and the program producer/engineer, my wife, Chris, and her assistant in the adjacent control room. No one could see us, so we dressed comfortably and had only microphones, earphones, and a telephone panel in the studio.

Obviously, a television studio is a far more complex, hectic setup, with much equipment and usually as many as a dozen people operating the cameras and attending to the various technological chores. On the set we had to dress appropriately and wear makeup. I wondered how George would respond to all this.

Over the preceding twelve months, he had gained so much self-confidence that he was almost looking forward to doing the television show—a big change from just a year before. Of course, that's not to say George wasn't a little nervous about his television debut. But that was normal. To ease George's fears and to help him adjust to the television studio, we decided that our first program would consist of a conversation about his ability, something along the lines of our introductory radio interview.

The taping went smoothly, and when I viewed the show later, I saw that George had a very good presence. He made an excellent appearance, answered questions clearly, and did not seem the slightest bit uneasy, despite his frequent off-camera protestations to the contrary. The director, crew, and I were all pleased with George's debut, but the real question remained: Could George actually do readings on television? There was only one way to find out.

"George," I said one day, "guess what we're going to try on TV next week?"

The look on George's face told me that he knew what was coming.

We hoped that George would be able to read callers over the air eventually. In the meantime, though, our first subject would appear with us in the studio. Elise was a twenty-year-old listener I had met several months before. A very pretty young woman, she appeared to be the picture of health, but as we became friends, she told me that she suffered from systemic lupus erythematosus, a chronic hereditary disease that affects the body's autoimmune system. In those who have the disease, a uniquely shaped white blood cell, the LE cell, causes the body's immune system, which usually protects against invading organisms, to turn on itself, leaving its victims weakened. Lupus primarily afflicts young women and may affect virtually every organ in the body, as well as the joints. For these reasons, in the past it was frequently misdiagnosed initially as arthritis or similar diseases. There is no known cure for lupus, and the effectiveness of treatments, primarily steroids, is limited. Despite the fact that Elise's case was advanced, her appearance offered no clue of her illness: She did not have the emblematic butterfly-shaped rash on the cheeks and across the bridge of the nose.

She had heard George on the radio but had never met him. I asked if I might impose upon her to become the subject of George's first TV reading, and, after some reluctance, she agreed. We made sure that George and Elise did not meet or even see each other before the taping. Only when the show's director called for us to take our places on the set did she join us. She sat between George and me.

"Good evening, welcome to *Psychic Channels*. I'm Joel Martin, this is Psychic Medium George, and tonight we will experiment in the world of unexplained phenomena as George attempts to receive communications from spirits on the other side of the veil. Our subject is a young woman whom George is meeting at this very moment for the first time. Her name is Elise."

Turning to my right, I said, "Hello, Elise. Is what I said accurate? Have you ever met or spoken to George before?"

"No," she replied. "I've never talked to him."

George, already absorbed in his automatic writing, was not looking at either of us. A camera was positioned behind and to the side of George so that the audience could see him scribbling across one sheet of paper after another. From where I sat, it was impossible to decipher exactly what George had written.

"I see blood around you," George began. "Do you have a health problem involving the blood?"

"Yes," Elise answered.

"Does it affect the joints and the bones? Arthritis-like?"

"Yes."

George drew a simple sketch showing two bones, and, where they met, he made several short vertical lines to indicate the connective tissue. He held the drawing up to the camera, and Elise acknowledged that the sketch accurately represented what he had described as "arthritis-like."

"Is something wrong with a certain cell in the bloodstream? Something like leukemia, but it is not leukemia."

"Yes."

George drew a second picture of what he was seeing psychically. The drawing showed a blood vessel with blood cells going through it. He drew the blood cells as small ovals, but among the ovals was a much larger, peculiarly shaped cell. He held up this drawing to the camera for another close-up.

"I'm being told that the disease is rare," George remarked, "but I can't make out the name. Whatever they're telling me from the other side, I cannot figure it out. I don't think it's a condition I've ever heard of before."

"Yes, it is rare," Elise replied.

"I see an iron deficiency."

"This is probably true. I haven't eaten much for the past two weeks. I was sick."

"Do you take the name Lydia?"

"Yes."

"Mother vibration. Grandmother?"

"My great-grandmother," Elise corrected.

"She's saying that she had the same illness you have."

"I know," she said, "my grandmother just told me that a couple of months ago. No one else knew. She felt guilty about it and told only me. I may have inherited the disease from my great-grandmother. My grandmother made me swear never to tell anyone else."

"Did your great-grandmother die young from this disease?"

"Yes, in her mid-thirties, from a heart attack caused by the disease."

"She's guiding you and says keep dealing with your illness the way you are. Don't let the doctors treat you without good cause. Be very cautious about what they say," George said, passing on Elise's great-grandmother's advice.

"I will."

"Do you take the name Helen? I think I hear Helen speaking another language, so it is hard to understand her."

"Yes."

"Mother vibration."

"Grandmother."

"She sounds like she's speaking French," George remarked.

"Yes."

"Do you have severe pain?"

"Yes."

"I see a particular cell in your bloodstream doing something it's not supposed to do. It's not a clot. And it's doing the opposite of what it's supposed to do."

"Yes, it's a white blood cell, which is a kind of leukocyte that destroys its own kind. The body destroys itself. The cells cause the self-destruction of the body."

A number of other personal communications for Elise, unrelated to her health, followed. All were accurate. They went to relatives and included one complex and correct message from Elise's late grandmother about a family inheritance. Then George concluded the reading, saying, "That's it. The energy is fading now."

Following the taping, several members of the program crew cautiously approached Elise to ask her if what they had just witnessed was real. Several were visibly touched by George's reading. Elise assured them that the demonstration was genuine, that this was her first personal contact with any psychic or medium, and certainly with George. She also admitted to being as stunned by his accuracy as they were.

As usual, George seemed unimpressed by his display, and later told me that he thought he could have done better. In fact, though, it was a remarkable reading, even for him. Now that it was clear that George's abilities were not compromised by the busy television studio setting, we could proceed.

George's reading of Elise was quite typical of the kinds of communications he receives. Spirit communications come through George via clairaudience, clairvoyance (of psychic symbols or projections), sympathetic pain, and clairsentience. He may receive the message through one method or a combination of several or, as in Elise's case, any or all of them. George then "records" his various impressions through automatic writing. While in some instances he may receive an important symbol—such as the star of David during my first reading—in others he uses the writing to take notes on what he's seeing, hearing, and feeling.

There are no "rules" (at least none that we know of) as to which spirits communicate, when, why, how, or what their messages concern. In describing George's readings, we rely on such words as "usually" and "generally," because, while taken as a whole the readings do follow certain patterns, the spirits are individuals, and there are always exceptions. Most readings involve several spirits. One spirit may wish to deliver greetings, offer advice to the subject, or apologize for something he or she did while on earth, while another may wish to offer just a breezy hello or congratulations on an event as relatively mundane as the purchase of a new home.

Understandably, the most valued piece of information in any message is the spirit's name. For many, this is the final, definitive proof of George's authenticity. Often the spirit "speaks" his or her name, which George receives clairaudiently.

But the spirits don't always give such simple information so easily. During a public reading at a local school, George called out to a woman in the rear of the room, "A young woman close to you passed?"

"Yes," the woman answered.

"Tragically. Vehicle-involved."

"Yes."

"Is this a daughter to you?"

"Yes."

"Around twenty, or early twenties."

"Yes."

"Ma'am," George began, "no disrespect. I know this sounds funny, and I don't mean it to be, but I see the cartoon character Wendy the Witch circling your head."

"Yes, George, I understand," the woman answered. "My daughter's name was Wendy. She was twenty-two when she was killed in an auto accident."

Another time, George said, "Woman close to you passed on."

"Yes."

"Sister, that's what I'm hearing."

"Yes."

"I see a spice rack."

"I don't understand," the subject replied.

"The spirit is telling me," George said, "that the spice rack is a symbol for her name."

"Oh, I understand now," the subject replied. "She was called Ginger."

At times it seems as though the spirits "reach into" George's mind and call up an image whose meaning he would understand.

"Has your mother passed?" George inquired of a young man in one reading.

"Yes," he replied.

Suddenly George saw a scene from one of his favorite operas, Verdi's *La Traviata*. It was the first act, in which the character Violetta sings her main aria. Assuming that the spirit was indicating that she was of Italian descent or perhaps had enjoyed the opera in her mortal life, George didn't bother offering this information aloud. After the reading, however, he asked the subject for his mother's name. The subject replied, "My mother's name was Violet. In Italian, that's Violetta." So the spirit was there, and her message was correct. The problem was in the receiver, George.

Considering how easily George can become confused by the roundabout way in which some spirits communicate simple messages, it's amazing how often he is accurate. One day George had no idea how to interpret a vision of Disney World. He knew that it applied to the spirit of a man who was trying to give George a clue as to his name, but where did Disney World fit in? Following his logic, George tried to think of who—or what—associated with the amusement park would have a man's name.

"Was his name Donald?" George asked.

"No."

"Was his name Mickey?"

"No."

"Was his name Walt?"

"No."

George was stymied; everything else he'd given out was acknowledged as correct, and he'd exhausted all the obvious possibilities. "Okay," George said in frustration. "I give up. What was his name?"

"Orlando." Only then did George make the connection: Disney World is in Orlando, Florida.

When George saw American Indians dancing around a male subject's head, he asked, "Is there any reason why I'd see American Indians circling you?"

"Not that I know of," the subject replied.

"You're not a native American Indian?"

"No."

"Why do I see American Indians circling you in a war dance?"

"My last name is Geronimo," the subject offered, "like the American Indian chief."

George sometimes picks up names through a vision of a

famous person who had that name. For example, a vision of
Theodore Roosevelt usually means that the spirit's name was
Ted or Teddy. But it isn't always that simple. George may be
shown Franklin Delano Roosevelt when a spirit wants to communicate to the subject that there is "nothing to fear but fear
itself," one of Roosevelt's most famous quotes. George has
seen Roy Rogers for a spirit named Roy, a scene from the film
Gigi for a spirit named Maurice (Chevalier), Rudolph the Red-
Nosed Reindeer for a spirit named Rudolph, a Peter Paul
Mounds candy bar for a spirit named either Peter or Paul, or
the spirit's name spelled out in letters that appeared to float
before George "like skywriting." Again, context is everything.

We can assume that spirits retain some sense of humor.
George once got a spirit's name when he showed George a
frankfurter that he recognized as coming from Nathan's, a
famous East Coast fast-food chain, over the head of his
nephew, the subject. The spirit was Uncle Nathan.

One time, a widow's husband's spirit kept singing, "Every
little breeze seems to whisper Louise." It made no sense to
George, but when he told the woman what he heard, she
laughed and said that her husband's pet dog was called Louise.

"Sometimes," George says philosophically, "you just can't
see the forest for the trees. My mind may reject the most
logical interpretation and go for something far more complex. I
don't know why. I guess it's just human nature or my inability
to believe sometimes that things can be presented so easily.
More than once I've rejected or disregarded a spirit who claims
to have a very common name, like John or Mary. I'll say to the
spirit, 'Come on, everybody has a deceased Aunt Mary. You
don't have to be psychic to know that.' But every time I've
done that, sure enough that is the spirit's name. To this day, no
one is as skeptical about this as I am."

This raises the question of how the quality of George's
messages might change if, for example, he were not well-read
and exceptionally intelligent to begin with. Would his medical
readings be more specific if his knowledge of medicine was
more extensive? Would he be able to deliver additional information if he understood all the foreign tongues he sometimes
hears the spirits speaking in? Would his repertoire of symbols
and references be different if he'd been raised in a different

part of the United States, with a different religion, or in another country altogether?

How and why do some entities transmit their messages clairaudiently rather than by projection or visuals in spirit or symbol forms? That is as mysterious and important a question as any that could be raised about the mediumistic process. The symbols pose an especially fascinating, complex, and enigmatic problem that calls for further study and careful scientific investigation if the process is to be better understood. Why do spirits transmit messages through some of the most cryptic representations imaginable, which then require careful interpretation? Do they choose which methods to use? Do they have any control? Are the symbols part of a universal language? Does the repetition of these symbols from those who spoke foreign languages when on earth point to a set of universal symbols or a form of interdimensional telepathy that transcends all spoken language? If the symbols are communicated from the other side to George's subconscious and then interpreted by his conscious and rational mind, is the process similar to the interpretation of dream symbols? Or, as one psychologist suggested, more akin to a psychotherapist's interpretation of a patient's language, dreams, and so on? Why do the spirits sometimes communicate their messages directly but at other times use symbols?

We know that the spirits frequently transmit their messages by clairaudience, as well as in visible form, but most often it is a combination of the two, along with some clairsentience and sympathetic pain. When the transmission is clairaudient, George listens patiently and writes down what he psychically hears.

"The voices usually sound far away, like from opposite ends of a tunnel, and yet the two worlds run parallel," George explains. "Sometimes you can hear the chatter of five discarnate entities at one time. It's like several people in a room all speaking at the same time, or on a party line. Generally, they wait their turn, or I separate them. Sometimes the entity with the most forceful personality will dominate. But usually each speaks for several minutes, and then they let the others take their turn communicating from the other side, to loved ones here."

Spirits who wish to give out information about their cause of physical death can do so through clairaudience. George will hear gunshots or the sounds of an auto crash, an explosion, or a tree crashing if these sounds were related to or were heard at the time of the spirit's physical demise. He may hear more pleasant sounds, such as pealing wedding bells "rung" by a spirit telling of a celebration or offering congratulations. He might also hear music, which can indicate that the spirit or the subject is involved with music; or it might have symbolic meaning—for example, that there is a need for harmony in someone's life.

Through spoken words, George gets clues about the spirit's state of mind and often picks up on such idiosyncrasies as tone of voice or particular expressions. It's not unusual for a subject to say of a spirit who has communicated clairaudiently, "That's just how he would say it," or "That was one of her favorite expressions."

Although we have yet to discover how these processes occur, George and others have theorized that however and wherever the message is received in the brain, the "normal" auditory channels and process of hearing are irrelevant. When George's hearing was impaired by a serious ear infection, the communications' clarity and volume intensified. The transmissions are not always clear and are sometimes hampered by what George terms "interference." "It could be compared to the interference we sometimes experience when listening to a distant radio station," he explains. "In one reading I remember hearing from the other side a spirit calling out what I thought was the name Bessy. So I repeated it to the subject. It turned out the name was Becky."

One summer evening George was in the middle of a reading when a bolt of lightning crashed down from the sky during an electrical storm and cut his clairaudient reception. "The communications from the other side stopped for several minutes. It was as if the ability was cut. I could not hear or receive anything. Then a short while later, the ability resumed and the communications were working fine again."

The incident opens up many questions about the nature of the energy on which the communications travel. What is it? Is it electrical or electromagnetic? Current knowledge and technology have been unable to solve these riddles so far, but tests conducted later did suggest some interesting paths of future investigation.

Generally, the spirits seem most concerned with making themselves known to the subjects, and they use some very remarkable methods to get their information across. During a reading on the TV program, George discerned the spirit of a young man whose message went to a woman in the studio audience. He correctly identified the spirit as the woman's late brother, but he was confused because all the information came through exclusively in visual symbols.

"I wonder why he's not speaking to me," George said. "I don't know why I'm not hearing anything at all from your brother." Nonetheless, the reading continued, with George receiving everything through visual symbols, including what appeared to be sign language.

At the end of the reading, the woman told George that her brother had been mute. Could he have had the ability to communicate with George clairaudiently after death? Or was he intentionally not "speaking" to let his sister know that he was her brother, presumably the only spirit who would come across mute? We do not know. To this and questions like it, the spirits either cannot or will not reveal their secrets to George.

The visual component of George's messages are psychic projections. These fall into two categories: spirits and symbols. How does George know what projections are spirits rather than symbols? The spirits show themselves to him as actual manifestations, which he literally sees as they appear before him. Sometimes they appear as ethereal beings or occasionally— perhaps through sufficient energy, we suppose—as more solid forms. This may occur when George's specific physical description of the form will help the subject identify the spirit. The entities manifest anywhere from several seconds to as long as several minutes.

During a group demonstration at a local high school, George spotted a man for whom he'd recently done a private reading. The man's nine-year-old daughter had been brutally assaulted and murdered, and, although almost everyone who has a reading with George is comforted, this man's understandable bitterness about his daughter was made clear in a cynical, challenging attitude. In front of the entire group, the man said to George, "If it's really my daughter's spirit, what was she buried with?"

"A teddy bear," George replied without hesitation.

"Yeah? And what was around its neck?"

"A ribbon."

"And what color was the ribbon?"

George closed his eyes for a few seconds, then replied, "Red."

The man slumped into his chair, then said softly, "Thank you, George." Later he told me that George was correct and that there was no other way that he could have known those details.

What the spirits intend to communicate by materializing is not always clear to George or the subject. In one of our early readings, George accurately described my late grandmother in such detail that even I could not confirm everything until later, when I spoke to my mother. At one point George said he saw my grandmother as an elderly woman sitting in a chair. He remarked that she appeared to have only one leg, and assumed that she must have had an amputation. That didn't make sense to me, for I knew that she hadn't. My mother, however, knew that what George had been referring to was my grandmother's lifelong habit of sitting with one foot tucked under her long skirts and only one leg showing.

Symbols, on the other hand, are just that. Transmitted from the other side, their purpose is to provide clues as to the spirit's message or identity. Like symbols in a dream, or a secret code, the spirit symbols often require "translation" by George's logical, rational mind. Some of the common symbols are used repeatedly and generally have only one or two possible meanings—the white lace celebration that often indicates a wedding or birth, the offering of roses in apology or congratulations—while others are unique and personal, relevant to and understood only by the subject and the spirit. The "language" of the symbols is similar to a verbal language in that any word, or symbol, can have several meanings, depending on its context. The information we have collected thus far about psychic symbols forms a primitive sort of glossary that is constantly expanding.

One example of a personal message with dual meanings that only the subject would know or understand occurred in 1982. I had just finished taping an interview with a middle-aged Englishman. He was very distinguished in appearance, and anyone meeting him for the first time would probably assume that he was an upper-class London businessman. Nothing in his manner of dress or speech betrayed his true roots—working-class Liverpool of the forties and fifties. I asked the man, whom we'll call Justin, if he cared to meet George. Justin was interested in mediumship in general, though that was not what we had discussed in our interview. He agreed to speak with George that evening. When George arrived, I simply said, "I'd like you to meet a friend of ours from London."

The two had no sooner exchanged greetings than George was staring at the man with a look of puzzlement.

"Since my friend is returning to Europe in the morning, is there anything you can tell him about himself now?" I asked.

George immediately began his automatic writing, but as he looked at Justin, his eyes widened. "There's a spirit of a man behind you. He's wearing wire-rimmed glasses, and he's holding a guitar—" George stopped, as if he couldn't believe his own eyes. "Wait a minute . . . it looks like . . . no, it can't be." He stopped again.

"What is it, George?" I asked.

"It looks like John Lennon," George replied, astonished.

"It does?" I asked.

"Sir, is there any reason why I see John Lennon's spirit behind you? He's saying, 'I know him.'"

"Yes," Justin replied.

"Did you personally know John Lennon?" George inquired.

"Yes, I did."

Justin then asked if he could speak with George in private. They went into an empty room, and when Justin emerged about half an hour later, he said that George had been very accurate. Then he added, "George said that John's spirit was telling me, 'Remember the ice, remember the ice.' He was reluctant at first to tell me that. He said he heard John's spirit saying something that George didn't think made sense. George seemed to be talking to the spirit. He was telling the entity which was invisible to me, of course, 'What? I won't say that. It sounds silly.' Then he said John's spirit was insistent. So George finally said to me, 'Remember the ice.'"

"Did it mean anything special?" I asked.

"Yes," Justin replied. "The first time John Lennon and I met, a long time ago, was at a party. When I arrived, he and the other guests were having fun by throwing ice cubes down each other's backs. That is the first thing I remember about John, even before we were formally introduced. The last time I heard from John was when he rang me up in England from his home in New York City. John was very enthused to play over the telephone for me a new song called 'Walking on Thin Ice.' He was especially proud of Yoko Ono's work with him. 'Walking on Thin Ice'—it was their last together." Justin's voice trailed off into a sad silence.

Generally, symbols play a very large role in the messages George receives. Some experts who have observed George believe that the symbols are somehow projected into his subconscious mind and are then processed in his conscious mind, much like dreams. It's not uncommon for a spirit to offer a symbol that George will overanalyze, or interpret according to that symbol's meaning in previous readings or its personal meaning to him, and be told, sometimes quite sharply, by the spirit to basically mind his own business and just deliver the message.

In fact, one of the most common problems George has in interpretations is that he often assumes that a symbol's meaning is consistent from one reading to another. Roses, for example, are symbols of apology, thanks, or congratulations in the majority of readings. However, that doesn't preclude their use in relaying a more personal meaning. To an elderly woman, they were part of her late husband's message about a rosebush he'd planted for her; for a young man, they predicted his lover's apology (which he received three days later, written in a greeting card bearing a picture of roses); in another reading they symbolized the spirit's name, Rose.

Receiving messages through symbols is often a time-consuming, frustrating task. George has expressed his fear that people might feel he is "fishing," "guessing," or "playing twenty questions" when he hands out an unfamiliar symbol or a message that just doesn't seem to make sense to him. Usually, however, once the meaning of the first symbol is confirmed, it establishes a context for the reading—or at least for one spirit's message—and everything else generally falls into place.

Because the spirits seem to present George with symbols that they know he will understand (for example, the scene from *La Traviata*), and because George often does have to interpret for himself, what happens when a spirit communicates some message that is personally abhorrent to George? Do his personal religious beliefs in any way color his interpretations of the messages he receives? Though George is deeply religious, he does not proselytize. However, there appear to be both spirits and symbols that are clearly religious in nature and that provide him with communications for subjects of readings. Often these manifest themselves to George as the spirits of saints. But they are purely for his personal interpretation, and the subject need not be Roman Catholic, or even Christian, for these projections to manifest. George describes the saints who appear to him in spirit form as "the real thing. It's quite a sight, really. The saints appear with burning, transparent white light surrounding them. It's like I'm looking at unmelted snow on fire."

For example, the spirit of St. Francis of Assisi, who devoted his life to the care of animals, indicates to George that the subject is cruel to animals or an unsportsmanlike hunter. Even though George disdains hunting and loves animals, he does not allow his personal reaction to the content of a message or what it reveals about either the subject or the spirit to influence him. George has been warned more than once by the other side to keep out of the readings, to not become emotionally involved.

Once George saw the spirit of St. Florian psychically pin a medal on a man he was reading. To the individual, of course, the gesture was invisible, but its meaning soon became clear to George.

"I see St. Florian around. Are you a fireman?" George asked.

"Yes."

"Did you recently perform a specific act of bravery or heroism?"

"Yes."

"It involved a rescue of someone from a fire, they're telling me."

"Yes."

When George did a reading for a former Franciscan brother, he saw a spirit, which he recognized as St. Paschal Baylon, a sixteenth-century Spaniard whose physical body has never decomposed (an example of an unexplained phenomenon known as incorruptibility). George could clairaudiently hear the saint saying, "I am this man's guardian angel saint." George told the man that the saint was also saying, "You chose my name in your religious life as a brother."

"Yes," the man confirmed. "My name was Brother Baylon when I was in the religious order."

When a saint appears, the spirit may be telling us that the saint's association or significance applies to him, to the subject, or to someone close to the subject. For example, St. Peregrine's appearance would suggest that someone—the spirit, the subject, someone near the subject—has had or will have cancer. If George views the spirit of St. Lucy, patroness of the blind, or St. Clare, patroness against sore eyes, and receives a message about a subject's health, it indicates concern about an eye condition. George's seeing St. Joseph, patron of the happy death, will tell the subject that the spirit passed peacefully to the other side. St. Patrick's appearance usually indicates that someone concerned is of Irish descent, though one time it referred to the subject's father (who may not have been Irish), who had died forty-two years earlier and was named Patrick. When George sees the spirit of St. Anthony dressed in gray, it indicates poor health in the present or future. When St. Anthony appears in black, it is a sign of physical death around the subject—the death of a loved one on earth or the subject himself. If the forewarning of the passing is meant for the individual, George will not give it out, unless he is told by the other side that the subject can avert that fate through his own actions. Overall, though, it is very rare for George to receive any message regarding an individual's demise. He believes that, in such circumstances, he is not meant to know.

One saint whose appearance is usually welcome is St. Gerard, the patron saint of expectant mothers. But the saint's message cannot always be easily acknowledged. In the course of reading a young woman on the radio show, George asked her if she was pregnant or had children. She emphatically denied both, saying that parenthood was the furthest thing from her and her husband's minds. George explained to us that he saw St. Gerard and what he believed it meant, but in the face of the caller's denials he had to let it go. A couple of months later, the woman called us at the station with the news that she'd just discovered she was pregnant and had been at the time of her reading.

The symbols appear before George much the way images appear to us on a television screen or as visions in his mind. Sometimes he sees a single object or symbol, while in other instances he may see a whole scene, like a scene from a movie, as in the case of the murdered pianist Jean, or Ellen, who had been so badly burned in a fire. The symbols may strike George as being so off-base or just so silly that he can't believe them. An interesting aspect of the symbols is that they often refer to or play on familiar clichés or figures of speech. For example, a ripe apple would indicate that the subject is "ripe," or ready for something.

Of all the means the spirits use to communicate, sympathetic pain is the most "testable." Because we know that pain results from nerve stimulation and the brain's perception of that stimulation, we can detect evidence of pain using currently available technology, such as thermography (the process whereby a heat-sensitive instrument registers differences in body heat caused by injury, illness, or disease in various locations). Sympathetic pain occurs very rapidly, lasting just as long as it takes George's brain to register the type of pain and the area of the body affected. Somehow, the spirits stimulate part of George's brain, which allows him to feel the sensation. Sympathetic pain may refer to past, present, or future illness or injury and is the means by which George obtains information in many health-related readings.

One such reading was set up by a physician. His patient, a young woman with no visible signs of illness, would be diagnosed by George. Only the woman, her physician, and her mother knew of her illness. She was instructed not to speak with George at all, not even to say hello, and certainly not to acknowledge messages. George proceeded to correctly describe and sense the specific physical locations of the disease. The doctor confirmed each point as accurate. Then George described a symbolic vision that he was certain was being given to him as a clue about the woman's disease.

"It's a scene from the movie *Resurrection*," George said.

"Can you be more specific?" the doctor asked.

"It's the scene in which the woman with the healing powers cures a crippling disease called dys—, dys—, dystonia."

"That is correct, George. This woman suffers from dystonia musculorum deformans."

Here, even though the name of the disease came to George through a vision of a movie with which he was familiar, the information about the patient's physical suffering came exclusively through his sensations of sympathetic pain.

The most fascinating information that George has obtained through sympathetic pain concerns what it feels like to die, physically. Describing the sensations of a man who died after being struck by lightning, George said, "My body feels as if it has gone numb, but at the same time I feel like I've received a tremendous electric shock. I feel both sensations at the same time. It's very painful."

In another reading, George relayed, "I feel tremendous pain and pressure. It's as if my entire body is being compressed. Literally squashed. I feel like my internal organs are bursting. It's a horrible feeling. In fact, this is one of the worst episodes of sympathetic pain I've ever experienced." The spirit was that of a man who had been killed when he fell into a shaft and was crushed by a freight elevator car. Another spirit, who had drowned, also communicated it through George via sympathetic pain. "I feel like I'm filling up with some kind of fluid. My whole body is overcome with a chill, and I feel a bursting sensation. It's as if my insides are filling up and bursting. At the same time, I can't catch my breath."

More common causes of physical death are communicated as follows:

—Heart attack: sharp pains over George's heart.

—Stroke: numbness in George's arms.

—Coma: George feels a painless death.

—Sudden death: George describes being "shocked out of the body." This is typical of a spirit whose physical death was instantaneous, following a car accident, for example.

—Choking, strangulation: George feels as if his air is being cut off and he can't catch his breath.

—Stabbing: sharp, piercing pains in various parts of his body.

—Drug overdose: George gets the feeling that something "foreign" is going through his body, often accompanied by sensations of nausea, dizziness, and faintness.

When George felt a painful crash of something onto his head and heard what sounded like a tree limb breaking and falling simultaneously, the subject confirmed that her nephew had been fatally struck on the head by a tree limb during a storm. Another time George said he felt badly bruised all over his body, followed by a painful sensation, as if all of his bones were being crushed. The spirit turned out to be a young woman who'd been beaten and bludgeoned before her killer hurled her body from a bridge overpass onto the sharp rocks below.

Not surprisingly, in the last year or so George has done a number of readings for people whose lives have been touched by AIDS. During a reading on television, George told a young female subject that he felt "blood cells going crazy" and had difficulty breathing, "like pneumonia." He then described feeling his lungs fill with fluid, followed by general sensations of pain, weakness, and finally coma. After that, George told us that the spirit was spelling out the cause of his death. "He just spelled out the word AIDS in front of me," he said, which the woman confirmed.

George continued, "The spirit says he crossed and he's okay. He's glad it's over with. He says he's happy on the other side. He's fine and at peace. He's freed now from suffering. He says there was a purpose for him to go through what he did and then pass on. He's fulfilled a mission and thanks you for being such a good friend to him right after the point of transition known as death. Because he says he's not dead."

Obviously, loved ones of those who do come through with sympathetic pain can find these parts of the readings upsetting. However, the spirit's message is almost always one of comfort. This is a typical statement George receives from a spirit following such an exchange:

"The spirit is telling me from the other side that he did not suffer long. He's saying there was only momentary pain and then he left his body, and the pain was gone. He's telling me he was brought into the light and now he has adjusted to the other side. He wants you to know that he is at peace."

Seven

Having known George for a couple of years now, everyone on my show was accustomed to witnessing some rather interesting things. Although George long ago had learned to block out messages when he is not doing readings, there still are times when he is literally overcome by what he sees, hears, or senses about someone.

My friend Joan surprised me when she called to ask if we could meet sometime in the next couple of days. Joan said only that she had something to tell me, and we agreed to meet for lunch at her hotel. We really hadn't kept in touch since she and her husband moved to the West Coast two years before. I assumed that she was on Long Island to visit her parents, who still resided there, and she said nothing that would indicate otherwise.

The morning after Joan called George underwent a series of tests designed by a computer specialist to determine the probability that George could accurately foresee groups of numbers both before and after they were randomly generated by a computer. In other words, could the computer aid us in determining if George was precognitive (able to predict which numbers would be generated before the fact) or telepathic (able to know, without using any of the usual five senses, which numbers had been generated). For the two precognition tests, the specialist established that George had one chance in a hundred of guessing the correct number. Out of twenty randomly generated numbers, George could be expected to correctly guess four. In fact, however, he was correct in predicting nine out of the twenty numbers in both the first and the second rounds of tests. In the tests for telepathy—a paranormal ability we had long suspected that George was no better at than the average person—he scored lower than average on the first round (he got three of an expected or average four) and slightly higher than average on the second round (five, one more than the average four).

These tests, while preliminary, taken along with the information we'd collected in the actual readings and post-reading interviews, confirmed that George was not reading minds. Where did the information come from? We still could not say. Now we could add one more item to the list of what George's ability was *not*.

Following the tests, I invited George along to my lunch with Joan. We left for Long Island, and at the hotel, I rang Joan's room on the house phone and said we would be waiting in the lobby. No sooner had I hung up than George asked me if my friend had just experienced a great tragedy. I replied that I honestly did not know. Then we saw Joan descending the carpeted staircase into the lobby. He discreetly whispered to me, "I see black all around her. That's my symbol that there has been a tragedy or death. I'm sure of it."

George's remark was unsettling, but since there was no tactful way to confirm or deny it, I let it pass. Joan greeted me warmly, and I introduced her to George. She seemed genuinely happy to meet him. From all appearances, Joan was fine, but I couldn't put George's remark out of my mind.

Once we were seated in the coffee shop, Joan and I spoke, but the conversation, while pleasant, was superficial. I asked her what she'd wanted to tell me, and she replied that we'd talk about it in a while. A few minutes later, our sandwiches arrived. As soon as George took his first bite he began moving his head from side to side, all the while holding his neck and throat with one hand.

"George, what's wrong?" I screamed in panic.

"I feel like I'm choking," he answered hoarsely.

"Are you okay? Did you swallow wrong?" I asked.

Joan was now staring at George as he grabbed at his throat with both hands. He suddenly turned toward Joan and the choking seemed to be over. "Ma'am," he said, "I don't mean to intrude or seem impolite, but as soon as I saw you walk into the lobby before, I felt there was a tragedy around you. I just had to say it."

"George—" I snapped.

"No, Joel, let him speak. It's okay, George. What tragedy do you sense?" Joan asked.

George resumed tilting his head back and forth and from side to side, and his fingers moved along his throat again. "Well, to tell you the truth," he said, "it feels like someone choked. That's what I'm feeling. A choking sensation."

"Please, George, continue. What do you feel it is?" Joan inquired with no discernible trace of emotion.

"A woman close to you pass?"

"Yes."

"Mother vibration. Has your mother passed on?"

"Yes."

"Did she pass tragically?"

"Yes."

"Recently," George stated.

"Yes."

"Did she choke, somehow?"

"Yes."

George paused. He was responding to some sound or voice that only he could hear. "She's saying, 'I passed by choking, but—' Wait. I hear a crashing sound. Something came crashing down."

"Yes."

"Wait. I think I understand what she's saying now. She's showing me what she means."

"What, George?"

"Did she take her own life?" George asked.

"Yes."

"That's what she shows me. She committed suicide."

"Yes." Joan was pale but otherwise expressionless.

"George," I asked, stunned by the news, "what was the crashing sound you heard psychically?"

"Was your mother standing on something when she took her life?"

"Yes."

"Because it sounds like something she was standing on came crashing down. Furniture? A table or chair."

"Yes."

George again placed his hands back on his throat and twisted his head from side to side.

"Joan," I said, "I didn't know any of this. What happened?"

"That's what I wanted to tell you today because you knew my mother. It happened only last week. George, can you tell me why she took her life? Does she tell you?"

"Forgive me if I'm treading anywhere I shouldn't. But did your parents have a difficult marriage?"

"Yes."

"She says, 'I did it to get even.' I don't know what she means," George added apologetically.

"Yes, I understand that," Joan acknowledged.

"Your mother is saying she was very depressed. She couldn't take any more. There seems to have been a great deal of friction with her husband—your father. There was a great amount of arguing, disagreement, shouting, and tension. It seems that they fought badly."

"Did your father find her?"

"Yes."

"That's what she says. But she knows now this was not the way. She's apologizing for what she did."

Joan just closed her eyes and nodded in reply.

"Did she or you lose a dog?"

"Yes."

"Was it her dog?"

"Yes."

"Because she says the dog was there to greet her when she arrived on the other side. That was a comfort to her."

"Yes, she loved the dog. Does she call out to my father?"

"Well, just to say that she should not have done this as a way to even the score, so to speak. She understands the burden he and the family carry now because of this."

"Yes."

"Do you have a sister?"

"Yes."

"Your mother is calling out to a daughter. Younger than you. She's concerned for her, especially."

"Yes."

"She's sending your sister the same message: 'This was not the way, suicide was not the answer.'"

I interrupted reluctantly. "George, I thought people who take their own lives, suicide victims, don't progress or adjust quickly or well on the other side."

"Yes," he answered, "that's true. But she seems to have done well, considering. That surprises me, too."

"Joan," I said, "I had no idea about your parents' marital difficulties. What was George talking about when he said your mother was getting even with your father?"

"Mom and Dad were getting along very badly. Arguments and fights. When Dad got very angry he would threaten that one day he would kill himself, and he would say that when Mother came home one night from her office she would find him hanging. That was *his* threat to her. He said that would make her feel guilty. She turned the tables on him; she did what he only threatened. Dad came home, after a particularly ugly fight they had earlier that day, and he found her hanging."

George and I sat in silence, moved by Joan's tragic story.

"Is she at peace?" Joan asked quietly.

"Yes, remarkably, considering the circumstances. She's remorseful for what she did, of course; she apologizes. But she seems to be adjusting well, given the situation. She says her dog meeting her helped make the transition easier."

Joan smiled.

"Pray for her," George said.

"Okay."

"I hope I didn't say anything to upset you. I know you didn't expect me today."

"No, George, quite the opposite. You've been a great comfort. You answered several questions I was wondering about."

The three of us talked for a while longer before it was time to go. As we got ready to leave, I noticed George's automatic writing on the paper placemat. I must have become so accustomed to his doing automatic writing that apparently, without even thinking, I had handed him my pen during the reading.

In his reading for Joan, George was typically accurate. We knew that George was correct most of the time, so we turned our attention to trying to establish patterns and repeatability.

One of the biggest problems faced by parapsychologists, and mediums in particular, when dealing with the scientific community is the question of proof. What really does prove that what George is doing is what he says it is? If he delivers a thousand genuine messages, one each to a thousand people, does this comprise sufficient evidence? At this point, he had done approximately six hundred readings for anonymous strangers over the radio and on television (and countless others in public group readings and private readings), but for some critics that still was not enough. Yet such large numbers alone ruled out guessing, and even ESP or telepathy. In one test conducted live over the radio by a psychologist, the odds that George could correctly determine two facts about each spirit—its sex and its relationship to the caller (father, sister, etc.)—in thirteen calls was 1 in 6,044. On that show, George's accuracy was the usual 85 to 90 percent.

But what if George, doing readings for people who were in some way related to the communicating spirit, or spirits, got essentially the same information but in different readings, for different subjects, over a period of time? Considering the number of readings George does, even if he saw all of these subjects in person, he could not possibly guess the same messages correctly with different subjects. No offense to George, but like many people with psychic abilities, his memory is not good enough to allow him to remember information from one reading to the next.[1]

Over the summer and into the early autumn of 1982, George did a series of three readings that served as a "test" of sorts, although they were not all planned. Two of the three readings were done on the live call-in radio show, and neither George nor I knew the callers. The third, a private reading, involved four of the spirit's family members and one of his friends. Back in June, George had done a private reading for the spirit's

---

1. An amusing example of this occurred when George did a reading for co-author Patricia Romanowski. At this point, he had known her for over a year and had been speaking with and seeing her regularly in connection with the writing of this book. In the middle of his reading for her, he stopped himself and laughed. "I can't believe this, but I was just getting ready to tell you that I saw books around you and ask you if you had anything to do with writing. Wake up, George!" he said, admonishing himself.

parents; the couple did not attend any of the three subsequent readings. Only one subject—the spirit's older brother—participated in two of the readings. And one subject never knew the spirit and knew of his family only after his death. The common thread among them was that each had some relationship with David Licata, the young hit-and-run victim whose story opens this book.

Following George's initial reading for David's parents, Barbara and John Licata, he had no contact with the family. Almost a month had passed between then and the evening of July 4, when an anonymous young man called.

"Hello," he said.

"Do you recall a friend crossed over through a car or violent type of accidental death?" George asked.

"Yes."

"Before the other lady came on [referring to one of two female callers who preceded this young man], somebody came in and said, 'The first male caller will go to me.' That would be that 'I passed on in a violent car accident or some type of violent passing.' Is it a car accident?"

"Sort of."

"A vehicle involved, in any case?"

"Yes."

"Very close to you?"

"Yes."

"By blood."

"Yes."

"Why is there something different about it? Without telling me, can you understand what he means? There are question marks about it."

"Yes."

"Was he hit with a car?"

"Yes."

"That's what he says. Hit-and-run. Was it hit-and-run?"

"Yes."

"A young person?"

"Yes."

"Is it your son?"

"No."

"Like a son to you?"

"No."

"He keeps on saying— Does he have a son?"

"No."

"I don't know why he keeps saying that. I'll let it go. Not too long ago, this happened?"

"No."

"He is related, though. I can't remember if I asked you that."

"Yes."

"Have you not gotten over it?"

"Not really."

"Because he says, 'Get over it, I'm not dead. I'm over here.' Why does he keep saying 'son'? Do you have a son?"

"No."

"I don't know what he means. He keeps emphasizing something about a son. . . . Are you in contact with his parents?"

"Yes."

"Can they handle this? Then I'll say that. He's asking that you tell his parents that you've heard him. That he's okay. That he's on the other side. The name David mean anything to you?"

"Yes."

"Is that him?"

"Yes."

"That's what he says. 'My name is David.' He says, 'Please tell my parents that you have heard from me and that I'm over here and that I'm fine.' Was he very fond of animals?"

"Yes."

"Because I keep seeing a lot of animals around me. And he tells me he works with animals on the other side. Animals and children. Very close to his mother?"

"Yes."

"Are you his brother?"

"Yes."

"That's what it is. That clears it, then. He says, 'You're my brother.' Also he knows there's a lot of hostility in you about— He says do you know who did this to him?"

"Yes."

"It was a male?"

"Yes."

"But he forgives him. He says, 'Why can't you do the same?'"

"It's hard."

"I know, but that's what he's saying from the other side. He also—something else he's trying to say. I'm losing it. Is your mother's maternal grandmother still on this side of the veil, on earth?"

"Yes." (Note, however, that David's mother's maternal grandmother is Rose, and that she was in fact deceased. In this and other readings, David calls out to Lucie, who is David's maternal grandmother, who is still living. This is the kind of error that George has trouble clearing when the subject is nervous and answers incorrectly, not uncommon for people who become self-conscious knowing that they are on the radio.)

"Were they very, very close?"

"Yes."

"He calls out to her. 'Please tell her you've heard from me.' He's trying to remember everybody. I think you have a sister as well?"

"Yes."

"He's trying to keep everybody in mind so nobody's forgotten. Also, was he young, a teenager?"

"Yes."

"Had to be no more than sixteen."

"Yes."

"I see a young male in front of me, no more than sixteen, a big kind of kid, though."

"Yes."

"Broad shoulders, athletic-looking?"

"Yes."

"Dark-haired?"

"Yes."

"Boy, he's really strong in this room. He's appearing right in front of me—it's wild. Are you older than·he?"

"Yes."

"Because he says you're the older brother. He says, 'Please relay all that,' and says, 'I have to go back now,' so apparently, he's signing off."

"Thank you."

After the caller hung up, George and I just looked at each other. "That was wild!" George exclaimed. "That message came on right before the second caller. Somebody just appeared to me in that room and said, 'The first male caller you

have will be for me.' The interesting thing is that he kept
emphasizing 'son,' and every time he said, 'No, it's not my
son,' I couldn't figure out what he was talking about.''

I was confused myself. "I don't understand," I said. "The
moment you heard that guy's voice, no matter who he
was—?''

"Instant apparition!" George replied. "He appeared right in
the room instantly and started giving me all the details.''

"You're telling me that the second you hear a voice that
says, 'Hello, George,' you can see instantly a violent car accident?''

"That call I could. As I said, even before you hit that call.
The second caller we had was a lady. When I heard a woman's
voice, I was to hit her with the message, and the young man
that just spoke to us came and said, 'I don't go to her. I go to
the first male caller that you receive on the line.' I heard the
male's voice, and he said, 'That's him, that's him!'"

"Immediately, you had the sense of a violent car accident?''

"Yes. Hit-and-run, he told me hit-and-run. The thing that
intrigued me, he said, 'My name is David,' and I kept ignoring
it.''

After the show we learned that the caller was Darrin Licata,
David's older brother. Darrin's call lasted only a few minutes,
less than one-tenth the time his parents had spent with George
several weeks before. Even in that brief period, however,
David's message to Darrin contained eight pieces of information that had appeared in Barbara and John's reading. In both,
David mentions and sends greetings to his maternal grandmother, mentions that there is some mystery (George remarked
on the question mark symbol) around his death, calls to his
parents, calls to his sister, indicates his approximate age, mentions that a vehicle was involved in his death, and mentions
that it was a hit-and-run.

The eighth similarity, and by far the most striking, was
David's expression of concern over the way Darrin was handling his death. In both, David mentions Darrin's anger and
hostility and asks Darrin to forgive the man who killed him, as
he has. In June, George had said to the Licatas, "He [David]
has a brother who is very hostile. David is saying he shouldn't
be hostile. 'I forgive, so should he.'" To Darrin, who, again,
was one of several anonymous callers that night, George said,

"He [David] says, 'You're my brother.' Also he knows there's a lot of hostility in you . . . he says, 'Do you know who did this to him?'" After Darrin replied yes and it was confirmed that the suspect was male, George said, "But he [David] forgives him. He says, 'Why can't you do the same?'"

On August 16, 1982, Chris arranged with George to do a group reading for five people. George had never met them before and was not introduced to them until after the reading was completed. Even I did not know who these people were. As we learned after the reading, they were Darrin Licata; his younger sister, Diana Licata; Cory, David's friend; David's maternal grandmother, Lucie; and David's Aunt Linda.

Not until we began work on this book did I learn the whole story of this particular reading. Barbara Licata, David's mother, did not attend the reading herself but drove her mother, Lucie, her children Darrin and Diana, David's friend Cory and his Aunt Linda to the radio station and dropped them off. Chris had instructed Barbara not to come inside the station to ensure that George would not see her and possibly connect her to the other five people. Conceivably, Chris could have told me who they were, but the fact is that she did not. These tests were designed to prove George's ability to me as much as to anyone else. Chris frequently arranged these readings without our knowledge, just as she would screen phone calls or help set up emergency appointments for people who wanted private readings.

But, to answer the skeptics, even if Chris had told me who they were, neither she nor I could possibly have known even a fraction of the information brought forth in the reading. In addition, despite the impact John and Barbara Licata's first private reading with George had on them, Barbara, as we will see later in the chapter, continued to pray for other signs from David that he was still alive. David's brother Darrin, for personal reasons, had been reluctant even to attend this particular group reading, and had secretly designed his own experiment to try and trick George.

That David's death continued to have a profound effect on the family is clear, and in the case of Lucie, his grandmother, her grief and the emotional intensity of the reading resulted in her answering several questions incorrectly. This fact is pointed out here, because many times the experience of the

reading itself is overwhelming and causes many subjects to
inadvertently give confused or incorrect answers. For this reason George not only permits but encourages people to record
their readings by making notes or using a portable tape recorder. In fact, he is one of the very few mediums I've known
who permits recording.

The reading began with the five sitting around a room and
George, paper and pen in hand, scribbling. George can never
predict or control who comes through, and this particular reading started off with "interference" from a spirit several of
those in the room might have identified if they'd been thinking
of her. As it was, they could not. Even so, George proceeded.

"Was she strangled? Was she injured in the throat?"

"No," they replied.

"Can anybody else take this at all? Just to make sure I'm not
getting somebody else's. Okay. It's got to stay. It means something," George said.

"Possibly a scream?" someone asked.

"It's more than that. I don't know if it goes to you. I may be
getting cut off. Anyone here know anyone who passed on with
a condition in the throat? It's got to mean something. It's too
strong. It keeps coming back. They keep insisting."

When no one could acknowledge, George said, "All right,
I'll block it."

Linda, who believed at the time that this might have been
David's friend who was murdered by strangulation shortly before David passed, made a note of it. Although she did not
know enough about the girl's case to acknowledge, she felt it
did mean something. As it turned out, she was right. The girl,
Dawn, was eighteen at the time of her passing, an important
fact, because she will later bring up the difference in her and
David's ages as a form of identifying herself in the reading.
After a pause, George began again.

"Does Francesca mean anything to you, or anybody else in
the room?" George asked Lucie.

"Yes," she replied.

"Passed on or living?"

"Passed on."

"Family member?"

"Yes."

"I felt something around you before, but I wasn't sure. She's related to you by blood?"

"Yes."

"Do I go back with her, many years?"

"Yes."

"I put her in grandmother, great-grandmother category. Not saying that that's the identity, but that's the area of family I'm going back to."

"Yes."

"I'm just curious as to how I got the symbol, how I got the name. I saw St. Frances Cabrini next to you, and her first name was actually Francesca, and they said first name goes to her," George said, pointing to Lucie. "A male close to you passed on?"

"Yes," she answered.

"She knows him? She knows him over there."

"No."

"She passed on before him?"

"Yes."

"Because she was there to meet him when he came over. Tragic passing?"

"Yes."

"That's what she says. Did you know this Francesca personally?"

"Oh, yes."

"Did she have a nice sense of humor, a very pleasant way? The reason I ask that is— I'll give you the message. When she said that about the male close to you is over there with her, that she met him, she said, 'Can I be selfish and say I'm glad to have him over here,' so to speak."

"Yes."

"That's what she meant. She said it with a smile. I figured she was kind of kidding you. Was there any violence involved in his passing?"

"Yes."

"I don't understand this. From another source?"

"Yes."

"Because I could see a hand come over you, and it's a symbol. I don't want you to think— Do we put a *great* or *grand* before her name? Like great-aunt or grand-aunt, or just aunt?''

''To that one that passed on. Francesca.''

''To the male that passed over, she would be a great-aunt. She says 'aunt' to me, but she also says 'great-aunt,' 'grand-aunt.' And she wanted that cleared as well. I realize now that that can be a clue. They can give me aunt and grandmother and they're telling me it's like grand-aunt, and that's why I get both identities. Did she speak another language?''

''Yes.''

''Italian?''

''Yes.''

''With a name like that, it's obvious. Well, it could be Spanish. I guess with Mother Cabrini there, too, it's rather obvious.''

''What did you say, St. Frances of what?'' Lucie asked.

''No. I said St. Francesca Xavier Cabrini, Mother Cabrini, was there to clue me as I saw her appear, a vision of her, so I would immediately point to her name as that identity. Is this your son?''

''No.''

''You haven't lost a son? Do you have a son?''

''No.''

''You never had a miscarriage or something?''

''No.''

''Did someone in the family lose a son?''

''Yes.''

''Oh, okay. Because there's someone coming in here saying, 'I'm the son that passed on.' You're saying, 'No,' and he's saying, 'Yes,' and I'm going crazy! Did he pass on tragically?''

''Yes.''

''Would he know Francesca?''

''No.''

''On the other side?''

''Yes.''

''That's it. I'm getting that feeling from the other side. Any violence with his passing?''

''Yes.''

''Bloodshed?''

''Yes.''

"Because I see bloodshed in front of me—violence. Did he pass on quickly?"

"Yes."

"He comes through. Were you worried about him being in pain or suffering? He says, 'I wasn't. I went quickly. I was out of the body instantly and was here just as fast.' He was— Were there any loud noises? I'm hearing loud noises, crashing sounds."

"Yes."

"He says to me it did frighten him, but this Aunt Francesca was there and she came right up to him and put him at ease. Because when he got to the other side, he just said he wandered screaming, he didn't know what had happened. He was terribly frightened, and she came right over to him and helped him, brought him into the light, so to speak. Very religious woman again? Strong faith maybe a better word?"

"Yes."

"Because I say religious, I don't necessarily mean going to church every day, whatever. I don't know if what I'm seeing is meant as a symbol or to be taken literally: Was an auto involved?"

"Yes."

"That's what it is. I hear two cars crashing. Are you related to this young man?"

"Yes."

"Why does he keep on saying 'son'? Is it your grandson?"

"Yes."

"Okay, I'm glad you didn't say anything. He came back again and he started pushing that 'son' bit to me and then he said, 'I'm her grandson.' I have to remember that all comes in on the same vibration. Was your grandson very young?"

"Yes."

"Teens. Because he seems to be a teenager."

"Yes."

"No more than sixteen."

"Yes."

"I don't know what it means. I think it's something personal for you. Did he have very dark hair?"

"Yes."

"Beautiful dark hair, I should say," George added.

"Yes."

"He's standing right next to you, he keeps appearing every now and then. Very athletic?"

"Yes." With that, Lucie, who had been very close to tears several times during the evening, broke down sobbing.

"I don't want to be a pain," George said gently to Lucie, "but please try to control yourself or I get just as emotional, and the vibrations in here are really heavy." A moment later Lucie had calmed down, and George continued.

"Is he into basketball?"

"No."

"Baseball or something?"

"No."

"Maybe it's just a symbol for athletics."

"No, he is in athletics," Lucie replied. Then, as if to correct herself, she added, "He was."

"Oh, okay. Good size boy for sixteen?"

"Yes."

"Was he hit by the car?"

"Yes."

"Because that's what he says to me. He was hit by the car. He wasn't in a car, it wasn't a car accident where two crashed. He was hit by a car, hit-and-run."

"Right."

"Because he says to me, 'Hit-and-run.' Do you know Rose?"

"Yes."

"Passed on?"

"Yes."

"She's there also. Is it his other grandmother?"

"Great—"

"Okay, I'm getting grandmother vibration again. Is it your mother?"

"Yes."

"Okay, that's what she means. She passed on before him?"

"Yes."

"Because she says she was there to meet him when he came over along with the aunt as well. Did he have a really striking smile?"

"Yes."

"I keep seeing that clearly. He's got a good vibration over here. He can actually appear. I can see him appear at different intervals. He's a tall, athletic-looking guy, no more than sixteen, dark hair, good-looking, striking eyes, very prominent smile, very sensitive vibration, very warm person, good-natured, nice young man for his age. I'm not just saying that because he's your grandson. It's honest. It's the feeling I would get from him if I met him in the flesh instead of in the spirit. Is his name David?''

"Yes."

"That's what he says. I didn't know if he was giving me someone else's name, because he said, 'It's David, it's David.'"

"How do you see him?" Lucie asked.

"I can't explain it."

"No, I mean, how do you see him? What does he look like?"

"From that description I gave, from what I can see, he's in light. He's surrounded with light, which is my clue he's in the light on the other side. He's well progressed, and if he can communicate this accurately, he's very well progressed. But your mother and your aunt are there just to make sure that everything runs smoothly for him. They say to me they've been a tremendous help to him over there. He says he knew you were coming today. That's why, when I came in, I immediately zeroed in on you. I felt something around you first, and he has a very, very positive spiritual vibration. He just says to me that—he's kind of laughing—he says, 'You kept me waiting all day.' He says, 'I was waiting all day for you to get here.' He was very anxious. Again, he says he has spoken to you before. As long as you know what it means. His parents still living?''

"Yes."

"They believe in this? Because he asks for them both. He says, 'Please tell them you have heard from me.' There is a girl next to you now. A young girl that passed on."

"I know her," Lucie said.

"You know who she is?"

"I would say."

"Is she related?"

"No. When you say young, about what age?"

"I would say at least young enough to be on his—maybe a little older."

"I don't know her. I know *of* her," Lucie said, clarifying her earlier statement.

"Because she's less than thirty. Okay, that's the thing. She's less than thirty. Her circumstances of passing similar to his?"

"Violent."

"That's what she says. She passed on before him, though."

"Yes."

"Because she was there to meet him also when he came over. Were they related?"

"No."

"Just very good friends?"

"Yes."

"That's what she says. But she was like family almost? There was a closeness there, or she certainly feels it on the other side. Does she know—does he have any brothers?"

"Yes."

"Does she know one of his brothers?"

"Yes."

"She keeps saying, 'Hello, brother. Hello, brother.' I don't know what she means, but I'll leave it with you. Again, this is a double symbol, so I'll just ask. Would a vehicle be a symbol of accidental sudden death? Or was there a vehicle involved in her passing at all?"

"I think so," Lucie replied. In fact Lucie really knew very little about the girl's passing. This was incorrect, and provides an interesting example of how failure to acknowledge correctly can influence the reading. For George a vehicle is also a psychic symbol for an accidental passing. If Lucie had replied that a car had nothing to do with the girl's death, George would then have concluded that the vehicle was being used as a symbol for something besides the obvious. Since we've seen from experience that a series of correct acknowledgments seems somehow to help the spirits communicate more clearly and quickly, we might conclude that the girl's spirit "left" because of lack of response from anyone in the room, a common occurrence.

"She seems to identify with the same circumstances. I don't think I even have to ask you this, that you pray for him, because he's acknowledging it."

"Oh, yes."

"The name Charles mean anything to you?"

"Could be."

"Passed on?"

"No."

"Would your grandson know him?"

"Yes."

"Anything to— Do you know this person fairly well?"

"Yes, very well."

"Any reason for concern around him at all?"

"Not that I know of." (In fact, George was correct. There was concern for Charles's health. He had been paralyzed for many years.)

"Your grandson gives me his name and asks you to say hello to him." George then paused for several seconds before asking David's grandmother, "Do you know Dominick? Are you sure you don't? It seems to push more to you."

"No."

"Think, go back. The name goes to you. I'll just ask you to keep it in mind."

Again, Lucie's emotional response to the reading experience was affecting her ability to acknowledge correctly. As Barbara informed me while we were preparing this manuscript, Lucie did know a Dominick, a relative of Lucie's husband, Joe. Dominick had passed on many years earlier.

"I think your grandson is back now," George said. "I'm laughing, he smiles at you and says your prayers are best because they come with great faith.

"Again," George continued, looking directly at Darrin, "he says he's spoken to you before. He impresses me to question you in the past tense. Have you forgiven yet? For his passing?"

"You mean, have I gotten used to the idea?" Darrin asked.

"No. He says to me, undoubtedly, he passed on at the hands of somebody else behind the wheel and he wants to know, have you forgiven that person?"

"My mind is blank," answered Darrin, who was somewhat nervous and not very happy about even being there.

After a moment's silence, George continued. "David is back, but he seems to go around the room. Without telling me who, is there someone else in here related to him?"

"Yes."

"He says, 'There's someone else in the room.' He doesn't want them to think he forgot them or doesn't know that they're here. Is there more than one?"

"Yes."

"He says, 'A little family gathering here tonight,' he says."

"Is he happy about it?" Lucie asked.

"Oh, definitely. Vibration is very clear. He just keeps kidding, 'You kept me waiting all day. You kept me waiting all day.' Did he have a sense of humor?"

"Yes."

"I'm getting that impression. That's the way he comes in. He's saying to me, 'You kept me waiting all day. We do have things to do over here! We don't just sit around!' Does he have any brothers? Is one of his brothers present here?"

"Yes."

George looked at Darrin and Cory. "Is it one of you two over here?"

"Yes."

Pointing to Darrin, George asked, "You? Because he seems to be going over to that side. You're older than he, right?"

"Yes."

"Has he spoken to you before?"

"Yes."

"Because he says he has. Again, that's the message. 'I've spoken to you before.' The same questions again, 'Have you forgiven yet?' He has asked you once before. I wouldn't say a fanatically religious young man, but he's spiritual, sensitive, a sincere young man."

"Yes."

"Again, not the type that if he missed Mass on Sunday, he would cry the blues. But I think internally he's very spiritual, yes. His vibration is very spiritual. He keeps saying, 'Forgiveness is greater. Forgiveness is greater.' He seems to impress it more on you," George said, addressing Darrin, "because you seem to be more hostile, more vindictive. He says, 'Just reflect on what I'm saying.' In order to experience soul growth, you need to have forgiveness. I don't know if you understand what I mean here. Were you called by a nickname?"

"Sometimes," Darrin replied.

"By him. I can't say it, but I can feel it. Again, he called you by it. I hope I'm not getting personal, but did you feel guilty when he passed on?''

"Yes."

"He said you did. He writes out the word. He keeps saying, 'Why? Why? Why do you feel guilty? Why do you feel guilty?'"

"He was supposed to go out with me that night."

"It seems that you're holding it on your conscience about his passing. He says, 'It's not true, it's not true.' He says to relieve yourself of it. He asks if you feel responsible for his death in a way?''

"Not that much."

"Because he's kind of kidding you. First of all, he says, 'I'm not dead. So you shouldn't feel responsible.' Was he very fond of children? Children and animals?''

"Yes."

"Do you have a pet at home?''

"Yes."

"More than one?''

"No."

"Is it a dog?''

"Yes."

"Because he comments about having a pet dog at home. 'Give the dog a hug for me,' he says, although he's around often enough. Did he have his own room?''

"Yes."

"Did the dog ever wander into his room?''

"All the time."

"Because he says, 'The dog knows when I'm in my room, because the dog comes in.' He says, 'When you see the dog go into my room, you'll know I'm there.' Like a sign that he is present for a reason. He's being a gentleman and stepping aside because I seem to be getting . . .'' George paused again. Speaking to Darrin, he asked, "Do you ever bicycle ride? Do you have a motorcycle or minibike, something along that line?''

"No, but I know somebody that does," Darrin replied, thinking of a friend of David's who rode a dirtbike.

"Your brother speaks to you about caution on a motorcycle or minibike. Somebody to be cautious on it. I'll leave it with you. I don't know what it means. I'm taking it for something to happen maybe—"

"One of his friends does."

"Is he reckless on it?"

"He gets in his moods."

"He's warned to be . . . According to your brother, he says, 'Warn him to be cautious on a minibike or motorcycle.' That there is—I'll be honest with—that it seems there could be an accident or he could hurt himself severely. So if his friend is hip to this, and you can speak to him about it, he . . ." George's voice trailed off. After a few moments, he continued, saying to David's grandmother, "I know your grandson is back in the room to say goodnight because I'm getting David again, present in the room again."

"Does he acknowledge any of the others that are here besides me?" Lucie asked.

"Does he have a sister here?"

"No," she replied. (This is obviously incorrect; Diana was sitting right there. But it was nearing the end of the evening, and the reading had clearly taken its toll on David's grandmother.)

"Does he have a sister?" George persisted.

"Oh, yes. I'm sorry, I thought you said, do *I* have a sister?"

"No. When you didn't acknowledge anybody else, he said, '*My* sister.' And you said no, and he just blanked. 'What do you mean, no?'"

"Does he acknowledge anyone else?"

"Either of his parents here?"

"No."

"But they do believe in this, because he again calls out to both mother and father, both living on the earth. Any other brothers?"

"No."

"Did he have any other brothers?"

"You're just the only one?" George asked Darrin. "Your mother ever lose a child?"

"No. Is this person on this side?"

"No, your brother seems to give me the impression of another brother. I'll leave it. I don't know what it means."

"Could it be like a brother?"

"I'll take it. Definitely. He says, 'Brother,' like a brother in the family sense."

"If you could look at a person, would that give you any kind of clue?" Darrin asked.

"I don't think at this time," George replied. "He's fading. He's going."

Darrin's last question was asked for a reason. He had David's friend Cory accompany him not because Cory was especially interested in attending a reading, but because Darrin wanted to try and trip George up. Perhaps, he assumed, George would think that Cory was David's brother, or that they were both David's brothers or David's friends. In fact, though, George spoke directly to Darrin at several points, making it very clear that David acknowledged Darrin as his brother.

But Darrin also had another trick up his sleeve. Following her first reading with George back in June, Barbara had wondered about George's physical description of her son. He had said that David was appearing before him (as he did with Darrin's telephone reading and this group reading), but the details, while numerous, were pretty basic—dark beautiful hair, nice smile, dark eyes, and so on. Barbara wondered how clearly George had seen her son and devised an experiment to test him. She and Darrin gathered photographs of three of David's friends. Each was about David's age at the time of his death, had dark hair and dark eyes, and basically fit the description of David that George had given earlier from the apparition. The fourth photograph was of David.

At the end of the reading, Darrin approached George, showed him the four photographs, and asked him which of the four boys was David. George immediately picked out David's photograph, then, laughing, said to Darrin, "You set me up."

This third reading, the second to include Darrin, contained sixteen facts in common with Barbara and John's reading and ten facts in common with Darrin's. One part of the message—David's asking Darrin to forgive his killer—appeared in all three. The information George received in Barbara and John's reading and the group reading were David's acknowledging their prayers, mentioning the pet dog, indicating a sense of humor, showing his appearance to George, indicating that he suffered little and passed quickly, mentioning maternal great-grandmother Rose by name, indicating being athletic, mentioning being met on the other side by the murdered girl, indicating that she predeceased him, calling to parents, calling to sister, indicating approximate age, indicating a vehicle was involved in his death, mentioning that the accident was hit-and-run, and asking all to forgive his killer.

The information that comes through in Darrin's reading and the group discernment includes David's mentioning his name (something that George seemed to be on the verge of getting right before Barbara mentioned it in the first reading), identifying himself as someone's son, and mentioning his work with children and animals on the other side. Another fact both readings share is that, before each, David appeared to George and told him that someone would be contacting George for him. In addition, there are the five pieces of information common to all four readings: David's calling to his parents, calling to his sister, indicating his approximate age, indicating that a vehicle was involved in his death, and mentioning that the accident was hit-and-run.

One new piece of information that couldn't be repeated was David's telling George that he had spoken to Darrin before. This part of the message indicates that the deceased do have an awareness of things that happen after their physical deaths. In other words, discarnate consciousness is not just a collection of information gathered during the spirit's physical life and somehow accessible to people like George. Many times, the spirits have spoken of their deaths, whom they met on the other side, and other such details. A skeptic could argue that certain preconceptions about death—for example, which deceased loved ones will be there to greet us—might be well set in our minds before we die. But when a spirit reveals information about something that occurred only after the physical death, it suggests that there is constant awareness from one stage of life to the next. The next reading concerning David Licata would prove this point conclusively.

One evening in late September, George took an anonymous call from a woman and immediately confirmed a male presence.

"Don't tell me anything, just say yes or no," George said. "Is there somebody you know that he's closer to?"

"Yes."

"That's what it is. He's using you as the go-between. Is he related to that person?"

"Yes."

"Because he's definitely giving me 'relative.' Did he pass on from an illness?"

"No."

"Was he in great pain?"

"I don't believe so."

"Any type of trouble in the chest? Accidental type of passing?"

"Yes."

"Anything in the chest at all—that's why I thought illness at first. I'm getting pain in the chest."

"I don't know."

"Generalize the word 'vehicle-involved.'"

"Yes."

"Okay, automobile, specific because vehicle could mean plane, boat, whatever. Killed in auto crash?"

"Yes."

"Young?"

"Yes."

"Are his parents still on the earth?"

"Yes."

"He calls out to them. If you have any contact, he says, 'Please tell my parents you have heard from me. I'm okay.' Do you know anything about his family at all?"

"Yes."

"Has one of his grandmothers passed on, prior to him?"

"I don't think so."

"I'm getting the presence of a woman with him. It comes in on a mother vibration."

"Yes."

"I'll have to say grandmother, maybe great."

"Probably great."

"She was there to meet him when he came over."

"Yes."

"Was he in his twenties?"

"No."

"Younger?"

"Yes."

"Wow. I didn't think he was that young, but he looks pretty young."

I asked, "Was he young-looking?"

"Yes, very," George replied. "I just saw a flash for a second of a young male but he looked as if he could be close to twenty. Was someone else involved with his death?"

"Yes."

"Was he in the vehicle?"

"No."

"Because he says he was not in the vehicle."

"No."

"He was hit."

"Yes."

"Somebody else is responsible for his passing."

"Yes."

"Hit-and-run."

"Yes."

"That's what he tells me. Are you somebody close? Would you know of a young woman who passed on prior to him?"

"Yes."

"Because she's here with him also."

"Yes."

"It's not the same circumstances, but it's a sudden type of death as well. It's not a car accident or whatever, but a sudden type of death."

"Yes."

"Teenager, this person?"

"Yes."

"Now that I see him again, about sixteen, seventeen?"

"Yes."

"Does the name—you don't know his relatives—he's saying to me the name Rose."

"Yes, yes, that's his great-grandmother."

"That's who was there to meet him when he came over. Rose, he says, 'Rose was there to meet me when I came over.' Now, is someone— Are you in any contact with his family at all?"

"Yes."

"Do you have any idea if there's a birthday coming up soon of a male member of his family?"

"It was recently his birthday."

"Oh. He's saying something about a birthday. 'Happy Birthday,' whatever. His mother's father still on the earth?"

"Yes."

"Do you have any contact with him at all? That would be his grandfather."

"Yes, I know them."

"He says, 'Papa.'" (This, we later learned, was David's name for his maternal grandfather, Lucie's husband, Joe.)

"Yes."

"He says, 'Please tell him you have heard from me, that I haven't forgotten him.' I don't know why. He says, 'Please tell him you have heard from me, and also Linda.' Does the name Linda mean anything to you?"

"Not to me, but it might to them."

"Any relative of his by the name of Linda?"

"I wouldn't know. That I don't know."

"Very athletic person?"

"Yes, very."

"Soccer have anything to do with it?"

"Yes. Yes."

"I keep seeing a soccer ball in front of me."

"Yes."

"He's holding a soccer ball."

"Soccer has a big thing to do with it."

"Well, that's the thing. He's holding a soccer ball out to me."

"It has something very big to do with it."

"He's holding it out to me and he says, 'Relay it back.'"

"Yes, yes. Very much so."

"Again, I don't know how his family feels about it. Undoubtedly, they aren't too pleased, I'm sure. But he says, 'I have forgiven the person who did this to me, please do the same.'"

"Yes."

"Are you—"

"I can't give you any input at all, can I?"

"No. Not at the moment, not now. Wait till he's finished. He's coming in loud and clear. Are you a neighbor? In-law or something?"

"No."

"He knows you, though."

"Only—not," the woman replied, then stopped, obviously confused about what to say.

"He knows who you are," George said.

"He doesn't know me from the earth. He knows me now that he's passed on."

"Oh, okay. Does he have a younger sister?"

"Yes."

"He calls out to her. He has another brother?"

"Yes."

"Calls out to him. Calls out to his parents."

"Yes."

"All the relatives. He says, 'I haven't forgotten anyone.' He keeps saying, 'Linda, Linda, Linda,' over and over again."

"I don't know. My name is Lauren."

"No, it's not you. It's somebody else. Does he have an aunt by that name?"

"I don't know. He might."

"Well, you find out."

"Yes."

"Does the name Barbara mean anything to you?"

"Yes, that's his mother."

"Then he must have an Aunt Linda because he says to me, 'Barbara is my mother, and Linda is my aunt.' That's who he's calling out to. Did you know this girl that passed on? Did she pass on before him?"

"Yes."

"Did they go out or something?"

"No. They knew each other."

"Very good friends at least?"

"Yes. They knew each other."

"Because I could see, and she had to be a teenager also."

"Yes, she was."

"Did she pass violently?"

"Yes."

"She related to you at all, or just a friend?"

"No. I don't even know her."

"Funny, but she— Is his name David?"

"Yes."

"He says his name is David, the boy I'm speaking to."

"Yes."

"And then he says—this girl comes in and she sends out

love and regards to everyone. She says, 'Please tell everyone you have heard from me.' It seems almost as if—did someone kill her?''

"Yes."

"That's what it looks like. It looks as if she's being murdered in front of me.''

"Yes, she was."

"Because she says the same thing, that she's fine over there. She passed on before David, though?''

"Yes."

"Because she says, 'I met him when he came over here.'''

"Yes, shortly before."

"And she says—she's sending back regards to everybody and says that they work very well over there on the other side.''

"What do they do?'' the caller asked.

"That's a very good question,'' I added. "I'm going to have to move on to another call. But I love the questions.''

George replied, "They're both very much at peace, first of all.''

"Do they progress?'' I asked. "Do they age?''

"Sure,'' George said.

"Do they get wiser, literally, as they get older?'' I wondered aloud.

"Yes. Because you have to realize there are no restrictions earthwise, so they can progress stronger. There's no temptation. They unite themselves fully with God, they can do the utmost.''

"Can I say one thing before you—'' the woman asked.

"Sure.''

"Now that it's through, can I give you the input that I wanted to?''

"Yes.''

"The reason that I had contact with David, was that after he passed away—not knowing him—I set up with the school a scholarship fund in his memory.''

"Oh,'' George said. "I understand.''

"It was a soccer scholarship.''

"You knew David, who was killed by the car?'' I asked.

"He was killed. He was hit by a car,'' she answered.

"It's funny," George remarked, "he held out a soccer ball to me and said to give it to you."

"Yes."

"Why soccer?" I asked.

"I never knew him in this life, but I took part in—"

"Wait a minute," I said, interrupting her. "You did not know him in this life?"

"No. I didn't know him when he was alive, but after he died, the whole story hit me so that—"

"But," George said, "the thing that flips me is this information was given to me before we went on the air."

"Really?"

"A young man appeared to me as we were sitting, waiting to go on the air, and he said to me, 'The first female caller that comes on will be for me.' And when I heard a male first, I disregarded it, and he came back again, and then we skipped a line or something."

"I was supposed to be the first person on the air," the woman said.

"That's right," I said.

"The lines got screwed up and you couldn't—"

"Yes, exactly. You were supposed to be the first caller, and something fouled up. I just have one more question that I don't understand," I said. "What does soccer have to do with it?"

"He played with the Commack Soccer League. He was very big into soccer. After he passed on, we set up a scholarship through the Commack Soccer League in his memory to benefit other students. It's going to be going on for years now. Other students who are graduating will receive money for their college."

"This is giving me the chills," George stated, hunching his shoulders as if he were shuddering.

"Yes," I agreed. "This is giving *me* the chills. What's your first name, dear?"

"It's Lauren," she replied.

As you may recall, Lauren was the young woman who, without ever having met the Licatas, phoned Barbara to tell her about George. This last reading was especially interesting for several reasons. First, Lauren's role in the reading was spelled out very clearly by David: she was not a relative but a go-between. Second, when Lauren could not acknowledge certain information—David's chest pain (which also came up in Barbara and John's first reading) and his Aunt Linda's name—George insisted. A medium with less integrity could have easily picked up on Lauren's suggestion that David meant Lauren, not Linda, for example. But George did not. Third, George not only stuck with Linda but gave out Linda's relationship to Barbara and to David.

But perhaps the most amazing part of the reading was David's indicating that, although he had not known Lauren while on the earth, he knew of the soccer scholarship. All his previous indications that he was athletically inclined (in two of the three earlier readings) were nonspecific, yet for this one David showed George the soccer ball and said that it should be relayed to Lauren. He knew of the scholarship and Lauren's association to it. This reading contained the five facts in common that all four readings shared (as listed above), plus five other pieces of information that appeared in both Barbara and John's and the group discernment (mentions deceased maternal great-grandmother Rose by name, asks all to forgive, mentions being athletic, mentions meeting girl on the other side and that she died before him), one piece of information that also came up in the group reading (that the girl had been murdered), and one piece of information that appeared in this reading, Darrin's, and the group's (his name, David). Finally, George was, for the third time, informed by David that there would be a call for him.

We do not know why so much information that was confirmed in the four readings was not always repeated. In the case of Barbara and John's reading, perhaps they didn't need to be told that the spirit was their son, David, something he mentions to all the others. What we do know is that of 22 pieces of information in the group's reading, 17 appear in Barbara and John's reading, 10 in Darrin's, and 14 in Lauren's. Five appear in all 4, 8 appear in 3 of 4, and 13 appear in 2 of the 4. These figures, combined with the nature of the information, such as specific names and relationships, knowledge of things that happened after David's death, the consistency in repeated messages, and especially his message of forgiveness to Darrin, leave no doubt but that David was speaking to friends and loved ones through George.

However, the story does not end there. In late October,

George gave a public demonstration for approximately three hundred people at Lindenhurst High School. During a reading, he began receiving messages from David. At this point, the trial of the man accused of killing David was in progress, which David acknowledged, saying he had attended the trial. George delivered messages he received directly from David. These contained information he could not have known. David identified his maternal grandmother by her given name, Lucie, asked for his father, John, by name, mentioned his grandfather, Papa (as he had done in the reading with Lauren), and called out to his Aunt Linda. And, as always, he sent thanks to them all for their prayers.

By this point, George knew the Licata family by sight, so we might play devil's advocate and disallow this reading. However, after this, and for the next several years, David continued to contact his family through George. On December 27, 1982, George was working at his desk at the phone company when David's spirit appeared before him. George heard David say, "Send my mother roses," and "dictate" the wording for a card to accompany the flowers. That day George went to a florist and ordered a bouquet of mums, daisies, baby's breath, and six roses. He wrote the message David requested on the card, signed his own name beneath David's message, and instructed the florist to deliver them to Barbara Licata.

When she answered the doorbell and saw the flowers, Barbara assumed that a neighbor had sent them as a belated Christmas gift. Then she read the card: *I love you Mom and All. Love Always, David.* Barbara looked at the six red roses and began to cry, then she understood what had happened. On December 23 Barbara had begun saying a novena, a series of special prayers that are said for a period of nine days. Her novena was to Saint Thérèse of the Roses. She had been praying that David's dog, who had played ball with him in their backyard and had died that month, was okay and with David on the other side. She also wanted a sign from David that he was still doing fine. Barbara called George, who then related the story of the flowers. Through George, David had answered Barbara's prayers.

Four years later, in 1986, Barbara went to George for another in a series of readings. During the course of one, George psychically heard David say, "Tell my mother what you see, tell my mother what you see."

George was seeing muffins, which he assumed had to be a psychic symbol. The idea of seeing muffins was just too ludicrous to take literally. He said to Barbara, "You're surrounded by muffins. Do you bake?"

"No," Barbara replied, laughing. "That was our dog's name, Muffin."

Apparently David was letting his mother know that he knew Muffin's fate and that he was there with him on the other side. Although David had alluded to the dog in readings, the dog's name had never been mentioned. In fact, Barbara never even told George that the dog had died. And—a note to skeptics—if she had told him, wouldn't it make sense for George to have brought the dog up in any of a number of earlier readings and not four years after the dog's death?

At the 1986 reading George delivered to Barbara the following message from David: "I got a new job. I'm counseling young people who cross over." He explained that he made the decision to do this and that all of the family's and friends' prayers had helped him to grow on the other side. Toward the end, he joked, "I earned my wings."

Eight

After years of hosting a radio show, you begin to regard your listeners not as strangers but as a group of friendly neighbors. While you may actually meet only a few dozen in person, through letters and calls, hundreds become known to you. It was through one such interested listener that I met Dr. John Gschwendtner. The caller had been one of his physics students, and was impressed by Gschwendtner's discussions of the paranormal in his science classes. Dr. Gschwendtner seemed unperturbed by his colleagues' closed-minded objections to his deviation from "orthodox science."

By the time we met in 1982, Dr. Gschwendtner had served on the faculties of three New York City area colleges, including Columbia University. He had earned his doctorate in physics from the prestigious University of Vienna in 1940.

I liked Dr. John, as I called him, immediately. Though past sixty-five years of age, he was in excellent physical condition, the result of years of practicing meditation and yoga. His handsome, lined face was framed by short gray hair and a neat beard and mustache. A man of obvious intelligence, he was always charming, articulate, and witty, so much so that it was impossible not to find him entertaining and quite likable, even when we disagreed.

During our first conversation, Dr. Gschwendtner spoke enthusiastically of his quest for answers to questions about the paranormal, despite its elusive nature and its many controversies and paradoxes. His greater frustration was the lack of a public forum for the expression of his ideas and philosophy about science and the paranormal. He graciously accepted our invitation to appear on a forthcoming radio program, where I could introduce him to George.

Once on the air, Dr. Gschwendtner and George conversed briefly about George's ability. Dr. Gschwendtner offered his opinions about science and the paranormal, explaining that not only were science, mysticism, and the paranormal compatible, but that "one cannot exist without the other." In fact, he said, thousands of years ago, the ancients seemed to understand systems that we are only now slowly beginning to rediscover. He admitted, however, that within our current systems genuine psychic or mediumistic functioning "cannot be explained by present scientific, physical, or psychological explanations." He added, "A legitimate psychic or medium is outside of science. He is, by that definition, paranormal."

Dr. Gschwendtner then asked George if he might demonstrate his ability, with himself as the subject. As always, there was no way for us to know what to expect. The doctor said nothing about his personal life, and there was nothing in his manner to indicate that he was particularly eager to hear from anyone on the other side. George began writing. He looked up momentarily at Dr. Gschwendtner and then shook his head.

"There's a spirit of a woman standing behind you, doctor," George said.

"Yes," the doctor replied.

"Is there any reason why she would appear in a nun's habit? It looks like the type worn many years ago."

"Yes."

"Has your mother passed on?"

"Yes."

"Would the woman in the nun's habit have any reason to say she is your mother?"

"Yes."

"Your mother was a nun?" George asked, thinking it highly unlikely.

"Yes, before she left to marry and raise a family."

"Doctor, there's also a man standing near your mother. Your father has passed, because that's who I feel it is."

"Yes."

"Is there any reason why he would be wearing the garb of a priest or a brother?" It was obvious that George found it hard to believe that both parents would have been involved in religious orders prior to marrying.

"Yes."

"Your father was a priest?"

"A monk," Dr. Gschwendtner replied.

"Both your parents are standing behind you in the dress of the Roman Catholic clergy," George explained.

"Yes."

"Your father is saying that you turned out well. He's not disappointed in you at all."

"Thank you."

"Your mother is urging you to go to church."

"Okay," he replied, seeming to understand the message.

"Were you in the military?"

"Yes."

"Because I see military symbols."

"Yes."

"The German military. I see the swastika," George explained.

"Yes."

"Were you an officer?"

"Yes. I was an officer during the Second World War. Who is telling you this, George?" Dr. Gschwendtner inquired.

"I see two spirits behind you. They appeared as soon as your parents' spirits left. One is wearing a green uniform; the other is in a brown uniform."

"Yes," the doctor responded instantly.

"Do you take the name Hans?"

"Yes."

"He's one of them. He's blond, nice-looking. In his early twenties, I would say. He's wearing the green uniform. The other spirit shows himself in a brown uniform. But, he's got a darker complexion and darker hair."

"Yes."

"Is there any reason why they would be apologizing? Hans is. But he's saying you have no reason to feel guilty about what happened," George said. "They're saying it wasn't your fault."

"I understand."

"Do you feel responsible for their passing? Because they're saying not to feel guilty."

"Thank you."

"Now, the soldier who identifies himself is holding something up for me to see. It looks like a drawing or a shape of some kind. He says you'll understand it if I draw it for you."

A few seconds later George held up a sheet of paper on which he had drawn an upside-down triangle. Dr. Gschwendtner looked at it for a second, then acknowledged it. At that, George was bouncing up and down in his chair. "Hans is telling me it's a code of some kind. It's a code. I never got a code before," George said excitedly. "Doctor, does the code have something to do with your military service?"

"Yes."

"They're telling me that you got out of the military."

"Yes."

"I hear dogs barking. Vicious dogs."

"I understand."

"Did you try to or ever escape from the military service?"

"Yes."

"Hans is saying the code has something to do with your escape. The dogs are related to your escape also."

"Yes."

"They're telling me you made an escape over a border to safety. It looks like a miracle that you escaped."

"Yes."

The reading continued for a while longer, and George provided other accurate details. I was amazed to learn that the man whom I had known only as a scientist and teacher had escaped from the Nazis years before.

Dr. Gschwendtner corroborated George's reading as he gave us and the listening audience an incredible account of his early life. He was unwillingly conscripted into the German military early in the war, but because of his scientific background, he was assigned to the meteorological service of the German air force, the Luftwaffe, where he achieved the rank of captain.

In 1942 he made a bold but dangerous escape from Germany to neutral Switzerland. His treacherous journey took him through the heavily guarded and fortified German border patrolled by soldiers with attack dogs. Capture, of course, would have meant certain execution as a deserter. That he eluded the

Nazis was miraculous. However, once in Switzerland, Gschwendtner was not a free man. The Swiss detained and interrogated him. To prove that he had nothing to hide, Gschwendtner revealed to the Swiss certain technical details about the German military, including some secret codes. The inverted triangle George had drawn was part of that code, the meteorological symbol for a rain shower. "What George referred to was not a secret symbol in and of itself," Dr. Gschwendtner said, "but where it happened and its context were secret." The Swiss authorities' acceptance of the codes and other secret information became, in Dr. Gschwendtner's words, "my passport to freedom."

Gschwendtner then clarified the roles of the two soldiers George saw psychically. Hans, the blond officer in the green uniform, was accidentally killed when he failed to follow Gschwendtner's flying directions. The darker-complexioned soldier George saw was an Italian whom Gschwendtner met in Switzerland, who was killed trying to escape from the Swiss, which Gschwendtner refused to do. He told us that he had long felt responsible for both of these deaths.

John Gschwendtner acknowledged that there was no way George could have had prior access to the information he brought forth during the reading. For example, the chances that not one but both parents had been in religious orders before marrying were infinitesimal, especially in those days.

"He finds out things no one else is aware of except the person he is doing the reading for," Gschwendtner said. "There is no way he could have known these facts about my life. They are not the kind of memories one talks about readily. I can tell you there were things George told me that no one in the United States ever knew, things I never told anyone since I came to this country in 1960. The probability of escaping from the Nazis was rare. The probability of George's knowing is even more rare."

I asked Dr. Gschwendtner if he had any theories to explain George's capabilities.

"It is my opinion," he replied, "that George's insights cannot be explained by our present scientific, physical, or psychological explanations. He is outside of science. He is paranormal. George is seeing a picture of the events he is describing. One theory is that he may have access, somehow, to our unconscious minds and to our memory banks. The information is coming to him."

"Could George have had access to the memory banks of those who have passed on?" I asked, referring to one common theory.

"Certainly. I see no reason why not. Yes, he could see and project disembodied entities—but there is no way of proving it. On the other hand, there is no way of saying no. I have no way of saying there are no disembodied entities. But parapsychologists have so far not been able to substantiate it. Telepathy is easier to follow than disembodied entities. Telepathy is beyond a doubt."

"How do you suggest that George is able to provide messages about future events?" I asked.

"There is no past, present, or future in the way you're describing them. This is my metaphor: the book is already written. Even if you have not yet read the final chapter, it is already written. Similarly, the future is already here, even if we haven't gotten to it yet. Time is a fiction."

"What happens when we leave this physical body?" I asked.

"We go from one home to another. There is an indestructible energy. I don't think this energy changes so much. We hope it develops."

"That energy could be the soul?"

"Yes. George sees the souls of the dead."

"And, doctor, after we pass on from the physical world, can the souls or spirits communicate back to us?"

"We cannot prove it with our present systems of knowledge, but I personally give it a high probability," Gschwendtner answered.

"Doctor, I'm curious. Why your interest in the paranormal?"

"From the time I was a young boy I had faced that in this world there are things that exist which are not in physics books. So I began to pursue this systematically. I've had a lifelong interest beyond the limits of orthodox science.

"Carl Gustav Jung, the great psychiatrist, wrote a doctoral thesis about parapsychology. Jung's system of psychology includes the concept of meaningful coincidence, or synchronicity. Jung was interested in nearly all areas of the paranormal, searching for causes and explanations. Jung was both a psychiatrist and a philosopher. He was Swiss. I met him in Switzerland. He was like a patriarch to those who learned from him. He was always talking to himself and letting us listen. Jung had an open mind. He was an honest man who used psychic phenomena in his own practice,'' Gschwendtner explained.

"What would you hope people today consider when they approach the paranormal?'' I asked.

"I hope that someone using me as a role model begins to rethink his ignorance. You must educate people. Open their minds. Wake their brains up!'' Gschwendtner replied.

The on-air reading with Dr. Gschwendtner and the two private readings that follow provide good examples of one pattern we've observed. There seems to be a clear correlation between the tragic, unusual, or very emotional circumstances at passing and the strength, clarity, and specificity of the spirit's communication. Why this is so, we cannot say for certain, but someone whose passing has left loved ones with questions, regret, or intractable grief seems to make an extra effort to provide private details and identifying facts. Interestingly, we also see the opposite whenever a subject is vague, unwilling, or unable to acknowledge a message. A subject's repeated denials of a message pretty much ensure that the message will end—however, usually not until after the spirit has made several attempts to get it across.

In contrast, if we look at a grandparent who quietly passed on at a ripe old age of natural causes and leaves a basically stable family arrangement, we get some idea of what the spirits may be thinking. Almost without exception, the spirit fortunate to have passed from such an ideal death has little to say. Of course, the message has profound meaning for the family, but spirits who pass under these circumstances seem the most likely to be concerned with a subject's job promotion, new car, change in residence, or upcoming birthday. That's not to say that these messages have no other content; they do. But they seem to lack the sense of urgency and high emotion of the more tragic or unusual cases.

The spirits' acknowledgment of prayer and statements of concern for us indicate that they somehow have knowledge of what we feel and, perhaps, think. There's no question that spirits seem to be drawn to those who need to hear from them, and once those people make contact, either through George or otherwise, the spirits' messages contain words of love, comfort, forgiveness, and reassurance. These particular points tend to be repeated often in the reading, as though, as George believes, the spirit knows how badly those left behind need to hear them.

It's very difficult to sit for hundreds of hours with someone like George and not be moved deeply and personally by many of the readings. In some sense, every loved one's passing is painful, but both George and I believe that there is nothing as devastating as a parent's pain over a child's death.

One day in the fall of 1983 I received a call from a man I had never met. He wanted to discuss the brutal murder of a ten-year-old boy that had occurred several years before in a nearby state. The crime was particularly shocking because it was committed not by deranged adults or a group of young hoods, but by two or three other kids, none very much older than their victim. The deceased, a young boy named Charles, was accosted by three other youths, demanding that he hand over his denim jacket. When he refused, they attacked him and then stuffed several cotton bandannas down his throat, choking him to death. From what I'd read of the case, three boys were being accused of the murder, but there remained some question as to what roles each of them played in the crime or even if all three were guilty. The man I was speaking to was the father of one of the accused boys. He had heard about George and asked me to help him arrange a reading. I promised to do what I could.

The next day George told me that the night before he had the strangest vision. For some reason he couldn't figure out, the spirit of a young boy who was brutally killed appeared before him. George vaguely recalled hearing or reading something about the heinous crime, and the spirit gave him a symbol. When George described the spirit and the symbol to me, I realized that the spirit was that of Charles, the young boy I'd discussed with the man just a day before. George still couldn't figure out why the spirit would appear to him. I declined to explain but made arrangements for the man to have a private reading with George.

The reading took place at George's home and began in the typical fashion.

"Whatever I say, just say yes or no; don't give me any details or information. Let me do all the talking." After a brief pause, George asked, "Is there tragedy around you, or has there been?"

"Yes," the man replied.

"Has been; it's finished."

"Yes, I hope so," the man answered quietly.

"Well, let's just say that the nucleus of it is over. In this world, anyway. Several years ago this happened?"

"Yes."

"It's over with, but you'll never get over it. That's what I'm getting at. Family member passed on in this tragedy?"

"No, not a family member."

"Somebody very close to you?"

"Not really."

George fell silent. This was unusual. "But there has been a death; a tragic one." On a sheet he had written out the word *redrum*. "Murder?"

"Yes."

"That's what I'm getting. Is the person passed on male?"

"Yes."

"But not close to you?" George was stuck. "I just don't understand why they're coming in. Not related to you?" he repeated.

"No."

Hoping to help clarify what George was receiving and rule out the possibility that someone else from the man's family might be coming through, I asked, "Is there anybody else in the family that he could be talking about?" The man shook his head no.

"I don't understand," George repeated. "It's very confusing. All right, we'll just let it go. Pass on kind of young?"

"Yes."

"Not related to you by marriage or anything on that scale."

"No."

"He's related to you in some way, I just don't understand how. Friendship?"

"No."

"You positive?"

"Yes."

"Was he murdered?"

"Yes."

"Because that's why I keep writing *redrum* out; murder spelled backward. Young person."

"Yes."

"Young male."

"Yes."

"Silly to say, but an unusual way of passing on?"

"Yes."

"It's not a murder I'd hear about every day, that's for sure. Does the name Benjamin mean anything to you?"

"Yes."

"It does? Because I keep seeing Benjamin Franklin overhead. I thought for sure you'd say no to that. Do you know a great deal about this person who passed on from the murder?"

"Now, yes."

"Okay, that's where I'm getting the relationship. You know who the person is, and you know enough about him. It's almost as if you've carried stories about him; you've done some work involving his murder."

"Yes."

"There's the relationship I was picking up on. Okay. You know the people connected with this personally. That's why I was getting the pull; he knows from the other side that you've been involved in his case. This is a very, very emotional case. There are a lot of tears around it, despondency, sorrow."

"Absolutely."

"Is this person Benjamin related to you at all?"

"No."

"Just a friend. Okay, he have anything to do with working on this case?"

"Yes."

"Because I'm getting the same connection you have, some sort of connection in that sense, not by family, but here's a close sort of connection. Do you do any type of writing?"

"Professionally, no."

"Investigation of any kind?"

"No."

"They're going to go crazy," George said of the spirits

whose messages didn't seem to be connecting. "In regard to this case, have you worked with this case, or something?"

"Yes, in a way."

"Investigated it, spoken about it?"

"Extensively."

"Okay, this is the connection. Did you know this person personally? You had no contact with him prior to his passing."

"No."

"Do you have any contact with his family?"

"Remotely."

"*Could* you have contact with his family?"

"Could I? If I wanted, probably."

"You're on good terms with this family?"

"No."

"That's an unusual thing. Do you know somebody involved in his case?"

"Yes."

"That's the connection, too. I don't want to say anything until I'm convinced that what I'm getting is correct. You know how this person passed on?"

"Yes."

"Was somebody you know involved with his death?"

"Not that I know of."

"Somebody you know was accused of his death?"

"Yes."

"Because when you said no, I got, 'No, wrong,' that there is involvement in it. Name Joseph mean anything to you?"

"Yes."

"Living."

"Yes."

"On the earth. Another young person, not passed on, though. Was he young at the time of this person's passing over?"

"Yes."

"Okay, that's what I'm getting. Well, I'll have to ask it: Is this Joseph involved in this murder? Because that's what this party from the other side keeps telling me; he says, 'I have forgiven Joseph.' Do you understand? As long as you understand, I'll just keep feeding. Is this Joseph away?"

"Yes."

"He's away from here, not in this area. I don't feel he's out of the state where this occurred, though."

"No."

"I would say in his mid to late teens by now?"

"Yes."

"Did this person that passed on know Joseph?"

"Yes."

"They knew each other personally, because according to him, 'We knew each other personally.' He says to me . . ." George paused, took a deep breath, and then said, "Well, I'll ask it: Is Joseph being accused of his murder?"

"Yes."

"That's what he says, 'Joseph is being accused of my murder.' Now the person I feel I'm in contact with, I'd say passed over at ten, eleven, very young, very tragic passing. Not a vehicle accident or anything like this; he clears me of any of those types of symbols. He says no. His parents still living, correct?"

"Yes."

"Because he keeps calling out to his parents, 'Please tell my parents that you've heard from me, tell them I'm all right.' He keeps saying that over and over again." George then continued having trouble with determining the subject's relationship to Joseph. "Now, is this Joseph related to you? Again, just working with this case or something? There's no relationship or friendship?"

"With a member of my family, Joseph is."

"Okay, okay. He's related to you through marriage?"

"No, he's not related," the man said, trying to clarify what he meant without giving anything away. "Just friendship."

"Okay, because there's some sort of connection with his family. I couldn't figure out what they meant. Is there somebody being accused who's related to you?"

"Not at this time."

"Could there be?"

"At one time there was."

"Because someone psychically points at you and then clears away, which means . . . a son? According to this male on the other side, your son was kind of picked out but released or pushed away from it, and he's not making any accusations. He's giving me the impression your son didn't have anything

to do with it. If he did, it was very, very minor; it was not to
the extreme of these other people involved.''

"True.''

"He's not in jail. Is it basically over with?''

"With him.''

"Okay, because I'm getting clearance. I think you're pretty
convinced of that anyway, but he says for you to put your mind
at ease; 'Your son had nothing to do with my passing.' He was
arrested, though, wasn't he?''

"Yes.''

"Yeah, I do see an arrest in front of me, and he had been
incarcerated temporarily, but he's been cleared. Does the name
Charles mean anything to you?''

"Yes.''

"Passed over, though.''

"Yes.''

"Not a family member.''

"No.''

"You don't have anyone named Charles in your family that
passed over?''

"True.''

"Okay, I just wanted to clear that, that there's nobody related to you who passed on. Is he called Charlie?''

"Yes.''

"At first he says Charles, then he says Charlie. Is he the
victim?''

"Yes.''

"He must be, because again I'm getting the calling out to
parents, 'Please tell them that you've heard from me, tell them
that you've heard from me, I'm all right, I'm all right, I'm all
right.' He keeps saying it over and over again. The name
William mean anything to you?''

"Yes.''

"Living.''

"Yes.''

"Involved with this.''

"Yes.''

"I'm getting the vibration of forgiveness again. Would William have been involved in the case?''

"You said he was cleared.''

"He seems to forgive this Joseph and William for involve-

ment in his passing. I'm only repeating back what I hear. The
party that was murdered says to me that one person definitely
had front-row involvement. And he seems to give me the name
Benjamin. He gives me the impression they definitely had
something to do with it. But he's forgiving. He keeps saying,
'I forgive, I forgive,' and again he keeps calling out to his
parents. Was he very close to his parents?"

"Yes."

"Must have been. Those two names come back again that
they were directly involved, whoever these two others are,
Joseph and Benjamin. Charles says, 'They were directly involved in my passing.' But he's not saying it in hostility, he's
saying it in forgiveness and realizes that it happened. Charles is
definitely the victim who's on the other side. Passed on
through this."

"Yes."

"I see a jacket of some sort, he shows it to me and says that
it has something to do with the initial problem."

"Yes."

"According to this Charles on the other side, there were
three altogether, with one ringleader, so to speak, and one
other party directly involved. Yours is like the third party.
There are two people actually being pointed to, actually being
involved. If I included your son as being accused, he would
make three, but I'm going to clear him away. That's what I
was driving at; I had to explain it. According to this Charles,
there were the two—one ringleader and one other, a hench-
man, so to speak. And he says that the third party accused has
nothing to do with it. And he was a youngster, too, had to be a
teenager, because he would be, like, what twelve, thirteen
around there."

"He just turned sixteen."

"Were the others older than he at the time of this?"

"No."

"Because he said, 'It's the one that was the eldest, had one
of the greatest age differences,' didn't seem to have any connection whatsoever. Whatever this case was, it just seems that
at the last minute, they were looking for somebody else to
accuse, and he just happened to be on the list, but they said he
has nothing to do with it, and he was cleared. This Charles
passed on as a child? The only child."

"Yes."

"That's what he says to me, the only child. Getting a very nice vibration from him. He seems restless only in the sense of he wants his parents to know he's okay, I imagine from the tragedy. He keeps calling out to his parents—'Tell them I'm all right, tell them I'm all right.'. . . In this case, was a weapon used? Stretch beyond that—not a knife or a gun."

"A weapon?" I asked.

"Yes," George replied, "but not a knife or a gun, because I see them x'ed out. Another form of weapon."

"Yes," I answered.

"According to this Charles, he says, 'I passed on,' but not from something I'd identify as a weapon. Was he red-headed? Do you have any idea what he looked like?"

"Yes. He had red hair."

"Very bright-faced; a pleasant face, from what I can see in front of me. Does the name Louise mean anything to this Charles?"

"Yes."

"Because he keeps calling out to Louise, 'Tell them you've heard from me.' Were they very close?"

"Yes."

"Related?"

"Yes."

"He seems very— There's a woman behind him, and I'd love to know who this is. Must be the grandmother or great-grandmother. She's kind of helping him to make contact. Louise is his mother?"

"Yes."

"That's what he says. Okay. She's very close, I imagine. He keeps telling me to tell his mother that I've heard from him, again and again. I assume they were close because he calls out, 'Mommy.' His father still living also?"

"Yes."

"I'm not getting a name, but he keeps calling out to him as well. 'Tell my father you've heard from me.' I don't know what they're feeling about this, but they must believe he's dead because he keeps saying, 'Tell them I'm not dead, I'm not dead.' He's like an anxious child, repeating it over and over again. It's the strangest thing: I keep feeling a pressure on my throat; did that have anything to do with his passing on?"

"Yes."

"Um, would somebody have—now listen closely to my question—would somebody have held him on the throat at one point?"

"Possibly."

"I feel like I'm being held on the throat, but I'm not being strangled. Not by the hand, in any case. I'm getting a gasping feeling—he must have been choked. He passed on through choking, something like that; not strangulation, though. There's something *in* my throat. It's the same feeling I had when I did a case where somebody choked to death, and I'll say that's the way they passed on, but not of their own accord. Was anything forced *into* the person's throat?"

"Yes."

"It's as if I feel something being shoved down my throat. Nowhere to go—horrible feeling. I have to clear that quickly. . . . Getting a lot of headaches. Would you know if this person had a lot of head pressure before passing on?"

"Possibly."

"I'm feeling a tremendous headache, like, whew, blood is swelling in the top of my head, from whatever happened in the throat. Are both of these people incarcerated?"

"No."

"One is, though. One more on the way," George stated. I interjected, "You tell us."

"It's a very strong possibility."

"We don't know," I said.

"There is one in there now, he tells me," George explained, accurately, as it turned out. "I keep seeing a big, black stamp that says 'guilty.' If he's innocent, I get told that; if he's guilty, I get told that as well. There might have been a lot of controversy about it, but they're holding their ground and saying 'guilty' on the first one. Now, he says to me there are definitely two guilty. Yours, no, but the other two, definitely. The one in jail now is involved directly, the other one might have been a part of it, or might have stood there and watched. I see two males around another male. I think if anything your son might have been around at that time, before this all began, and because of fear ran away, I don't know.

"The party that has passed on says that your son had nothing to do with his death. If anything, you might have had your chops busted by the police, I'm getting that you were put through the mill by the police department, but I'm not getting any evidence. Nothing, a clear flow of water in front of me, which means clearance, and a zero, which means no involvement. That's why I have to hold my ground about what they say about the other parties. I'm getting a big 'guilty' stamp in front of me.

"Besides this Charles passed on, is there someone living close to him by the same name, because he repeats the name?" George continued. "Oh—I understand now. He says he was named after somebody; a Charles senior, so let's assume it'd have to be his father; that's my first choice. Because he says, 'I'm the junior; my father has the same name as I do.' Okay. I don't know if anybody has any contact with his parents, but he certainly would like them to hear. He keeps telling me, 'Tell my parents you heard from me.' Again, 'Please tell my parents you've heard from me.' That's all I keep hearing. Definitely a young person calling out, 'Mother. Mommy. Tell Mommy I'm all right,' that sort of thing. They stopped. Contact is broken."

After a few moments' silence, George and William's father discussed the reading. Each name given was correct, as was George's account, through sympathetic pain, of the act that killed Charles. Everything that George had said about the case proved to be true. His son was the third suspect, and had been found not guilty by the courts. Of the other two suspects, both were found guilty as charged. At one point, George told William's father, "It was interesting; the minute you sat down, I started seeing that scene out of *The Shining*, where they were saying 'redrum.' Somebody kept repeating it over and over, and they kept writing it. That's murder spelled backward. And I said, 'Ah, so now I know what this means, this must be a murder case.' And I saw black over your head. But it was gray, which means the worst is over, it's clearing away. It's just a bad memory, so to speak. I thought somebody had something to do with movies at first, and then I figured, then I saw the blackness, I said, no, it has to do with murder."

For William's father, the reading brought a message of comfort for him and, if he ever discussed it with Charles's parents, for the murdered boy's family. Unfortunately, we have no idea if they ever heard about this.

* * *

Generally, people come to George seeking answers. Did their loved one suffer before dying? Did he or she know that after their physical deaths they had a grandchild, or that a spouse was suffering with a health problem? But every now and then, people come to George to learn about someone who might still be on the earth and, in the rare case, to find out whether a loved one is on the earth or has already passed to the other side.

One evening George was contacted by a young couple whose little girl had been abducted. It was an unusually complex case, involving a custody battle and an out-of-state adoption of questionable legality. George attempted to read them but was unsuccessful, coming up with nothing. We wondered, could the fact that everyone was alive—the girl's parents, grandparents, and most relatives, as well as the girl herself, and the abductors—account for the lack of communication from the other side?

One of the saddest readings I ever witnessed took place with the parents of a man who had been reported missing in action since early February 1973, just eight days after the treaty ending the Vietnam War was signed. Stationed in Laos and before that in Thailand, he flew out as part of a routine reconnaissance mission, his plane was shot down, and he was, they believed, taken prisoner. After over a decade of searching for answers—from the government, other former POWs, and various organizations—they were no more certain about their son's fate.

His mother, Lila, explained after the reading was finished, "Four were killed in the crash and four were captured. They first said Matthew was missing, then they said he was killed, and then we later found out he was captured, and they have voice recordings of the enemy talking about the capture. So we don't know if he's dead or ali—" She paused for a moment, as if she couldn't finish. "That's why I've always wondered, is he dead or alive?" They came to George for an answer.

The actual reading with Lila and Anthony, Matthew's father, ran for over an hour, during which time a number of spirits came through, including Lila's father, uncle, and aunt, each with messages that were acknowledged. What follows are excerpts that pertain specifically to Matthew. The actual reading is too long to include here in full; however, several things happened in the reading before Matthew broke through.

For nearly the first fifteen minutes of the reading, Lila's father was speaking. He gave a long series of clues that were later acknowledged—a map of Europe, addressing George as a young man, interest in medicine (although he was not a doctor)—but were initially denied by Lila and Anthony, who were "interpreting" all the messages in terms of how they would relate to their son. When George asked, "Is it your father?" Lila said no. Then George said, "He told me I was going to get a no on that. He said, 'They'll misunderstand you.' It's either a father or a father figure." After it was finally determined that the first spirit was Lila's father, not her son, George reported that the spirit had said to him, "I'm her father. You're going to get a no, they're not thinking it's me."

This proved to be a classic case against telepathy. Obviously, if George's source of information was his subjects, and if the readings were essentially the product of his reading their minds, he would have come up with Matthew, not his grandfather. Further, George later relayed other information from Lila's father, such as a nickname—which George repeated to Lila, using the same Swiss-German pronunciation her father used—she hadn't thought of in years. Still, early on, and later as well, George stuck to his message, even when he could have easily "followed" his subjects' leads. Perhaps as a result of the early confusion, Matthew goes to great lengths to offer proof of not only his identity but of his death, by speaking at length of several events in his parents' and siblings' lives that had occurred after he was reported missing. Again, at this point, George does not know who Lila and Anthony are—their names or their relationship to each other—or why they are there.

"Did you lose a child?" George asked.

"Years ago," Lila replied. "A miscarriage."

"Okay, that's what I was looking for," George replied. Then, turning to Anthony, he asked, "You didn't lose a child, did you?"

"Yes, I lost a child," Anthony said softly.

"Okay, wait a minute—don't say anything. A miscarriage?"

"Yes, yes. I didn't answer it right," Lila said suddenly.

"Not a miscarriage? It's not a miscarriage. When you said miscarriage, it didn't click."

"When you said child," Lila explained, "I'm thinking little one—"

"No, they mean that there's definitely somebody who claims to be your child. Your uncle brings him in."

"All right," Lila answered, understanding.

"This is funny. When you said miscarriage, it was like, 'no, no,' then they leaned on you," George said, indicating Anthony, "and then they said you lost a child, he told me to go to him, that he would understand. The child was grown up."

"Yes."

"Okay. Still pass on kind of young by today's standards?"

"Yes."

"Yeah, that's the thing I'm getting. Very close to you."

"Yes."

"Still is."

"Yes."

"Very sorrowful passing?"

"Yes."

"Did he pass on after your uncle?"

"Yes."

"Did he know your uncle at all? If not, he met him over there, because— Is he your son, by the way?"

"That's him, but he didn't—"

"Okay, but he met him over there, your uncle was one of the first people to meet him when he went over because of the fact he's so close to you. Did he know your father?"

"Yes, he did."

"Because your father met him also. Did your father pass on before him?"

"Yes."

"Because I'm getting who met whom when the other came over—that's what's throwing me off."

"That's a question right now," Lila replied. "I don't know."

"Okay. He met your son or your son met him, one or the other. It *is* your son, right?"

"Yes."

"He was over sixteen when he passed on?"

"Yes."

"Okay. Is this who you thought it was when we first started?"

Lila replied, "When you first talked to him [meaning her father], yes."

"He says to me, 'You thought it was me.' But he wasn't ready to come through yet, that's why it was your father and uncle first, and he watched them to see how they did it, and as soon as he realized how they were doing it, like he learned from it, he took up on it . . . he was definitely adult, he was at least in his twenties or older—"

"Yes."

"Did he wear a uniform?"

"Yes."

"Because he's appearing in a uniform right behind you. Flipped me out. Did he pass on in the military? Or in this uniform?"

"In the uniform."

"Just bear with me. I'm jumping to conclusions on military—it could be policeman, fireman, something else—but he passed on in uniform."

"Yes."

"Okay, I'll just stay with it. I have to keep my logical brain out of it and just listen. Okay, he says he passed on in uniform."

"The military," Anthony interjected.

"Do you have a picture of him at home in uniform?"

"Yes," Lila answered.

"Because he keeps saluting you in uniform, and he says, 'Yeah, you have a picture of me at home . . . in uniform,' and I could see it out, it's definitely on display. Do you keep something near it? A candle, a rose?"

"Yes," Lila replied.

"There's something to commemorate him there, he tells me and he's very pleased with it. A very sensitive young person?"

"Yes."

"Very strong, sensitive vibration I get from him." Turning to Anthony, George asked, "He knows you also, right?"

"Yes," Anthony said.

"He doesn't want you to think he's ignoring you, because the strength is going in this [indicating Lila's] direction. . . . All right now, I don't want to jump to conclusions. Was a weapon involved in his passing?"

"Yes."

"Okay, then it is correct. I didn't know if it was a symbol of military or if it meant something, but he said a weapon was involved in his passing. Is there any mystery about the way he passed on?"

"Yes."

"That's what he says to me, he puts question marks after the weapon. *A lot* of mystery, he says. Was he away from home?"

"Yes."

"Were there a lot of explosions around him?"

"Yes."

"Because I'm hearing explosions going off, but there's all question marks after it."

"That's right."

"Definitely there's something unanswered. Do you pray for him?"

"Oh, yes."

"Because he receives them loud and clear. Keep them coming. Do you say the rosary for him?"

"Every day."

"I can't believe this," George said, incredulously. "Son of a gun, he just holds the rosary up in front of me, and he says, 'This is what she says for me. Daily.' He says, 'Please keep it coming.' Just out of curiosity, are your rosary beads white?"

"Crystal."

"Oh, man. He showed me white crystal and he held them up in front of me." George's tone changed abruptly in mid-sentence. "Was he killed in an explosion? Or, apparently, he was killed in action? As far as we know, but yet it's not action?"

"That's right."

"This is what I'm getting. 'I was killed in action,' but not in the way I would interpret it as action. He's not in the battlefield. Or he's near a battlefield." George fell silent, trying to absorb the seemingly contradictory messages. "Do you understand what I'm driving at, without telling me anything? He's killed in action, but he says it's not—"

"Yes," Lila answered immediately.

"Not action, I would . . . when I get 'killed in action,' I know what I'm thinking, and he says, 'It's not what you're thinking.' Oh. Now has somebody written about him?"

"Yes."

"That's what he's saying, back before what your father was

saying, you understand, I understand, something's been written about him. Have you written about him?''

"Yes."

"Do you speak of him?"

"Oh, yes."

"Publicly, though?"

"Yes."

"Okay, now I understand. That's why I see you teaching. You're telling, you're relating the story of him to the public—okay, but I think that's what he means and he's trying to get across. Was he called by a nickname?"

"Yes."

"That's who the nickname is, okay. I can't pick it up because the mind is going to reject it; I've never heard of it before. You see, the problem is that sometimes when they come in all at once, I get confused. I don't know really who I was speaking to at first. And then your father fortunately came in and he must have been a strong-willed person, he dominated the interaction and he explained to me what was happening. Then your uncle came in and he explained why I was feeling the mellowness, and then your son came in and said that, because we both seemed to think that was who I was referring to in the beginning and he hadn't come in yet. Is there a sister he's quite close to?"

"Yes."

"That's the other female he speaks of. Younger than he?"

"No."

"Does he have any younger sisters?"

"Yes."

"Well, when you said no, he said, 'Yes, younger sister,' and he said, 'There's another one as well.'"

"Possibly. I thought he was closer to another one."

"Well, there's a reason why it's coming out that way. . . . He was definitely overseas when this tragedy occurred—"

"Yes," Lila answered.

"Okay, because he says, 'I'm over water.' Well, I don't think you have to be psychic to know. Was it Vietnam?"

"Yes."

"Yeah, it would have to be, because that's the most recent according to his age—"

"Well, that's not—no it's not what happened."

"Oh, it didn't. He *was* in Vietnam, though?"

"No," Anthony said.

"No, not at the time. No," Lila concurred.

"But in that part of the world?" George asked.

"It's the right part of the world," Lila responded.

"No, but he said to me, 'Southeast Asia.' Maybe the reason he did that was so I'd pay attention, otherwise I would have ignored it. Does the name Tommy mean anything to you? Thomas?"

"No, not Thomas."

"You're sure? Tommy actually is what I got. It means something, maybe not a name, but it's put in quotes. Well, I'll leave it."

"It could be something else," Lila offered, "but I won't say it."

"He says to me, 'Say Tommy and put it in quotes, and just say it.'"

"No, I don't—"

"Okay, I'll leave it. Do you know a Scott living or passed on?"

"Do I know Scott that passed on?" Lila asked. "Living definitely."

"Does your son know him?"

"Oh, yes."

"Your son asked for Scott. Are they related, very close?"

"Yes."

"Scotty? Is he called by a nickname or something?"

"Scott," Lila repeated.

Anthony answered, "I don't know if they'd call each other nicknames."

"It's just—I don't know, it seems he was close, he says, he asked for Scott. He says, 'Please tell him you have heard from me,' that's he's all right over there, he's at peace and so forth, and he certainly appreciates the prayer you've been sending. That's what kept him at peace and helped him. And your uncle, you pray for your uncle, because he certainly has helped him tremendously over there. He's very spiritually aware. Was he near water when he passed on?"

"Not to my knowledge."

"Ships of any kind? Any other military installations?"

"I wouldn't know," Lila said. "Possible."

"Could you say he was murdered?"

"That's possible. Stretch the word, yes."

"Stretch the word that he was murdered," George said.

"Definitely," Lila said.

"I don't feel intentionally, though, you know. It's just like he was a victim of circumstances."

"Possible," Lila answered.

"Yeah, it's possible," Anthony concurred.

"Were you given any type of medal for him or something?"

"Yes," Lila said.

"Commemoration of any kind?"

"Yes."

"Of any kind from the government?"

"Yes."

"Some bigwigs, because he speaks of that, he says some sort of medal you received or commemoration, now I'm not saying it is—"

"Well, there's a commemoration, and also a medal," Lila interjected.

"I'm not saying that this is what it is. I see a Purple Heart in front of me."

"Yes."

"Is that what it was?"

"That's one."

"Oh, okay—sorry, fella," George said to the spirit before turning back to Lila and Anthony. "He showed me a Purple Heart, he says that's one of them, and I just thought it was being used as a symbol."

"No."

"Very, very distinct smile?"

"Yes."

"Every now and then I see him appearing in back of you, very distinct smile. I mean, that stands out foremost. Did he fly at all?"

"Yes."

"Because I keep seeing these planes all around here, he says he flew them or at least he worked with them or he has worked with them or something. Ah, let me clear this now. He wasn't a Marine, was he?"

"No," Lila answered.

"But did he work with the Marines or—"

"Not to my knowledge."

"Or maybe some kind of contact with them?"

"That's possible."

"I keep hearing something—"

"Oh, I know," the mother exclaimed suddenly.

"He's singing 'From the Halls of Montezuma,'" George said, clearly not understanding its significance.

"I know, I know," Lila replied quickly. "Okay."

"That's the Marines."

"Okay."

"Okay, as long as you understand. He just says something about the Marines."

"Yeah."

"Now, did he fly?"

"Yes."

"He knew how to fly planes, because he was the pilot of these planes—" George said, following his symbols and clues to the most logical conclusion.

"No."

"No?" George asked, surprised.

"No," Lila repeated.

"No? He worked on it or something?"

"Yes, or in it."

"I see him in a plane, and it looks like he's working something, that's why I assumed he was the pilot."

"That's correct."

"Oh, okay, as long as you understand. He worked military—what's the right word?—he worked military equipment on the plane."

"Yes."

"Oh, okay. That's it exactly, I'm seeing something like this, I figured he was steering, but now I think I know what he means. . . . Was he in the plane when he passed on?"

"We don't know."

"Was he captured by somebody?"

"We think so."

"Because that's what I'm getting. He says, 'I've been captured.'"

"Right."

"Again, I'm going back to Southeast Asia, he says he's

been captured. Now, would he have been captured in Southeast Asia, in that area?''

"Yes."

"Because he says definitely—and he's showing me Indochina, which is in Southeast Asia—in that area. Now, do you know for a fact he's passed on?''

"No."

"I'm getting the impression he is. I'll be honest. But he would have been like—I'm seeing in front of me an MIA, so he was missing in action or whatever. But I will be honest with you—now, I can be wrong—but from what I've seen so far, he has made the transition. That's why I think he said he was murdered, not in the sense of—what's the word—"

"Combat?"

"Yeah, exactly. Victim of circumstance because of world conditions—"

"Yes."

"Very easygoing guy?"

"Yes?"

"You know—has no grudges or animosities toward the other side except, like, well, it happened, it happened, you know he's very much alive and so forth, and he's very happy to have peace over there, but he's not holding any hostilities. Was your uncle very . . . I guess 'Christian' is the word to use.''

"Yes."

"Because your uncle has had an influence on him, telling him that when it occurred, and he went over there in fear, your uncle put him at ease and said that he has to forgive and grow here. Your uncle was definitely well suited for the spiritual life . . . he passed it on very easily to your son, and your son was quick to learn it. Anything around what used to be Cambodia? Kampuchea, I think they call it now.''

"Not far."

"Well, I'm seeing Laos, Cambodia—"

"What do you see?"

"I'm near the border of those two countries—"

"That's right."

"That's why I'm seeing both of these, like the border of Kampuchea and Laos—"

"Bingo," I said.

"Whoa—I tell you, you'll never convince me that praying for the so-called dead doesn't help. You're praying for him, but you're also praying you'll get an answer."

"Yes," Lila said softly.

"He says, 'Your prayer's been answered.' I think you've got the answer. He says, 'She prays for me, but she prays for an answer. Tell her her prayers have been heard. She's getting her answer now.' And he says to me that you can rest well now, you can put your mind at ease knowing that indeed he is alive, but not in this world. Could he have been shot down?"

"Yes."

"Was it actually during the Vietnam War this happened?"

"No."

"Okay, that's what I wanted to know. The war is not going on in the sense of how I know it. That's what was throwing me off all the time. Then he came to me and he said, this was like almost what you'd call a reconnaissance mission or something like that—"

"Yes."

"He's doing something like that, he says to me, and we are not at war with whoever shoots them down, so to speak. That's why when I said before, you were killed in action, but you're not killed in action, and he said, 'Now you understand what I mean,' because we were not involved. The war, it seems, had been well over. Did he work with computers or something—"

"Yes."

"Some sort of technical equipment of some sort?"

"Yes—"

"It was definitely a lot of technical equipment in some way, on the planes and around the base and so forth. Now, at the time he was stationed overseas, correct?"

"Yes."

"He was stationed in Southeast Asia."

"Yes."

"Okay, that definitely is where he was stationed, in Laos or Kampuchea."

"No," Lila said.

"But he keeps showing me that border again—"

"That's right. I understand."

"He keeps telling me, 'Go to the border of those countries.'

. . . Did anybody else pass on with him? As far as you could know?''

"Yes," Lila replied.

"Definitely. At least two other people. Two other guys—"

"Yes."

"In the same experience. Thailand involved in this at all?"

"Yes."

"I see Thailand in front of me now. Interesting. He shows me *Anna and the King of Siam*. And he says, 'Now, what's it called today?' Was he based in Thailand?''

"Yes. That's where he flew out of," Lila said.

"That's what he says, based in Thailand. He flew out of Thailand, and went up near those borders or something—"

"Yes."

"Then that's what happened. . . . Your birthday coming up soon?"

"Yes."

"I'm not going to be able to sleep tonight. He just wished you a happy birthday and handed you roses, that it's coming up soon. He says better early than late. This gives me the creeps. Do you— Is there a memorial to him or something?"

"Yes."

"He shows me, like, a grave, but he says it's not a grave, it's a memorial—"

"Yes," Lila said quickly.

"To him, and you've been to it recently, you have it someplace, and he compliments it. Do you, have you put flowers there recently? Or something, or flowers left there?"

"No," Lila said. "Wanted to."

"Because he says something about flowers at the memorial, in commemoration there, something of that kind. . . .Very affectionate young man?"

"Yes."

"Very warm person, definitely nice vibrations. Am I safe to say this is Mommy's boy, definitely?"

"Yes."

"That's what he says. . . . Does the name Matthew mean anything to you?"

"Yes," Lila replied.

"Passed on?"

"Yes."

"Have we—just say yes or no, don't tell me anything—have we spoken to him yet?"

"Yes."

"We have. He says, 'You've spoken to me already.' Now I have a choice of three. Which one are you?" George asked the spirit, laughing.

"Are you able to tell?" I inquired.

"Ah, it's funny," George said. "No, not yet. I'm just going to let him go, he just says to me, 'Tell her Matthew is here and you have spoken to me already.' Would you spell his name differently?"

"No."

"Matthew know your father?"

"Yes."

"It's not your father, though, is it?"

"No."

"He says, 'I know your father and it's not your father.' Oh, I understand, they're saying your father would have spelled it possibly differently, or maybe known a different version of the name. He would have spelled it in German or something?"

"Possibly, but I never—"

"No, you had no reason to, but I understand what he means."

"It's very possible," Lila said.

"Does the name Anthony mean anything to you?"

"Yes," Lila replied.

"Matthew know Anthony?"

"Yes."

"An interesting symbol. I saw Saint Anthony in front of me, and he said, 'Take the name, not what you've seen.' Let them do all the talking, it helps them, too. You said your first name was Lila. Okay, you know Anthony, too."

"Yes," Lila said.

"This is Lila," George said, "this is Anthony. Is Anthony very close to you?"

"Yes."

"It's interesting, because I like to let them do it with symbols, I keep learning how to interpret them and let them take their time so they can show me a symbol that I can identify with," George explained. "Is Anthony your husband?"

"Yes," Lila answered.

"This must be your son, then, Matthew," George said.

"Yes," Lila said.

"Yes, because he says, 'Anthony is her husband, my father,' so it must be the son, then. Oh," George said, as it suddenly dawned on him, "you're Anthony. He said to me, he says when he started speaking of grandfather, his name had to be Matthew because he spoke in the grandfather sense, so it wouldn't be your uncle. Called Matt?"

"Yes."

"Yeah, he's just writing it out now. . . . Do you have any trouble with the eyes?" George asked Lila.

"Yes."

"Your son says, 'Have you looked into it?'"

"Yes."

"Keep an eye on your eyes, I see Saint Lucy over your head and that speaks for itself. And your son backs me up that it's for real. Have you had an operation?"

"Yes."

"He says you have some sort of an operation, you've had it already."

"Yes."

"Because he said that your father again was with you, your father comes back and he was with you then, your uncle was with you, and you're fine now, though, right?"

"Yes."

"Yeah, because he says it's clear again, I see clearance in front of me. Were you praying to Saint Lucy at any time? Oh, okay, I just wanted to know, I see her over your head, and that's usually my psychic symbol for eye problems. Have you had any work done with the retina?"

"Yes."

"That's what he said to me, work done at the retina. What was it, a detached retina?"

"That's right. That's right."

"A detached retina. Now, did you have this *after* you assumed he had passed on?" George asked.

"Yes," Lila replied.

"The reason I'm asking is that to me it's double proof that he's on the other side, because your uncle and your father are definitely aware of it, and he says to me you had a detached retina, and I kept seeing a laser in front of you, and that usually means a detached retina, doesn't it? Okay.''

"I'll answer that later," Lila said.

"Do you understand what it means?"

"I certainly do."

"Okay, because your son put it in front of you and he said, 'This had something to do with it,' and then he said, 'Detached retina.' . . . And it looks like I'm going to be closed off, that's the impression, I'm going down, I see the tunnel opening, so that usually means they're going in, they're going back to the other side. Well, I get the impression, he says to me, 'You're looking for peace of mind.' Definitely it was some sort of renegade communist-oriented group there that shot them down and took advantage and so forth. I might as well be honest, they were executed in a way by these scavenger types in the border area. You know, they would be very hostile toward Americans as it is. You know, this is why I think he says, 'murder' in quotes because he felt they were under attack, so to speak, when of course, there was no such thing."

"Do you get the feeling he was killed when the action happened, when he went down, or did he live for some time after?" I asked.

"I get the impression— No, he said to me he was captured. I feel he was first captured and then was executed or something. I could be wrong, but that's the impression he was giving me. Captured.

"One more thing. If this is right, I definitely won't sleep tonight," George said. "Did he have some sort of birthmark? Scar?"

"Not by birth," Lila said.

"All right, clearly, some sort of scar?"

"He had a scar."

"Was it not visible? In other words, clothing would cover it up."

"Clothing would cover it up," Lila confirmed.

"That's what he says to me. He says something about— He says, 'Ask them about the scar that was on me that clothing could cover it up,' or something. Was it from an injury of some sort?"

"One was."

"The one that was due to injury, he says. Was it like stitches?"

"Yeah."

"Yeah. That's what he says to me, the one due to stitches, he says the injury due to stitches from when he was a child or something."

"Yes," Lila said.

"That's what he says, from an accident when he was a child, or an injury when he was a child and so forth, he says, 'Accept that. I have to live with it there now, it's very nice. That must be the final message.' Definitely sending great abundance of love from the other side, more roses on your birthday, by the way. From your father, from your uncle, from your aunt, from your son. Okay, they sign off. They cut."

Right after the reading, George spent over half an hour with Lila and Anthony and they discussed the reading. Several things that Matthew brought up had occurred after his death—Lila's eye problems, Lila saying the rosary for him and having a photograph of him displayed in the home. He identified himself, his father, and one brother, Scott, a career Marine with whom he'd had friendly rivalry since he was in the air force; thus his singing "The Halls of Montezuma."

But Matthew also alluded to things with great specificity that he could not possibly know if he were still alive, and many of the indications of just how specific and correct he was are in the language. For example, referring to his death as having happened "in action" but not in action, or referring to his mother's going to a grave that's not a grave (as it turned out, a memorial stone at Arlington, where flowers are not allowed; the latter fact accounting for the mention of flowers). There were also other memorials—a gymnasium on the Isle of Crete named for him—and posthumous awards, including the Purple Heart, the Distinguished Flying Cross, and another. Earlier on, Matthew indicated that he knew that his mother spoke of his situation and that things had been written about him. Following the reading, Lila and Anthony showed military photographs of the scars to which George had alluded. In addition, there was information about Matthew's nickname (Kiwi), which George was sure he wouldn't get, and other details.

At one point George said, "If he were still alive, where did all the information come from?'' A valid question. Later Lila and Anthony learned that their son had been captured alive in the area George indicated. It was believed that he was later killed by his captors, probably with a machine gun (thus the "tommy" in quotes, a term Anthony, a career military man, would have recognized from World War II).

Lila and Anthony were basically convinced by the reading that Matthew was dead, but Lila, understandably perhaps, sought another explanation. Toward the end of the evening she asked, "How do you explain my feeling that he is still alive?"

"Because he is," George replied softly.

"Why did I hear him talk to me about a month ago and say, 'Hey, Ma, I'm going home'?"

"As much as he could come to me, he could come to you," George said.

"About three to six months after we got the word that he was killed, at two o'clock in the morning," Lila said to us, "Matthew was at the foot of the bed, in uniform, clear as can be. And he said, 'I just want you to know that I'm all right. You don't have to worry about me anymore.' And I heard that as clear as a bell, and I woke Anthony up and said, 'Matthew was here,' and then he went."

"I know you miss him," George said, "but he's with you. If you could be me for five minutes, you would have complete peace of mind that your son is at peace on the other side."

Nine

In the fall of 1983 Viacom moved _Psychic Channels_ to a new, larger television studio. Now, while we continued to tape most of the programs, once a month George did a live program with readings for a number of people phoning in and for several others randomly chosen from the studio audience. As with the radio program, we received a huge number of calls, phone lines were jammed, and studio tickets were in great demand. So many requests came in that we have had to limit ticket availability to those who subscribed to our cable system, and even then each person could get only two tickets. We had severed our ties with the radio station, so fewer people had phone access to George. The demand for private readings increased dramatically, and as early as 1984 there was a two-year waiting list.

At last tens of thousands of viewers could see for themselves that people of all ages, regardless of sex, ethnic background, or religious belief, were interested in communication with the deceased. They could also see that George was not your stereotypical "psychic." He was a well-groomed, well-dressed, well-spoken, intelligent young man with a quick sense of humor. Most important, people saw what happens during a reading. Any public reading is generally less intimate, particularly regarding very personal or potentially embarrassing matters. Sometimes it's the spirit who "censors" the message; other times it's George who may, for example, psychically learn of one partner's adultery but see someone who might be the subject's spouse in the studio audience. Despite this, the studio-audience readings provided the most dramatic visual evidence that what George was doing was real, that the messages held great meaning for the subjects. Transcripts cannot possibly do justice to those readings in which, for example, a frail, elderly woman receives a message from her late husband, and then, with tears in her eyes, cries to George, "I knew he would come through, I knew he would be here for me. Thank you, thank you." Or the expression on a father's face as his late son comes through and reassures him that he did not suffer long in his fatal car accident and his mother weeps into his father's hand. Or the look of relief and happiness when a young woman's father apologizes to her, through George, for his disruptive behavior and reassures her of his love—nearly fifteen years after his physical death.

On more than one occasion a die-hard skeptic has—inadvertently, of course, since the studio audience is as anonymous to us as any caller—been shocked to receive an unexpected message. Still, the most surprising aspect of the in-studio readings is that no matter how tragic the passing, or how much the spirit is missed by his or her loved ones, every subject ends the reading thanking George, appearing relieved and comforted, often smiling.

Our research was ongoing, and now that we had videotapes of each show, I could note two important elements. First was George's initial response when he hears the voice or sees the face of the spirit. How accurate is this first moment of contact? How precise is the information that follows? And how specific are the details that come forth? There are always those readings that start slowly, with George experiencing difficulty in picking out or understanding psychic clues. In those instances, is there a reason for the difficulty? Did the spirit commit suicide, or pass under unusual circumstances, or pass in a coma? And then there are those readings that literally begin before we even get to the set. Several times George has said, "They've told me that the first caller will be a male," or, "I was told to bring roses for a young man's mother. He told me she would be in the audience." And, of course, she was. Second, and perhaps most fascinating, is the reaction of the subjects in the studio audience. The look of surprise and amazement at George's accuracy, the confirmations pronounced aloud in expressions of joy or relief, the genuine looks of comfort and peace, the tears.

As time passed, George became increasingly comfortable and confident in his ability. He had resigned from his position at New York Telephone that summer and was devoting his full time to the readings. One result was that he started making statements instead of requesting confirmations during readings. When a subject failed to acknowledge, George was now more likely to insist. Following are highlights of some typical telephone readings conducted during a live television broadcast.

"Male close passed," George said.

"Yes," a woman replied.

"Woman close passed."

"Yes."

"They are related."

"There is a family connection," the woman acknowledged.

"You were close to him."

"Yes."

"It's your aunt's husband."

"Yes."

"Your uncle is calling out to her. He says he's in the light."

"It's an expression he used," the woman replied.

"He had a rough time before passing."

"Yes. He died one week ago tonight."

"There is litigation."

"Yes."

"About a dog bite."

"Yes."

"The dog jumped up and knocked you down."

"Yes. We went to court yesterday."

To another woman caller, George said, "Skin trouble? Rash or pimples."

"Yes," she answered.

"Three men close to you passed on."

"Yes."

"Dad passed."

"Yes."

"Father-in-law passed."

"Yes."

"I can't make out who the third male is," George confessed.

"Should I tell you?"

"No. A wedding coming up."

"Yes."

"The spirits say they'll all be at a wedding."

"Good."

"Your dad is sending you grace."

"Today would have been his birthday, and mine is coming up."

"Do you take the name Frank?"

"That was my grandfather."

"The third male I could not identify before!"

"Yes."

To a woman caller: "Emotional crisis around you. Personal. Sad and depressed."

"Yes."

"I see the symbol of knotted towels. Do you have trouble keeping your temper?"

"Yes."

"Your late father is giving me the message."

"Yes, he's passed."

"I see the symbol of a drink on the rocks. I take it to mean there is a romance on the rocks. I also see the symbol of a broken heart around you."

"Yes."

"Your father apologizes from the other side for abandoning you. He's your guardian angel."

"He died when I was very young."

To a male caller, George said, "Grandmother passed on."

"Yes."

"She shows me that you're in a uniform."

"I'm joining the Marine Corps. I've enlisted."

To a woman caller, George stated, "A recent illness or passing."

"Yes."

"Two passings. Two spirits present."

"Yes."

"Your dad passed."

"Yes."

"Passed within the last three years."

"Yes."

"He's calling out to Mom."

"Yes."

"Has his mom passed?"

"Yes—my grandmother, his mother."

"Well, she's with him."

"Okay."

"Your dad was very ill before passing. He's thanking you for staying with him before his passing."

"Yes, that's true."

"He's emphasizing 'weight.'"

"My dad—"

"He had a weight problem? He says—"

"Yes."

"I hear a second language, a foreign language."

"Yes."

"Your grandmother—"

"Yes."

"Do you take the name William deceased?"

"Yes."

"Did your father pass from a condition in the chest?" George asked, adding, "That's where I feel pain."

"Yes."

"Heart and blood pressure."

"Yes."

The evening that George had been told by a spirit to bring roses to the studio for his mother, he discerned the young man's spirit. Once it was determined that the message went to a woman, George said, "Young male killed tragically."

"Yes," she replied.

"Vehicle-involved accident."

"Yes."

"Your son."

"Yes."

George then went on to describe the young man's personality, age, and other details, which his mother acknowledged. At the end of the reading George rose from his chair and presented the woman with the roses he had brought. He told us that the spirit had said to him, "My mother will be in the audience. Give her these. They will comfort her."

Within a short time *Psychic Channels* was the most popular locally produced television program. Being on television had made us more visible, both literally and figuratively, and since we were no longer on radio, fewer people could get through to George. Being as—or probably more—curious about his ability, George welcomed tests, observations, experiments, and theories from experts and interested individuals. Working on Long Island proved to be a great advantage for us. Although generally considered a big suburb of New York City, Long Island is in fact large enough to be a state unto itself. Predominantly middle and upper-middle class, Long Island is home to no fewer than eighteen universities and colleges, and many technical schools, as well as the famed Cold Spring Harbor Laboratory and Brookhaven National Laboratory. The Island also boasts several technologically advanced industries, including aerospace. In addition, the population includes members of virtually every religious and ethnic group in America—from American Indians to Orthodox Jews. We have had in our audiences born-again Christians, Roman Catholics, Greek Orthodox, Russian Orthodox, Episcopalians, Unitarians, Quakers, Hindus, Buddhists, and Protestants of all denominations. We were joined on the air, both on radio and television, by an increasing number of experts and specialists—healers, hypnotists, physicists, psychologists, clergymen, physicians, law-enforcement officials, computer specialists, engineers, technicians, psychic researchers, magicians, educators, and even demonologists—who warned against the utilization of any psychic abilities.

George had been demonstrating his abilities in public for over three years. There had never been any question that something was going on, and there seemed to be no limit to the number of wild theories skeptics devised to explain it. One doctor, a psychiatrist with impressive credentials, observed George over a period of time and then gave us his findings. According to this man, George doesn't have psychic abilities, he is not talking to the deceased—it's all much simpler than that. George has access to a large computer system that is programmed with information about everyone George reads.

George calls up the data in advance of meeting the subject and then gives it out during the reading.

"You mean George memorizes all this?" I asked, incredulous.

"Sure," the psychiatrist answered.

"How does George have access to such a sophisticated computer?"

"Simple. The C.I.A. and other intelligence agencies would know. There are ways of getting such information. Obviously, since George can't be guessing, he has these connections," the good doctor proclaimed seriously.

"How about people who come to him anonymously or randomly?" I asked.

"He knows in advance who they are and has files on them."

"Do you know how complicated and complex that would be?"

"So?"

My mind was racing with a million possible answers. Where would George get information on such details as who was present when a person passed, a favorite nickname, relevant information on a criminal investigation that even the police had no knowledge of? The IRS? The Department of Motor Vehicles? The local obituaries? It was ludicrous, especially in view of the fact that neither George nor I had the financial resources to support such a system. And, again, this presupposes that George knows all of his anonymous subjects, every person whose one call is picked at random by the phone system from hundreds of others to get through the busy circuits, every detail of every crime the police ask for his help on. The police work is an excellent example. Although we cannot discuss the details of these highly confidential cases, we can say that George reveals information that could be known only by a victim or a perpetrator. How would that information be on a computer? And anyone who has ever dealt with the government's computers knows that if George relied on these sources, his reputation as a psychic medium would be shot. These were, I felt, all relevant points, but it was clear that the discussion had long ceased to be rational. All I could say was, "Doctor, no disrespect, but you need help."

Many of George's readings involved sympathetic pain. Unlike a factual detail about someone's personality, life, or physical death, sympathetic pain, any pain, can be monitored and checked. It was only a matter of time before someone came forward to test that aspect of George's ability. One doctor, a chiropractor, offered to participate and provide the anonymous subjects for just such an experiment. During the test the doctor brought in one patient at a time. Each patient would receive a private reading from George, and George would describe his or her physical condition—be it from illness or injury—based on what he perceived through sympathetic pain. It should be noted that George has made no attempt to gain more than a rudimentary knowledge of human anatomy and medicine. Once he mistakenly asked a woman subject about her "prostate." While on the one hand, a greater knowledge of medicine and anatomy might give George's health readings more specific details, we should regard his relative ignorance of such matters as further evidence that it is the discarnate entity, not George, providing the information.

Previous to the experiment, which took place in the doctor's Long Island office, he consented to a private reading. In the course of it the doctor acknowledged as correct several facts George brought forth, among them that the doctor's wife had suffered a miscarriage (which the doctor admitted only he and his wife knew about) and that his mother had passed from a stroke. George was even able to tell the doctor which of his mother's hands had been crippled. All the while, the doctor's young son kept insisting that George was a fake. The young man, a medical student, stated that what George was doing didn't fit into his definition of science and medicine, and so it could not be real. George remained calm; he'd heard all this before. But in the middle of the reading with the doctor's mother, George spoke of roses and suddenly the room began to smell of roses. Of course, this wasn't George's doing, it was the work of the son's grandmother, who was no doubt intent on showing her grandson that she was indeed there. Everyone present was amazed, but the doctor's son just wouldn't drop it. We moved to the tests.

The doctor set up a screen behind which one of ten patients would stand. There was no way for George to know which one or to get clues about physical appearance. Following are the results of the ten readings—George's response to each, with the doctor's diagnosis in parentheses: kidney pain (kidney problems, pain); lower back pain (lower back weakness and pain); arthritis-like pains, which George attributed to lupus since he also saw a blood condition (systemic lupus erythematosus); pain in neck, stiffness in jaw, difficulty in turning head and moving jaw (jaw and neck problems from accidental injury); pain in head, headache (headache resulting from whiplash injury); back pains (whiplash resulting in back injury); pain in arm and hand (bursitis in arm and shoulder); pain in back, backache (scoliosis, or curvature of the spine); leg pain (leg injury); nonspecific head pain (head, neck, and facial pain, with ear disturbance caused by injury).

Of the ten, the doctor accepted nine diagnoses; the tenth was not, he felt, sufficiently specific. Then the doctor went on to say that unless George could identify the specific vertebrae affected by the injuries or diseases, he would have to discount all of the other diagnoses as lucky guesses. Why the sudden turnaround? We had no idea, and the doctor wasn't saying. He had admitted being deeply moved by his private reading. Throughout the entire session, his son continued to badger George and made it clear to his father that he considered any belief in the phenomenon ridiculous. Could the doctor have been intimidated or embarrassed to say that George was right? We'll never know.

Others tried to do their debunking without our knowledge. A respected astronomer who had watched the television program for months felt that George had to be using some trick. To his credit, he analyzed a number of readings, searching the answers for patterns. Initially he assumed that the information George gave out was a result of deductive reasoning and run-of-the-mill generalizations. His theory would seem to make sense, except that at a certain point in nearly every reading, George would bring forth some information—a person's name, cause of physical death, allusion to the subject's personal life or relationship to the deceased—that simply could not be obtained through any other means but discarnate communications. When the astronomer finally told us about his investigation we were pleased, not only because he could not prove that what George was doing was anything but what we said it was but because of his honesty. He had used his knowledge and intelligence to create and test a hypothesis. When his findings no longer fitted, he said so. As he later told us, "My findings certainly throw off a lot of what I was taught and trained to believe.'' But did that make it automatically impossible or suspect? No.

Unfortunately, not all skeptics were as open, honest, or—to be quite frank—as bright. In the spring of 1984 I was contacted by a free-lance journalist who claimed to be researching a story on psychics in general and George in particular. I had known the writer's father, a local newspaperman, professionally for years but had not spoken with him in the last four. I found it unusual that the writer would phone me, since he could easily have phoned George directly (we gave his home number out during the television show, as we had done on radio). Naturally assuming that the writer called me to help get him an earlier date on George's crowded schedule, I promised I would do so and arranged for the writer to see George two weeks hence.

The appointed evening arrived, and we met the writer and his wife (whom we had not been told to expect). George sat in another room while I spoke with the writer, giving him information and background on George. Also present were my wife, Chris, my daughter, our friend Elise, and another friend who worked with computers. George then came in, did his reading for the writer and his wife, all of it tape recorded. In the first part of the reading, according to the story later published in *Newsday*'s Sunday magazine, George accurately described and gave the name of the writer's deceased paternal grandfather, determined that the writer's mother (who has a very Irish first and last name) was Jewish, and told him that he had had transmission problems with his car (which had occurred just hours before the reading). George then gave the man's wife's name, which was Ingeborg (and which the writer claimed in his article not to have said in George's presence). Turning to the wife, George discerned her late grandmother, gave her name, determined that it was the same as Ingeborg's middle name, that her grandmother had lived with her when she was younger, and that Ingeborg's birthday was coming up. Then George got the name Svien, who he said died young, at around twenty, from ''something to do with height.'' This was all acknowledged by the writer's wife.

We heard nothing further about the reading until the article appeared that fall. We opened the magazine to discover that George and I were being accused in print of fraud, collusion, and hiring private investigators to unearth information on the writer and his family. Certainly his family was not entirely unknown—his father was a local restaurant critic—but they weren't exactly public figures, either. This, however, mattered not at all. Although the writer admitted in print to being surprised by some of George's revelations, he wrote, "My first and last instinct is to remain skeptical. . . . I'd prefer to believe that there are logical explanations for the illogical."

We include this episode not to carp about a bad "review," but to give a textbook example of how not to try to debunk a medium and to show, again, that even well-regarded publications remain generally ill equipped to tackle this subject. If, for just one moment, we accept the writer's ludicrous assertion that George and I do "research," then it stands to reason that we can research only those people whose names we know, and that would include both the subjects and the spirits. Telling me his real name and his purpose *did* help the writer get an earlier appointment than the average person. Yet, rather than admit this in the article, he refers to me as "George's buffer against the public" and insinuates that George's waiting list was really not that long. He states in the piece that he spent an entire year doing research, yet he didn't contact George or me until a few months before the article was published. Why didn't he call George directly for an appointment earlier? He could have booked it under a pseudonym. Though he probably would have waited longer to see George, he would have protected himself from our "investigators." (Besides, George does not take last names for most appointments.) Better yet, why didn't he call and claim to have an emergency, or claim to be involved in a police case? If he'd been more familiar with the show and George, he would have known the names of several experts—all listed in the phone book—whom he might have approached about setting up an experiment. Suffice it to say, he could have pursued any of a number of routes to get to George without going through me and without revealing his identity.

Imagine how much better his "exposé" could have been if he had sent someone else claiming to be he in his stead, or brought along some other woman and introduced her as his wife, or accompanied another writer who would assume his identity while he posed as an interested friend, and then recorded George giving out the "research," which of course would all be wrong. Dr. Abrams, who showed up at George's posing as a drunk, and Stephen Kaplan and Max Toth, who had tested George by bringing along unexpected, anonymous subjects, had the right idea. Even coming to the reading as himself, he could have tried to mislead George by offering erroneous clues to draw him off the track. The local public library shelves are filled with books—pro and con—on the subject. A few hours of careful reading would have paid off in a wealth of debunker's tricks. Neither George nor I saw any used either before or during the reading.

Adding insult to injury, the piece was full of factual errors, including that the writer was introduced to George's wife and brother-in-law; George has never been married. The writer didn't appear to know—or at least did not explain to his readers—the differences among ESP, "something called psychometry" [his quotes], and other paranormal phenomena and the roadside palmists and fortune tellers he did the bulk of his research on. In fact, never once do the words "medium" or "mediumship" even appear. Did he really understand how George differed from the Tarot reader? It seems not.

The piece ended with the comment about George, "I mean, if he's really talking to dead people, why would he ever be wrong about anything?" But was George "wrong"? The writer admits that George is accurate on many points, and does not mention any errors. He complains of receiving a series of unfamiliar names yet does not say whether he followed up with the basic family research George encourages all his subjects to do for his benefit as well as theirs.

And, finally, we're back to one of those old preconceptions about discarnate consciousness. It's amazing how many people who dismiss even the possibility of discarnate survival and communication still insist on judging mediums according to some arbitrary criteria for entity behavior. They harbor expectations of how a "real" entity should act, even though they claim that such things don't exist. Here, the writer "reasons" that the dead cannot possibly be talking to George, but *if they did* they would always be right. Does this mean that, if George had brought forth *only* names that the writer recognized and if the writer had made his appointment anonymously, he would accept that George was genuine? There's no way to know. We must assume, then, that the writer believes (a) that the information came from our "research" and not the spirits of his dead relatives, and/or (b) that his dead relatives weren't bright enough to be correct about everything. Perhaps it was a hereditary problem.

Fortunately, despite the reluctance of many professionals in the sciences to publicly explore unexplained phenomena, there remain a few—though certainly a minority—who will come forward. Even before we began cohosting *Psychic Channels,* George had made dozens of public appearances, including demonstrations at the New School for Social Research, the Suffolk Academy of Medicine, the State University of New York at Stony Brook, Mensa, and other organizations.

By the time we held a psychic symposium, which was attended by many professionals from a variety of fields, in Suffolk County in 1986, there was no doubt but that science had begun to open up to questions about the unexplained world. In the eighties, syndicated columnist Jack Anderson was reporting on King Hussein of Jordan and his near-death and out-of-body experiences and running stories with such headlines as "Psychic U.S. 'Spies' Claim to Penetrate Secret Soviet Bases." *Woman's World* ran a spread on reincarnation, Whitley Strieber wrote a national best-seller, *Communion,* that told of his encounters with extraterrestrials. The venerable *New York Times Sunday Magazine* presented an essay entitled "Science on the Track of God." We were in the right place at the right time.

No one was as skeptical about the ability or as enthusiastic about tests and experiments as George. Unlike many psychically gifted people, George would freely undergo any test, participate in any experiment, under virtually any condition, provided no hypodermic needles were involved. Even the die-hard skeptics admitted that something was going on, and that George's ability presented a twofold problem. First, was he really receiving messages from the deceased? Second, if he wasn't, then where was the information coming from? In other words, no matter what the "source," George's abilities raised a series of secondary questions about the nature of consciousness, discarnate or "living," and the human brain. What could account for George's mediumistic ability? What is the process by which the spirit communications take place (in other words, is it in the "hardware" of George's physical brain or in the "software" of the mind)? Is there some as yet unexplained, undiscovered energy responsible? What makes George a conduit for these communications? How is it that he is a "human receiver"? And, if as George and others claim, physical death is just a transition to the other side, could we learn enough from him to build a working hypothesis, a foundation from which further scientific investigations into life after death could proceed? Was George's ability even "testable"?

The answer to the last question is clearly no. However, although we cannot test the ability, we can test its specific manifestations. We can compare readings and post-reading interviews to check his accuracy. We can present him with photographs of strangers from which he can pick out the entity he claims to have seen. We can study his crude drawings and automatic writing for words, names, symbols. And, thanks to tremendous strides in medical technology, we can test George for physical manifestations of such things as pain.

In 1983 we were introduced to a physician we will call Dr. John Bell. After observing George on several occasions and being the recipient of an emotional message from his late child, Bell conducted a series of tests on George. These tests, some using thermography, focused on sympathetic pain and psychic diagnosis. Dr. Bell appeared with us on several television programs and was always a welcome guest. He was the personification of open-minded skepticism, never jumping to any conclusion and stating often that these tests would have to be run not once or twice but twenty, thirty, one hundred times before he would draw any conclusion.

In February 1984 George underwent a series of thermography tests. Thermography is a diagnostic method that uses a heat-sensitive imaging device to measure differences in body temperature, which are then represented on a screen with different colors. A patient undergoing the procedure appears on the monitor as a multicolored silhouette, with white indicating the hottest areas and black the coldest. The room temperature and George's body temperature were stabilized prior to the test to ensure that the readings were true.

George stood before the thermography machine, a camera-like device, wearing only his undershorts. We were looking to see (1) if the thermograph would detect the area of George's body where he claimed to be receiving the sympathetic pain and (2) if that area corresponded with the anonymous subjects' health problems. Present, in addition to George and me, were two physicians, two thermography technicians, a computer specialist, a video camera operator (we later devoted two full programs of *Psychic Channels* to the session), an off-duty police officer, and two subjects chosen by Dr. Bell.

The tests went well, with George not only accurately describing each subject's specific health problems but also "lighting up" on the screen accordingly. Dr. Bell stated that George could not possibly create the hot spots voluntarily. One experienced thermography technician claimed to be seeing patterns of body temperatures she had never seen before. But George's accuracy went beyond anyone's expectations. In one case he accurately described a woman's myriad health problems—a back injury, a breast tumor that had been removed, and a degenerative neurological disease. Then he said that he sensed "a sharp pain" in the throat. We could see George's throat area heat up on the screen, but the woman's physician insisted that her throat was perfectly fine. The woman then confessed that she was so nervous that when she was called to enter the test room, she accidentally swallowed a large piece of hard sucking candy, which scratched her throat.

Sometime later George was tested for sympathetic pain. These tests were conducted on television. This time, a doctor applied a mild electrical shock to the body of a subject, a scientist, who sat off to one side of the studio. George sat several feet away with his back to the scientist, blindfolded. Each time the doctor touched the scientist with the electrode, George correctly stated where the contact had been made. In an attempt to trick George, the doctor did not apply the shock but said that he had. George fell silent for a moment, then responded, "I feel pain beginning in my right shoulder and going down my right arm." Of course, George was marked wrong on that one, but a month later the scientist experienced the sensation George had described. Tests revealed that he was suffering from the early stages of degenerative muscle disease. Had George sensed the disease before its symptoms manifested? Or had he gone into the future?

There is really no way to know. But George had experienced sympathetic pain before that could not be confirmed until weeks, or months, later. In the course of one very accurate reading, he told a woman subject that he felt pain behind his ear and was convinced that it related to her son. The woman replied that her son had no ear problems, but George insisted. Several weeks later the woman's son was standing on his front lawn when an unknown assailant shot and killed him in a case of mistaken identity. The bullet entered his skull directly behind the ear.

George has spoken—privately and publicly—of premonitions that have come to pass. One dream he had showed the scene of what he realized weeks later was the assassination of President Anwar Al-Sadat of Egypt. George could clearly see the scene—a military procession—and the colors of the various uniforms, but all of the faces were missing or vague. Another time he was extremely agitated and unable to stop pacing in front of a portrait of Pope John Paul II. The next day the Pope was shot. Were these premonitions or glimpses of the future purposely vague because the events were predestined and beyond human control? Even some very specific premonitions—like Tommy's grandmother's death—seem to suggest so. Other cases, and information George has received from the other side, suggest that while some future events cannot be altered, others can. While vacationing in a mountainous area, we telephoned George just to say hello. He was quite relieved to reach us and told us of a vision he'd had of our car careening over one of the steep mountain roads we were traveling. He urged us to have the car, specifically the steering mechanism, checked immediately. The next morning we took the car to a mechanic who, after checking things out, told us we'd caught a steering problem "just in the nick of time."

We have taken only the very first steps in finding out how George functions. Tests such as the thermography must be repeated many more times before any conclusions can be drawn. As far as George is concerned, while we may never know the why, the how is definitely worth pursuing. To that end, we have gathered pieces of evidence, observations that may or may not all fit together in the final answer. For example, Dr. Richard Resua tested George's pineal gland, a pea-sized gland in the brain whose total purpose is still a mystery. We do know that it synthesizes the biochemical serotonin, which functions as a vasoconstrictor and neurotransmitter and which may play a part in some mental disorders. The ancients regarded it as the "third eye," the seat of psychic abilities. Normally, the pineal gland functions only in the absence of light; George's functions in light as well. Dr. Resua also noted that George "had an unusual combination of cranial faults and an unusually shaped skull."

We have witnessed and recorded unusual phenomena in George's presence. Readings in which George has gone into trance have been recorded by highly sensitive microphones and when played back contain a staticky hiss no one present recalls hearing during the reading. In another instance two photographers, using two separate cameras and developing their own film independently, found unusual patterns on the film, areas around George's image that appeared to have been overexposed and make it appear as though energy or light were bursting from his head.

What does it all mean? Unfortunately, we cannot say. Perhaps one day after scientists have studied hundreds of the psychically gifted and discovered that the majority of them have overactive pineal glands or an abundance of cranial faults, we can put George in some perspective. Right now these seem to be just bits of information, not unlike facts in a reading, pieces of a jigsaw puzzle we try to assemble without knowing what the finished "picture" will be.

The absence of hard-and-fast scientific conclusions does not, however, preclude the development of theories. There is no doubt that the key to the ability, or at least to George's ability to use the ability, lies in his brain. Research into the brain has made greater advances in the last decade than were made in the century preceding that decade. We know, for example, that moods, even some aspects of personality, can have chemical origins.

Left-brain/right-brain theory is constantly being updated and refined. And a whole new generation of incredible imaging methods—magnetic resonance imaging, positron emission tomography, computer tomography—shows not only signs of disease and injury but charts brain activity. It is believed that in the near future magnetic resonance imaging will be able to trace chemical changes in the brain. What could these kinds of tests tell us about George?

For now the best, most logical theory takes us back to 1958, when George was paralyzed following complications from chicken pox and a dangerously high fever. It is well known that high fevers can affect, disrupt, and destroy brain function. We also know that the brain has amazing capacities for healing, often by accessing an undamaged section of the organ to assume the work a damaged area can no longer perform. Could not such a "rerouting" have occurred in George's case? Who knows what lies in the estimated 85 percent of our brains experts confess not to understand fully? Did George's brain "access" a psychic ability that lies dormant in all of us? Will we ever know?

Another of George's abilities we began experimenting with, and which he had been using frequently in police cases, was psychometry: the ability, through contact with or proximity to the object, to obtain facts concerning an object, its owner, or some person or circumstance related to it. A friend of mine named Harry was interested in testing George. One night Harry handed him a piece of cloth that had been folded into a small square, approximately two inches by two inches. George held it in his hand but, interestingly, did not rub it or try to make out the object's shape or size. "This is something from a uniform," George said.

Harry nodded.

"Something from a soldier?" Harry didn't answer, then George said, "Something from a foreign soldier."

"Yes," Harry acknowledged.

"I see blood, violence. Oh my God, it's a swastika!"

"Oh?" Harry replied, trying to sound very casual.

"This was your father's? I'm being told it's from a soldier he killed. It's from the first soldier he killed."

Harry then asked George if he could tell him what had happened.

"It happened around the time of the Battle of the Bulge. It was in the south of France, in late 1944, he's telling me." George then said that he saw a spirit's face materialize. It was the spirit of the German soldier from whose uniform Harry's father had taken the swastika.

"The German soldier is telling me his name is Fritz. He's saying there is no animosity to your father on the other side. 'We have met on the other side. This is an exchange,' Fritz said. Your father killed Fritz because in a previous life Fritz had killed your father. This is an 'evening-out' of karma, so to speak. In any event, they have met on the other side. They know each other now and they are friendly."

Harry confirmed the reading. His father, John, removed the swastika from the uniform of a soldier he killed in late 1944. John sent the swastika back to his wife with a letter saying,

"This is from the first enemy soldier I killed." A few months later John was killed in action. In 1956, when Harry was twelve, his mother gave him a number of mementos, among them the swastika.

The readings also had a lighter side. One evening during a live show, George experienced sympathetic sensation in what he gingerly terms "the private area." The woman caller acknowledged that she was having some gynecological problems in the corresponding area. When the reading ended, George said, "That's an interesting feeling."

"Yeah, I bet," I answered.

"You get right down and—zoop!" George said, laughing.

"Really, sympathetic pain?" I asked.

"Yeah, but where I would sense it, if you know what I mean."

The audience was laughing loudly at this point.

"I get the idea," I said.

"It's not that I'm getting turned on or anything," George said, smiling. From the audience's laughter it was clear that they didn't entirely believe him.

George's abilities have resulted in some rather humorous experiences. Once, at a party, George kept seeing one of the men there naked. Of course, the gentleman was fully clothed, but every time George glanced his way, he saw him as he would look nude. Finally George could no longer contain himself and started giggling. The man, who correctly surmised that he was the object of George's outburst, came over to inquire just what was so funny. Embarrassed, George explained that he was a psychic medium and told the man what he was seeing. The man began laughing, too. It turned out that he also had an unusual profession—he was a male stripper.

With the passage of time, we noticed that many subjects—callers, viewers, and those who saw George privately—were regarding the readings not as something unusual and bizarre but as a confirmation of feelings that they had always had. The following reading, with an anonymous female caller on the live television program in January 1987, is an example:

"Hello," she said.

"Female presence, female close to you passed on," George said.

"Yes."

"Strong female vibration. She is family."

"Yes."

"Family by blood."

"Right."

"Young when she passed on—or very youthful in her disposition. Young at heart."

"Yes."

"She passed on from health trouble."

"Yes," the caller acknowledged.

"It affected her chest, breathing."

"Toward the end, yes."

"I'm getting loss of breath, in the chest area. You took care of her."

"Yes."

"And she's very grateful to you. You might have felt, in fact, like you didn't do enough."

"Yes, that's true."

"Don't feel that way. She's fine and at peace in the next dimension and is very grateful for the help you gave her prior to her passing. You may have put yourself on a little guilt trip about it."

"I did."

"She says, 'Don't do that to yourself. Everything's okay.' Strong motherly vibration. Is that your mom?"

"Yes, it is."

"Because she says 'mother.' Very devout—spiritually, in her own way—whatever faith she was raised in. I feel tremendous devotion with her. Someone who would certainly know the power of prayer and would appreciate it in the next dimension."

"Oh definitely."

"Catholic. Is she Catholic?" George asked.

"Yes."

"Very devout with the Blessed Mother."

"Oh, yes."

"Because I keep seeing the rosary and symbols of the Blessed Mother in front of me. So, definitely, if you're saying the rosary for her, continue. She knows it's a very powerful form of grace."

"She said the rosary every day of her life," the caller said.

"Oh, great, because she wants it every day of her life there. I see white rosary beads."

"She owned a pair of white rosary beads, yes."

"Because she says, say it for her."

"I have them."

"Now you can put them to good use."

"Yes."

"Your dad's passed on also?"

"No."

"Health concern around him, because your mother speaks of your father."

"Yes."

"He has to live with it, basically, I think."

"I guess—I'm not sure."

"Okay. Because I don't feel there is anything I can tell you that you don't already know. But there is this concern that he has to live with it—keep alert."

"Right."

"He does have trouble walking," George stated.

"Not that I know of."

"He's told to watch where he's walking. Leave it. Could be circulation concern. Told to watch where he's walking. Did she speak another language? Because I hear another language with her."

"Yes."

"It's a romance language."

"Yes."

"Narrows me to four," George quipped. "Let's see." After a short pause, he said, "It is Italian. I hear prayers being said in Italian. I hear the Hail Mary being said in Italian."

"Yes, it's Italian. The Hail Mary was her favorite prayer."

"I guess it still is, because I hear it being said in Italian."

"And I always say Hail Marys for her when I pray for her."

"She's probably very pleased with that. I see you taking a trip, in warmer weather, within the year. More than likely over the summer. But you don't have to be too psychic to figure that out."

"That's good."

"There's a wedding or birth coming up, a gay occasion coming up."

"Oh! There *is* an occasion coming up. But it's not a wedding."

"But in any case, something festive. I see the white lace.

You're going to have a good time—happy, festive occasion. And she speaks of being part of it.''

"Shall I tell you?"

"No. Anyway, she'll be part of it.''

"You're so close!'' the woman exclaimed.

"There's a Maria or a Mary passed on. Aunt or great-aunt. You're married. Maybe on your husband's side.''

"Mary?'' the caller repeated. "I'm thinking. It's possible.''

"I'll let it go. There has to be—aunt or great-aunt. I'm sure you'll find one sooner or later.''

"Yes.''

"There's also Phyllis or Philomena.''

"Yes.''

"Passed on.''

"Yes. My goodness.''

"Mother figure to you—like an aunt or grandmother.''

"More like an aunt.''

"You—who has eye trouble? I see the symbol of Saint Lucy. Or someone in the family. Saint Lucy is the symbol of eye trouble.''

"Eyes. Well, I do a lot of needlepoint, and my eyes get blurry.''

"Could be. Seems to be concern around the eyes—you or an immediate family member. Like strain, one eye worse than the other. Not a big deal. Philomena spoke Italian. Was Philomena ever called Mina or Lina?''

"That's my mother's name—Lina.''

"Okay. That's my mistake. I could have sworn I heard someone say Mina or Lina. Does your mother have a weird first name? *Without* telling me.''

"Oh, yes.''

"Very Italian-sounding.''

"Very.''

"Is her name something like Pascalina?''

"You got it! Pascalina!'' the caller replied excitedly.

"I got the name from the book *La Popesa*. I saw the book in front of me. It was about Sister Pascalina. Now she said, 'You have my name,' but she didn't seem to like it very much, though.''

"Oh, she couldn't stand that name!''

"She said it reluctantly.''

"When we used to tease her we'd call her that name to get her mad."

"Now she can haunt you to get back at you," George said, joking. "But she also showed me a vision of Lena Horne and the book about Sister Pascalina. I recognized the book. Are you expecting money?"

"Yes."

"Not from work, though. Another source, your mother says, like an inheritance, winnings, gift, investment return to you or an immediate family member. You're entitled to it."

"Right. That's the truth."

"It's a question of red tape."

"Yes it is."

"Comes as a surprise. Felix the Cat equals good news, happy surprise."

"Okay."

"Did you lose a pet? Dog?"

"Yes."

"Because I hear a dog barking, and your mother says the dog is there with her, not to worry—keeping her company and her taking care of it."

"You're gonna think I'm crazy, but that dog appeared in my house before she died. I saw it. My daughter saw it," the caller said.

"I believe it."

"My mother loved that dog, and it was there waiting for her."

"The name Carmela, she says. Mean anything?"

"Yes."

"Mom calls out to her—concern with health. Mom calls out to Millie or Carmela. Carmela, keep alert to health."

"I feel my mother around me all the time. I always feel her watching over me."

Like many of us, the caller knew that her mother, though deceased, was still with her. Others, for whatever reason, may not be quite as clear about the presence of their deceased loved ones in their daily lives. As a message for a female caller on Valentine's Day, 1982, suggests, a spirit may be with us or attempting contact, and yet we may never realize it.

"Is there a male close to you passed on?"

"Yes."

"Related to you?"

"Yes."

"Close."

"Very close."

"You're hoping to hear from him."

"Yes."

"Because he just popped in. I just felt the male come in and say, 'She's hoping that she hears from me, and I'm here.' Did he suffer a great deal before passing?"

"Uh—"

"Or was there a lot of pain or something?"

"It's possible."

"Okay. Did he pass on suddenly?"

"Yes."

"Because he says sudden passing. Is it possible he might have kept it to himself?"

"It's possible but not probable."

"I feel pain within myself, but I want to keep quiet about it as well. Would he come in on a father vibration?"

"No."

"Grandfather, anything like that?"

"Husband," the caller replied.

"Is he a father, though?"

"Yes."

"Because when you said husband, he said, 'Yes, and father.' In other words, the children would be the ones to whom he's calling out. Was his passing an accident?"

"No."

"He passed on from an illness? Did he contract an illness?"

"Hmm." The caller seemed unable to answer.

"You see, the thing is, what I'm getting is not in the sense of a car accident, but it seems to be accident. He keeps saying, 'Yes, yes, yes.' Did he contract it accidentally, or . . .'"

"It's a very interesting thing. I don't know how much you want me to go into it—"

"In a little while we'll ask you," I said, "but not right now."

"Do you understand what he's driving at?" George asked.

"Yes."

"Because he seems— I'm getting accident but not the kind we would immediately identify with. Well, it won't sound silly to say that you're being wished a Happy Valentine's Day."

"Ah."

"Very thoughtful guy?"

"Extremely."

"I found it obvious, but he said, 'I'm very thoughtful and she'll definitely relate to that.' I see roses in front of you."

"That's true."

"Was that his favorite to give you?"

"Well, it wasn't unusual."

"Well, there are roses being given to you."

"And my daughter brought me a rose today."

"They're pink roses as well."

"Almost, it's like an orangish-pink."

"Okay, because I see pink. Do you have a son?"

"Yes."

"And a daughter as well. I heard you mention daughter."

"Yes."

"Because he calls out to the children. Did he have any trouble with his back?"

"At one time."

"Because I'm getting extreme pain up the back."

"At one time, but not related to his passing."

"I'm getting that pain. Would the condition have affected him from the waist up?"

"Uh. Within—"

"I feel hollow in my frame."

"Yes."

"Did he have any trouble breathing?"

"Yes."

"If your children are old enough to accept this, he just says, 'Tell my children you have heard from me.' Did he have trouble . . . would you understand why I feel such hollowness in my frame?"

"Yes."

"I'm not a doctor or anything. I can't describe it, but I feel it."

"Definitely."

"Okay."

"It's uncannily true," the woman said.

"Okay, you can explain. I don't understand, I just give it to you. Did you feel him near you recently?"

"Not particularly."

"I see him coming to you in a dream, or to someone else in the family."

"Possibly."

"I don't know, there's talk of a dream or a feeling of that coming through. Do you know Al, living or deceased, Alvin, anything along that line?"

"Alvin, yes."

"Would he?"

"Would he know—"

"Is Alvin living or deceased?"

"Living."

"Okay, would your husband know Alvin?"

"Yes."

"Because he's asking for him. Were they close or—"

"Friends."

"Okay, he just says, 'How's Alvin doing? Tell him you have heard from me.' He said that—"

"This is unbelievable. This is really unbelievable."

"The name Lynn mean anything to you?"

"That's me."

"Oh, I don't believe it," George exclaimed.

"This is unbelievable," she said.

"Because I was just going to ask you, if you had said yes, the message is, 'Love to you, Lynn,' and I was getting signed off."

"It's unbelievable," Lynn said. Then she told us of how she came to call George.

"What is the hollowness?" George asked.

"He died from acute leukemia, and he was on a respirator before he died."

"No wonder. I was having a lot of trouble breathing."

"And you say, did he contract it? There was a lot of question of how it came on. It came on all within two months from beginning to end," she explained.

"What did he do for a living?" I asked.

"He was a real estate broker."

"And you don't have any way to know whether that was something that happened because it happened, or whether it was—"

"No, because the doctors all asked us if he was involved with chemicals or if he was out of the country, and they just came up negative constantly," Lynn replied.

"It seemed to me," George said, "that he gave the impression that it was an accident the way he contracted the illness. I just couldn't understand it."

"Yes, it's really a freaky kind of thing. We still don't know. I have to speak to a doctor and request an autopsy report to see if that turned up anything."

"Sure, it's a hard thing, but it's just strange that George would ask a question about that when indeed—" I remarked.

"Is there anything that you read about the future at all?" she asked.

"At this point I would have to say I couldn't get anything, because I took it to be very obvious when I found out it was your husband and he said Happy Valentine's Day. I said to him, 'Give me something deeper than that.' And that's when he signed off after Alvin and said, 'Love to you, Lynn.' And good-bye for now and just signed off, so I'm not in contact with him anymore."

"Yes."

"How old was he?"

"Forty-three."

"That is your name, Lynn?"

"That's my name. And Alvin is my very closest friend, and he's in Florida."

"Well, he's alive and well over there," George assured her.

"Thank God for that."

Do deceased loved ones play a role in our day-to-day lives, and if they do, what is it? Back when George and I were doing the radio program, we allowed a limited number of interested people—journalists, researchers, experts from various fields—to sit in on the shows. Now and then a listener would call and be invited to join us.

A teenager whom we'll call Ricky asked if he could come down to watch a show. He said that he wanted to meet George. Ricky's father, an electrical engineer, drove him to the studio. Within minutes of their arrival, Ricky's dad made his position—and the real motive behind Ricky's visit—known. Claiming to be a skeptic, Ricky's father stated that his purpose was to protect Ricky from what he believed was George's trickery. George just shrugged, then entered the studio. It was air time.

Ricky and his father watched the proceedings through a large picture window that separated the studio from a hallway.

They could hear the broadcast through speakers. Toward the end of the show, George discerned a presence that went to Ricky. We hastily put Ricky on a microphone, and his reading began. The spirit George was discerning was Ricky's late grandmother. She gave George some accurate details, which established her identity, then she got to the point of her visit.

"Your grandmother is saying you're hanging around with the wrong crowd," George said.

"Yeah," Ricky replied.

Now Ricky's father was at full attention, watching the exchange from behind the glass.

"Your grandmother is saying you know exactly the trouble you got in already. I won't say it out loud here," George said. "But it's not too late to get away from the situation. She asks if you understand what she means and what you're to do."

"Yes, Grandma," Ricky replied, then quickly corrected himself. "Er, George. Yeah, I understand."

"It's up to you to change, she's saying."

"Yeah, I can. I will."

When the program concluded, Ricky's father was obviously a little upset and at a loss for words. He told us privately that he and his wife and school authorities had all but given up trying to get through to the boy about an especially bad crowd he was drifting toward. They also feared that he was dangerously close to getting into trouble with the law. Although Ricky's father had seen evidence of spirit communications, he was still unable to understand it. Nonetheless, his opinion had changed drastically. "I guess there are things that I don't understand," he admitted. Perhaps as a logical, educated man he found it difficult to accept. As a parent, however, he seemed very grateful.

Through the readings, George has been able to help countless people come to terms with a range of problems. This is not to say that the solutions to all of your difficulties lie in a reading—they don't. But in certain cases a reading can literally change someone's life overnight. Early on, George and I met Dr. Brenda Lukeman, Ph.D., a psychologist and psychotherapist, author (*Embarkations*, a book on coping with death and dying), and director of a Long Island–based educational organization called Courage in Crisis, which offers conferences and programs for all of those who deal with terminal illness, loss, and sudden change. She had discussed the relationships between psychology and psychic phenomena with us several times on radio and television. In spring 1987 she joined us on *Psychic Channels* to discuss coping with death, particularly teen suicide.

About midway through the program I remarked, "I'll ask you a question, although this might seem controversial to some of your colleagues. What about a psychologist, a psychotherapist, working with a psychic?"

"I love doing it," Dr. Lukeman replied. "George and I are good friends by now. Not only has George assisted me personally, enormously, with his readings, but he's assisted me as a psychologist. I did have a patient who came to me. Her sister had committed suicide quite a few years ago when they were both in their late teens, early twenties. The sister was fine one moment, the next moment she went over to the balcony, jumped off the balcony, that was it. She hit the ground and died immediately.

"The suicide's sister came to me. We were working on guilt . . . [which] had affected her entire life up to that point—I would say easily ten, fifteen years. It was as if she were living under a blanket of sorrow and guilt. She'd had a little fight with her sister just before her sister jumped. So we worked in many ways around the edges of this, and then I sent her to see George."

The result, Dr. Lukeman said, "was dramatic and beautiful . . . I told George nothing about her background, I just asked if he would see her. She went to see him, and her sister appeared in the meeting. George said, 'I feel someone here,' and he knew her name, he knew details about her relationship with her sister that she had not even told me; there were things that there was no way that he could possibly know. [My patient's] sister began to speak to her through George. She wept and wept for hours. Her sister said, 'I love you, I beg you to forgive me for doing this. I'm here with Father. I'm working through my painful karma that I've created as a result of doing this. It wasn't your fault.'

"It had such a profound effect upon my patient . . . she was so deeply moved on many levels. First of all, it just lifted years of guilt and sorrow from her. And then, on another level, it helped so much because she was so clear that there was something afterward."

Clearly, George's work could help people. Yet some continued to reject it on religious grounds. Monsignor Thomas Hartman, director of radio and television for the Diocese of

Rockville Centre, New York, had appeared on several radio and television programs with us. Soft-spoken and very easygoing, Father Tom, as we called him, became a good friend. In May 1987 he joined us for a *Psychic Channels* program entitled "Theology and Parapsychology." During the show he generously told the audience of his private reading with George, during which a priest under whom he had worked and whom he had cared for during a fatal illness came through. The whole conversation was fascinating, but we would like to end this section with two statements Father Tom made that, we believe, state beautifully the religious view of what George does. At one point, we discussed why the Church was so reluctant even to acknowledge the positive aspects of the work George and other gifted people do.

"I think one of the things that Church leaders are concerned about is, in our culture, faddism and commercialism," Monsignor Hartman said. "As I see it, life is difficult. Spirituality is difficult. Marriage is difficult. The commitment to any way of life is difficult. And if someone were to come to George, who has this gift, just as a panacea, as a placebo, to remove themselves from the struggle of everyday life, I think that they would be mistaken. What we're all trying to do is figure out, How can I take the spirit that is within and allow my spirit to become more important than anything else in my life? It's the spirit that energizes us. It's the spirit that activates us. It's the spirit that defines how we interrelate with other people.

"I never told you this," he had said earlier in the program, "but I had been wrestling with the idea, why do people pray for someone who's dead? If they're with God, and God takes full care of them, what more is needed? In the most spiritual moments of my life, I still need a hug and a kiss and all that. When people die and are with God, I believe they still need a connection with this world, to know that there are people who love them."

Ten

It has now been more than seven years since George and I first met. Those years proved to be an adventure, and one that appears to have no end. George does private readings three days a week and appears with me on *Psychic Channels*. Through his readings we have learned a great deal about discarnate communication and our abilities and possibilities as human beings. What has the ability meant to George Anderson as a person? How has it changed his life? What has he learned, through the readings and his own personal conversations with the other side, that he can share with us?

In July 1987, George and I spoke for a couple of hours about these questions. Many things had changed in all of our lives, but, rereading the transcripts, we could see that the work we had done in the previous seven years was probably only the beginning.

"Let's begin with some of the questions that people ask us all the time. Why do some spirits from the other side communicate and not others?" I asked.

"Good question," George replied. "I have no idea why some are discerned and others are not. It's happened continually in readings, where somebody doesn't come through for years, even though the subject comes back again and again. I've had it happen where they come to one subject and not another. It may be because they're not ready to come through, they're not prepared to come through, they're not certain how to do it. They may progress to such a spiritual level over there that discerning or communicating with this side of the dimension is not really for them. They may be involved in greater spiritual pursuits over there.''

"Where is it that we go when we die? Does the other side tell you where we're going?"

"Well, according to what they say, we go through the different levels of consciousness. We're working our way up. It's like, to go up to the twelfth grade, you've got to pass the first through the eleventh. When we pass on, we do go into the tunnel, we can go through these little darker levels, which can represent a form of hell or purgatory, because these are the two negative levels, or the darker ones. But if we've been a good person, we generally just seem to pass through them very quickly and then we go on to the third and fourth levels of consciousness, where average people such as ourselves go— not everybody can be a Mother Teresa, who would probably go higher up. When we go through these levels we meet our relatives and friends greeting us at the end of the tunnel, much as in the movie *Resurrection*, where they're there waiting and they lead us into the light. And there's like a form of spiritual rejuvenation, like a reunion, like a party, 'Hey, it's great to see you again.' We recognize each other by personality. As we all have individual, unique fingerprints, we each have a very singular personality. There's no physical body, but there's a spiritual body that may take on a physical form, but to tell you the truth, I think that's only during a reading, so I can see and describe what the person being read can understand.''

"Geographically speaking, where is it? Is it the stereotypical heaven, somewhere up above the clouds?"

"It seems that the next dimension is here, it runs parallel to this one. Making the transition seems to be more like a heavenly experience than a trip to the Hollywood-style heaven. I think that the reason we have the sense of being uplifted or believe that heaven is up is that we feel a sense of being uplifted in the next stage of life. When we become one in the next dimension, we feel that we understand everything, we feel spiritually and emotionally uplifted. That's probably where the conception of going up came from.''

"Can the spirits come right out and tell you what the other side is like, or do you have to put pieces together?"

"It depends on their degree of awareness and consciousness. Somebody may be having a different, subjective experience over there, so they would have a different interpretation of it. It's just as it is here with us. For example, I'll look at the sky today and describe the color as sky blue. Yet if there's a different shade tinted in it, or the sun moves a little, or you look up even five seconds later, you could say it's more turquoise, or powder blue. The same thing could be happening on the other side.

"I've never really heard any complaints about the other side, unless the person has gone over there and into the darker levels, for committing some serious crime, hurting people, or committing suicide. Generally, though, most spirits I've heard from seem to be very happy, very content, very much at peace, very aware and knowing of themselves, even if they were very negative and very unhappy here. They seem to be aware of a lot of knowledge and to understand it all there more than we do here.

"Learning and growing seem to be what it's all about there. And they are able to understand themselves, *if* they want to. I've been told by the other side that you have to make a prime decision over there. You have to face up to yourself and do something about it, otherwise you'll just flounder and you won't progress spiritually. That seems to be a very important issue, to recognize yourself, your positive qualities and your negative ones, and try to do something about it. I've also been told that they have tasks, jobs to do over there. For example, David Licata told us that he works with children and animals who have crossed over. It's like having a job here, you just take on a spiritual job in the next stage of life, where you earn your soul progression by helping others crossing over, by helping people here find their way spiritually, helping people there to find their way spiritually, to be involved in various sorts of things."

"Does it matter what level you're on to be able to communicate?"

"You might be inclined not to come to me if you're on one of the darker levels. I would not be attracting anything that would be negative, so if you're on the darker or the lower levels, unless it's for a specific spiritual purpose, I would not discern you. A

Hitler, to take one extreme, would put himself in such a state of darkness that he would literally not be able to communicate.''

"Will a suicide, for example, remain on that dark plain?"

"Not perpetually. Through their own free will, they can progress. This is why it's so important that people, no matter what your religious belief or persuasion, even if you're an atheist, remember to pray for those who have passed on. Because that embraces them in love and encourages them to progress. The problem that the suicide faces in the next dimension is that, when you do arrive in the next level, it's not the pretty sight that the average passing can be. Their problem is that they cannot forgive themselves. When someone comes through in a reading and is starting to make me feel as if they've taken their own life—"

"What do you feel?" I asked.

"You feel like you're in the presence of a ghost," George replied sadly. "There's a chilling feeling. And it's very important that those coming through acknowledge what they've done. It's like getting up and saying, 'I'm an alcoholic.' Coming forward and saying, 'I have taken my own life.' A friend of mine who had recently taken his life came through and did not know how to go into the light. I kept telling him to go forward to the light, but he was afraid of judgment. He couldn't forgive himself. Also, he was having a problem with the fact that after he had taken his own life, his spirit obviously lingered around the scene of the act. He could not overcome the memory of his father's discovering him, and that was haunting him emotionally to a tremendous degree in the next dimension. What he and many of us don't understand is that there is judgment there, but it is not done by God on a throne. Judgment rests basically with yourself. And we all know that the greatest enemy we can face is ourselves.

"It can take eons of time as we understand it before they go into the light. It depends on the person. You're in control. You hold the reins. Those who've come through those darker levels have said that they've had to face themselves and realize that if they don't shape up, in other words, learn more about themselves, they're not getting anywhere."

"Why are they able to face themselves on the other side if they weren't able to do so here? What changes?"

"One of the things that the higher entities in the next dimension say is that we can very easily cheat others, but we can never cheat ourselves or God."

"Supposing I went to one level and a relative of mine has gone to another level, how do we communicate?"

"Well, again, part of it seems to be a matter of progression. For example, if your mother's on the fifth and your father's on the fourth, your mother can come down to your father's plane, but your father cannot go up to her plane until it's earned. So a lot of souls are inclined to dawdle on the fourth or fifth plane until someone they love very much joins them and becomes equal with them on that level so that they can work spiritually together."

"Once over there, do we maintain the relationships we had here?"

"It seems that you might be inclined to be close to a soul over there that you were close to here because you're on the same vibration, or wavelength. For example, most of us have a friend who we feel is closer to us, more like family than someone in our own family. So do they, but they also seem to learn to love one another completely and equally, even though there may be a time when they're more attracted to a single individual."

"Now, some spirits may choose to remain on the other side indefinitely, while others return," I said. "When a spirit does come back, does it always come back to the same family it was with before, the same parents, the same loved ones?"

"We all seem to stay together with the same people that we felt close with—birds of a feather flock together. We may have different parents, our brother or sister could be our parent next time. But we do seem to stay with the same other souls that we feel a certain affinity with, or a good vibration with. This may explain why we feel closer with our sister than our brother, or why you feel more like your best friend is part of your family. I feel we've always been together with the same people from the beginning, but maybe we meet different people along the line, who would highlight, enhance, or play an important role in our lives at that specific point."

"Some come back over and some don't? What determines that?"

"Well, several things. They say it's best not to try to come back right away, they say it's best to hang out over there for a while, to rest, reflect, gain some knowledge and experience, so that you're more prepared for your next lifetime, and you'll be better able to fulfill what you want to accomplish. But they do say that it's up to you. A lot of the souls seem to go there and come back right away. Say you've been killed in a war and you feel cheated in your life. You want to come back here right away, but if you do, you could come back out of hostility and anxiety. It's better to throw off the negativity and come back in a more positive frame of mind.

"On the other hand, certain souls have said that they're going to wait out their time there. They have decided not to come back, even though it could take eons of time as we understand it to work out soul growth over there. On the other side you're not subjected to temptation, whereas here we're dealing with a positive and negative vibration of discord, which can be difficult, as many of us will attest. But a lot of souls I've spoken to have said 'no way,' they don't want to be tested to go into the flesh again, they just want to stay there and just work it out as long as it takes."

"If we continue to have what we would call human relationships, wouldn't we also have human emotions there? Do spirits who have passed on ever hold grudges, jealousy, and other negative emotions?"

"No, unless the soul was very negative when it went over to the other side and maintained that negativity over there. Most deceased spouses that I've had here have encouraged their widows or widowers, if they want, to go out and make somebody else as happy as they made them happy. They all say, 'The vow was till death do us part, and although I'm not dead, your life must go on, as my life may go on.' But that's up to them. There are those who've lost their spouses who will say, no, he or she was the only one for me. A spirit can have such a total affinity with a person here on the earth that, in the hereafter, they don't see the harm in the other relationship after that one ends. But that's their free choice."

"In many readings it seems that the spirits know a great deal about what's happening in our lives, how we feel, sometimes what we're thinking. Do they hear us all the time?"

"To a degree, I would say that they certainly can pick up our thoughts and voice and so forth. But they're not spending twenty-four hours a day listening to what we're saying. I think many of them are around in the sense of guardian angels, but they also have other missions to fulfill in the next stage.''

''Do the spirits sometimes communicate directly to the individuals?''

''Sometimes they do, they have mentioned it in readings. They can come to us in dreams or in what we understand as a dream state. They can give us a scent or a familiar sound or something about them. A lot of times people have reported that even though their father passed on, they've seen him in the house. They've smelled his pipe tobacco, they've smelled the cologne he used to wear, or the perfume a mother used to wear, especially during a time of distress. Yes, I think there are times when loved ones are near to us, if they really feel that we need them, they can somehow give off a signal that they're close by.''

''Who makes that contact? Is it the other side, or the person here, or both?''

''It could be a combination of the two. A person here could send off a signal, like I really need you, I need to feel that you're near me, and then the soul on the other side—your father, mother, child, whatever—is alerted to the need and, doing a spiritual good deed, comes to your assistance and lets you know that you're being comforted.''

''Does praying make any difference?''

''Praying and asking them to help? Sure. Because you're not only praying for them, you're asking them to pray with you to God to help things work out for you, and you're also helping them to earn spiritual growth. I highly recommend that people pray for those who have passed on. It says so in scripture and it's a good idea spiritually, especially for those who've had a traumatic passing or a suicide. You're embracing them with constant love and warmth, as you would here. You're sending them very positive energy that's helping them to find themselves and progress on the other side.''

''Must you pray in the traditional way? Must you go to church, a synagogue, a temple, a mosque?''

''Well, that doesn't seem to do any harm. I've had many spirits request the rosary, even if they weren't very spiritual, because they say it's a very powerful form of grace for them over there. But I guess you certainly could make up your own prayers. I know people say they think about them, and the other side will say, 'Think about us, yes, that's very nice, but pray for us.' There must be a difference in the level of energy between thinking and praying.''

"Is there anything people could do here to better develop their ability to communicate directly?''

"What I've been told from the other side is, basically, that we all can through prayer and meditation. I feel that we all have the ability to a certain extent. We can all discern or feel presences. I mean, who hasn't had an interesting dream, a feeling of intuition, precognition, something like that? Some people's abilities are a little more fine-tuned than others, but it seems like through prayer, meditation, if it's meant to be, it's going to happen. It's going to find its way.''

"All things being equal, would you prefer to be here or on the other side?''

"That's a hard question. I think I'd have to say that I'd prefer to be on the other side, because I think I'd have more of a chance to learn and to expand spiritually without all of the day-to-day nonsense we deal with here. Remember, I wouldn't be in the vibration of discord over there. It seems like the ability to learn and to grow there is tremendous and unending. This is not to say that it's Utopia over there, but if you want to tune in spiritually, and really, really get on the ball over there spiritually, your potential is infinite. You have unlimited capacities to learn and grow, whereas here you might be limited because, for example, a certain church tells you no, it's against the rules of this, this isn't right, this isn't permitted, and so on.''

"In general, do you think that most of us who are raised in the West, with our predominantly Judeo-Christian religious beliefs and influences, are well prepared for death, that we truly understand and accept it?''

"Some people do, but the majority that I have seen do not. Our religions seem to be concerned with concepts like hell, purgatory, damnation, judgment and punishment by an angry God. From the moment we can understand, we hear people speak of death as 'being six feet under.' In most movies and literature, the focus on death is on the suffering that precedes and follows it. Not surprising then that most people are afraid of death because they associate it with suffering. They'd rather go quickly, perhaps from a sudden heart attack or in their sleep. Personally, I'd rather pass on in my sleep—one, two, three. Most people really don't sit back and think about it, because it's a frightening thought. It's the unknown, and for many, sadly, death means termination, and people think, 'Well, this is the end. There's nothing further to me, to my life, or that of my loved ones.'

"But this is not the case. Death is a continuation. This mortal life seems to be the unhappy interruption of our natural state of being. When we pass on, we're continuing our lives forward. Life is life eternal."

"Knowing what you know, though," I asked, "are you afraid of death?"

"I don't think I'm afraid of death, per se. I am afraid of the circumstances of death, and I think that many people would probably agree with that. Unfortunately, that fear seems to overwhelm us to the point that most can barely even discuss it or think about it or truly help someone else who is dying."

"From what the other side has told you, how should we better prepare ourselves in this life for the inevitability of our physical death?"

"The other side says that acceptance is a very important virtue, acceptance of our lives. Now, this does not mean that we don't try to change things. If you're born in poverty and you want to work your way out of it, as long as you do it without hurting somebody else, that's fine. But acceptance is very important, because you have chosen to go through this experience. However, we can progress, we have to constantly move ahead, with positive thoughts, with positive attention, with loving thoughts and harmonious thoughts. It's just like when you're a child, you get knocked down, you get up, brush yourself off, and keep moving ahead. We try our best and we accept what we are and are not capable of doing. We also have to know that, even when we fail, we tried to the best of our ability."

"What does the other side say, if anything, about our funeral practices, our death rituals and rites?"

"Well, they have said that funerals are for the living. But they like the prayer that accompanies those services, they like the sentiment, the memory. Some souls have commented, 'I had a very nice funeral.' Many tell me that they attended their own funeral. If anything, many are upset by our grief. A lot of the souls still want to come out to us and say, 'Don't mourn me, I'm not dead, it's the shell you're burying, you're not burying me.' If anything, a funeral, a funeral mass, or a service where the person is prayed for or remembered is good. It is a comfort for the living and it is, to a degree, a comfort for those who have passed on.''

"If people are fearful of death—say they are afraid to leave children and loved ones—does that affect them when they cross over?''

"It can kind of hold them back a little bit. Yet, on the other hand, it can be a blessing, because once they're out of the physical body and their opportunity to be spiritual is unlimited, they could feel a greater ability to help those in this stage of life. What can be difficult is where someone passed over sees others here who think they're dead and there's no contact. It can be frustrating for someone passed over to see a child or a loved one in tears or upset, thinking they've been abandoned by the person who has passed over, when technically they haven't been.''

"What about different religions? Does it matter if here you've been a Jew, a Christian, a Moslem, a Hindu, a Buddhist?'' I asked.

"Everything goes to God anyway, so what difference does it make? It's just a different form of expression. Everybody feels that they have the one way, the one answer. The other side has told me that the answer, the one way is within yourself. For example, I use Catholicism as a spiritual foundation, and I would still affiliate myself with that church, but the true answer is within myself. God is not found in a building. God is right in the home. It's as Christ said, 'The kingdom of heaven is within.'''

"So it doesn't matter what faith you are? This is what the other side has told you?''

"They say God is within all of us,'' George replied.

"How has what the other side has told you over the years coincided with or deviated from your religious beliefs?''

"Well, as a spiritual Roman Catholic, it's helped me to better understand the spirituality of my religion. I disagree with certain man-made rules that have come into the Church over the centuries.''

"Have you ever considered a religious life for yourself?''

"Yes. I don't think it's for me. I think I'd do okay with chastity and poverty but not obedience,'' George said, laughing. "If I did select an order, it would definitely be one of the

Franciscan orders. At this point I would be more attracted to a cloistered life, but only after I felt I had fulfilled here what I was supposed to do.

"But I think that in a sense I am in the religious life. I think I'm doing something of a spiritual, religious nature, and this is why I don't go into the religious life, because being connected with a particular order, I might be restricted, whereas here I have the freedom of movement to do whatever I'm supposed to do. We're all here for a purpose. That's what I try to tell people who are very distressed with their life and what they're going through. They are here for a purpose. Maybe they don't know or discover what it is until later on. It's just as you go through something in your life that's so upsetting that you just can't see a purpose to it and then ten years later you realize what you were supposed to learn from it."

"Will we ever know some of the answers?"

"I think so. If we don't know here, when we get to the other side, we have a greater understanding."

"Who would give us those answers? Who would teach us?" I asked.

"I think we would understand ourselves, or the God self within us would help us to understand. But I don't think we get advice or help directly from God. We're all part of God, we're all in tune with the God within ourselves."

"Has anybody in a reading from the other side talked to you about God?"

"They constantly say that on the other side they are part of God and they praise God, but they don't tell me that God is some singular entity sitting on a big throne with a big beard and a scepter. God is a force, God is light, God is energy, God is everything. God is us, God is animals. That force of energy that has breathed life into us has breathed life into everything else. We are all part of a singular flow."

"Do animals have souls?"

"I don't know if they have souls technically, in the way we understand it and have been taught, but they certainly have life. God has put them on earth and brought them into life too. So I've had them come through from the other side, specifically if the animal is very close to a family member—a cat, a dog, a horse, whichever. They'll say that the force of life of the animal that we know goes on to the next stage."

"What does it feel like to discern spirits?"

"I get charged up. I'll feel like I'm shot with electricity. For example, say it's Tuesday. My first appointment walks in, I say hello and I tell him or her, 'Whatever I say to you, just say yes or no,' and I bless myself and I just wait, it seems like two seconds at most. It reminds me of the scene out of that movie *A Night to Remember* when the guy turned on the machine that would transmit the SOS. It's like all of a sudden I hear this whirring sound, like all of a sudden energy picks up and then I wait and then I feel the contacts and I start discerning. Most of the time what I feel is clairsentient. I sense right away, or discern, and then other 'psychic senses,' I guess you would call them, will take over. The clairaudience seems to be more powerful now.

"Then after the high, as I call it, comes down I'll be inclined to feel a little run down. It's like any job, you can get tired, you can have your moments when you need to break away from it completely. That's why I'm glad that those on the other side have always let me have the control of it. I can shut it off, I can turn it on. Technically, it's like any job. If you know that Monday you have to get up and go to work, you prepare yourself. For me, preparation simply entails knowing. I just have to know that a reading or demonstration will be expected. I condition my mind. I sort of say to myself, 'Okay, George, it's time to go to work, so put yourself in that frame of mind.'"

"What do you think is the value of a personal contact for the people who come to you? And how do you think it's different from getting messages from a single entity, as the so-called channelers do?"

"I don't know enough about channeling to really have an opinion. I can only talk about myself and mediumship. For example, I don't go into trance. I prefer for me personally to be in control. I don't want to be dealing with some sort of entity from twenty-one B.C. that I don't know anything about. And I think this is where people, even though they may be interested in the subject, feel a sense of a lack, or a piece of the puzzle missing, because it's much easier to receive a message from your late grandfather or mother or son than it is from somebody who died in the arena with Spartacus. Technically, you cannot relate to those people, you cannot relate to that time or that period. If I'm doing a reading for you and I say to you, 'Okay, my control or my spirit guide is Big Joe and he was a Russian cossack in his other life and he tells me that your father is here and that your father is saying this and that,' we're having a contact, impersonally, with your father through another medium. It is better that your dad comes in and says, 'Hello, I'm her father, my name is Bill, I passed on from cancer, she took good care of me.' There's that instant heart-to-heart contact which I think the subject being read can understand and feel better with. Then he or she can say and believe, 'My mother is truly here,' 'My father is truly here,' 'My child is here.' It also lets the person know that the soul has gone on, that the light, the personality that they understand, still exists—the physical body is dead but the person is not.''

''Are you always aware of the impact a reading of yours has on a person who is bereaved or a person who comes to you with any kind of problem?''

''Sometimes yes, sometimes no. I think a lot of times I feel I've disappointed a person, and then I find out later that they were so overwhelmed they didn't know what to say.''

''With something very moving, like the Licata readings, how do you react? These are very emotional situations,'' I observed.

''It's an interesting question, but the other side has always told me to keep my emotions out. I have found that once my own feelings interfere—say I get all choked up over a very intense reading—I feel my vibration wobble, like I'm going to lose contact. Especially when I see a parent or a family upset by a passing. In those instances it's best to try to stay out of it, to remain very formal. The other side says there's nothing wrong with being compassionate or sympathetic, but I should stay out of it, not let my emotions drag me down. With all the thousands of readings I have done—here in the house, in private—I've had grown men crying their eyes out over a suicide or the loss of a child. If I were to go with that emotional reaction in every case, I'd lose my purpose. I'd become just like a sobbing sounding-board, and that's not what my mission is. As the other side says, 'You're just there to help them out.' I'm the instrument.''

''We know how your ability has touched the lives of others. How has it affected your own?''

''I'll tell you the downer of it. George as a person may want to be someplace, but the George with the ability has to be some-where else. I may want to hang out with a friend on Friday night, go to the opera, or Broadway, or to a museum, but the ability has to be somewhere else to do something else. And the worst part is not being able to be there for everybody who needs it. Somebody may call up, and I'll have no room, but I squeeze him or her in. It can be done, but it can get to be overwhelming. It's difficult being only one person, because you can't help everyone. Those are my limitations as a human being.

"From a positive point of view, though, I feel that it certainly gives me the ability to comfort the bereaved, which, since we know so little about death and can't do much about it except live with it, gives people that personal connection that they need from one stage of life to the next. A reading can prove to a person that somebody is all right over there, has gone on, that there's no such thing as 'death.' So it's changed my life in the sense of bringing comfort to the bereaved, psychologically helping people, that I feel I can be of service to people in a very, very singular way.

"There's also the feeling of satisfaction that you have moved a person who felt so down and out over a passing or an experience. That feeling—you couldn't put a price on it. It's the most fabulous feeling to see somebody—a parent, a widower, anybody—get up out of this chair and feel he can go on with his life with a positive frame of mind. That you've left such an impression on him that he can at least feel good again and be stronger and feel more positive. What I do will never remove the scar, it will never remove the experience, but people are comforted by it."

"When you look back now on what was a difficult childhood because of the ability, how do you feel?"

"To be honest, there's a lot of unhappiness there, and I remember a lot of unhappy moments. And there's always that part of you that wishes you could go back and tell somebody off, but you don't want to hang your dirty laundry out in public, either. Because those people handled it in the way they thought was correct. I can't blame the institution of the Catholic Church for a few stupid people who were in it. There might have been something I had to learn and experience, such as how to have more confidence in myself, how to live with the ability."

"Do you ever get tired of people asking you to prove yourself? What do you say, or would you say, to the skeptics, the debunkers?"

"The only thing that I ask is that people meet me halfway. That's all I ask. I'm skeptical, I'm cynical about it. I want constant proof and reassurance that this is for real and it's really happening. You're not going to be able to please everybody, no matter what you do. I could walk on water, or change water into wine, and people are still not going to believe it. That's just a fact. It's the way we've been brought up, the way we've been conditioned—thinking that things of this nature cannot happen. But I say to those people, well, then, prove to me that the earth is round or that there is air. I know I'm breathing it, I see what it does, but I can't see it. No one, including me, really has any definite answers, and one theory is just about as good as the next. We can assume what we think it is, or how it's working, but the other side has said that it works off electricity. Look at what electricity can do now, what mankind has accomplished with it since we learned how to use it. Why would this not be possible where this ability is concerned?

"If we had listened to the people who said the world was flat, we would never have discovered America. If we had not paid attention to Thomas Edison, we would not have electricity in our daily lives. You can go around and debunk all you want, but the thing is, there must be something there, and until you can prove to me that it is *not* there, I still think it's worth investigating. I'm not talking about fortune telling or supernatural, Halloween mumbo-jumbo, I'm talking about a legitimate, scientific investigation of this. There's obviously some sort of electrical energy working here, and I don't think we've even tapped into it yet."

"To digress for a moment. On the subject of Halloween mumbo-jumbo, do you resent it when you see the supernatural trappings put to some of this? Does it bother you particularly?"

"Yes. I would prefer that this be looked at from a scientific and spiritual point of view. Unfortunately, I do resent the fact that when I say 'psychic,' everybody thinks that everything is supernatural and occultish. That has nothing to do with anything that I'm doing."

"Some people think that the other side should just tell you how it's happening," I remarked.

"Well, the other side may be telling me simply how it's happening, but my brain in its ignorance doesn't understand what it's being told. I certainly don't know anything about science; I was lousy in math and science, so I would be inclined to block out and not be able to understand. And then maybe, too, the other side expects us to find the answer because this way we grow and we learn.

"From what I can understand, there's something in the human brain or in the human anatomy—they tell me from the neck up—even in the upper chest area. The other side says that they are able to send what will be understood as an electrical charge, or an electrical signal, and from that it goes into the brain and it can be filtered and understood as a message. It can be put into the English language and the brain can begin to understand it.

"After years of being put down and being taken for a fool, it is very refreshing to find that there is something legitimately there, and that others see it, too. It does work, it does manifest itself. But now my attitude is, it's okay if it's there, let's investigate it, let's do something with it. Let's not worry about the past or what the future will hold. Let's try to figure it out."

"How does this differ from your attitude when we met in 1980?"

"When I first went public, I didn't understand what was happening myself, and I thought perhaps the answers were just good guesses. I even started to think that maybe people were so convinced themselves that this is for real before they came to me that they basically believed everything I said. I thought that subconsciously I had something like a trick and I just knew how to work it very well, without even realizing that I was doing it. When I went on the radio show for the first time, I was at the point in my life where I figured it could not be for real, so here's my chance to find out for myself. I thought, I'll walk into the arena, even if it might prove embarrassing, and I'll find out.

"But when I started to look over a lot of readings and experiences, I said, 'Wait a minute, where is this information coming from? Where could I get this?' I knew I couldn't guess correctly *that* many times, and people are not that gullible, especially not the skeptics I've encountered who seemed impressed. Something was happening psychically. Then, when I started to see physical evidence—like the thermography—of something happening, something I could see with my own eyes as could others, I knew it was real and I began to feel more confident about it.

"I admit I'm still inclined to be skeptical and cynical, and I think that is a healthy attitude to have. My motto in this field is still, Where does open-mindedness end and gullibility begin? It's something we should always keep in mind.

"Fortunately, people are far more open-minded about many subjects, and mediumship in particular, than they were even five years ago. But as refreshing as that is, I'm not certain that it's always for the best. I become a little concerned, for example, when people want me to tell them what to do in their personal lives, because they feel I am very responsible and I have this tremendous knowledge, like I'm some kind of guru up on the mountaintop. I will pass along advice from the other side, but the ultimate decision, the ultimate choice, must be made by the person. Everyone has to learn to grow through experience. You might as well be a puppet on a string if you don't want to find your own way, your own direction.

"It's important for people to understand that those on the other side don't have all the answers, especially for our lives and our personal problems. Many people here are inclined to think that just because Father has gone to the other side he has gained wisdom and he can tell them what to do. And they can't do that. God himself will not intercede. You've got to find your own way."

"So you believe in free will?" I asked.

"I technically believe in free will. I believe that we have chosen what goes on in our lives, we have kind of predestined ourselves through our own free will."

"Then how are you able to see into the future if there is free will? If you can alter something that's going to happen by seeing ahead and doing something to prevent it, is it or is it not predestined?"

"To a degree it is. There are certain experiences that we have to go through that are already predestined, but I think that what happens with free will is that we may hit what seems like a fork in the road, and the decision to make a choice of which way to turn—left or right—is ours. You can go into something that you have chosen to go into—for example, with a certain individual in a relationship—and all of a sudden when you're in it, you say, 'Hey, this is not for me.' Even though, spiritually, you might have chosen the situation to work something out, we have the choice to break away from it.

"For example, whenever I get away from the ability, it seems to find me again. It must be something I must fulfill; I have no choice. At one point, just before I was going on the radio, I was considering a move to Arizona, but obstacles came in my path to stop me from going. This seems to have taken priority."

"What do you think we should be doing with psychic abilities—our own and others'?"

"We should try to understand them better, we should try to utilize them more in our daily lives, to see where their origins are, scientifically. But we also have to make sure we don't let them take control of our lives, either mine or anyone else's. There are some people who are 'psychiholics.' They're obsessed. People just have to learn to take psychic ability as it is and accept it as far as it applies to their lives at that time. You have to know where to draw the line and to absorb only as much of it as you need. You don't go wacko over it. Even I don't seem able to tune in to it that much for myself, and they say that we should try our best not to call on them for help too much. It's good to do so, but we should always try to find a way to work out our own unhappiness here, too."

"Have they ever told you why you were chosen for this ability? Or, if you have a purpose in life, what it is?"

"They haven't given me any clarification. The only thing they have said is that I had to be a male, so that I would be taken seriously, which is a sad commentary on our sexist society. I have no idea why. I've asked, but I really haven't any idea. I don't know if I would really like to know. Maybe it's not meant for me to know. I'd rather just do it. They certainly don't seem to interfere in my life unless I ask for spiritual help or assistance. Technically, though, they haven't really told me why.

"As far as the purpose of it goes, I think that's pretty clear. My purpose is to give people a new interpretation of death, to comfort them, to remove their fears, to help those who are mourning to realize that death is not a termination but a transition. I believe that I am using my gift as it was meant to be used."

"Do you have any idea why you are so accurate?"

"To tell you the truth, I don't. I believe that this ability is a gift. We each have gifts, mine just happens to be this. Somebody like Luciano Pavarotti has a singular voice compared to other singers. I'm not putting the other singers down, it's just that Pavarotti's voice does stand out. Maybe he trained more, maybe he just had a special talent. It would be the same with me. I might just have been born with it, but we all have gifts. A friend of mine remarked on how great the psychic ability is, and yet I envy him because he's a wonderful musician. I might learn to play an instrument, but he has a gift for it, and I would never be as good at it as he is. I think that my ability is not unique. It's probably something that, theoretically, we all could do.

"I also think that I might have this level of accuracy because I constantly challenge the other side. If they tell me that someone's having an 'emotional crisis,' I say to them, 'Well, if you can tell me that, you can tell me more.' And I constantly challenge them to prove to me *and* to the subject being read that this is for real, especially to prove it to me. This could have something to do with it. Maybe they understand this and feel they have to work harder to send me the signals so that I can pick up more detailed information and be more accurate."

"Do you feel that you need any more proof to be convinced of what you're doing?"

"I don't think it's a question of proof. I think I would just like to have a better understanding of how it's working. If there's any scientific detail, for example, from which I could understand how to fine-tune the ability, I would like to learn it. If the ability can maintain an accuracy rate between 85 percent and 90 percent, then it must be capable of doing 100 percent. What might be limiting it, however, could be the human brain, my brain. The human brain is inherently lazy.

"I mean, I'm the person with the ability, and I'm not saying to skeptics and others, 'It's there, accept it or not.' I would like to have some answers, too. I experience this daily. I would like to have somebody say, 'We think it's this, we've discovered this, this is how it works.'"

"On the other hand, though," I remarked, "why is it necessary for us to understand why it's happening, if it is happening? I don't know that anybody's going crazy trying to figure out how Beethoven made music when he was deaf, for example. Why do we have this obsession that we must find out how it works? Couldn't we just accept it, or don't you think that's a good idea?''

"We could just accept it, but I think it's nice to have an explanation.''

"And you don't have any problem at all with those people who would question and probe you?'' I asked.

"No. Because I'm basically doing the same thing they're doing.''

"Do you feel that having your unique ability gives you a view of the world that's different from other people's?''

"To a degree. But maybe it's more because those people aren't ready to see the world any differently from the way they do now. What I see is my understanding of reality, what they see is theirs, but I don't really think it's that different. Remember, the psychic part of me is my 'higher self.' I still have my lower self to deal with. I can be just as negative or hard to get along with as other people. I'm a normal person, I'm a human being, with my limitations and talents, just like anybody else. I have my days, too. I don't want to make myself sound like some wishy-washy, syrupy saint. If another driver cuts me off, I'll yell just as loud as anybody else.''

"You're dealing with a lot of individuals, and it may be meaningful to me that my late grandmother came through, but it frankly won't be that meaningful to anyone else. And this is true for each person,'' I remarked. "Do you ever sit back and ask the other side, and try to view the larger picture? We're always on the verge of war somewhere, nuclear annihilation, the AIDS epidemic, the drug epidemic, people driving like lunatics, murder and violence—those things haven't changed since the beginning of time. They seem to be part of human nature. Do you ever ask the other side if there's any hope for change? Do you ever think that through your work you might get across a greater message, that we could all stop this madness?''

"Remember we are in a vibration of discord; there is strong negativity here as well as positive. But it's up to us to make the changes. The other side has said, 'Yes, we can change it, we can alter our future in the sense of wars and so forth.' Remember that wars, power, greed, things like that, are all negative vibrations. People feed into that evil, that devilish vibration, and they say that we can change things, but it doesn't look too probable, because most people will not turn around and learn to live with each other, and learn how to accept one another as they are, as individuals.''

"But does the other side ever ask, 'Why not'? Many times someone from the other side has said, 'Oh, I'm so sorry I beat my wife,' or 'I'm so sorry I was an alcoholic,' 'I'm so sorry I killed somebody.' Do they now know, on the other side, that there's positive from negative, or good from evil? Why can't that be communicated better to those of us here?"

"The temptations to be negative here are very powerful. Money is the root of all evil. People will strive for that. We've also been raised to think that you must be a success financially. Because people do not feel they have a greater awareness of their own life here or hereafter, they're inclined to just follow what they can understand. But it's also true that we have to understand that these are lessons being fulfilled.''

"In other words, here, in preparation for going there?"

"As I've been told from the other side—although I sometimes find it hard to believe—there are no accidents of the universe. Everything has a purpose, a mission, a meaning. And for the parent who loses a child tragically in an accident, the child was fulfilling his or her mission; the parent was fulfilling that mission too. The parents are in that circumstance to learn a lesson. Maybe the lesson was patience, love, acceptance, understanding, comfort of others. It can be a number of things.''

"Does the other side say anything about what's going to happen regarding dangers such as nuclear war?"

"In my case they haven't really reflected on that. I'm inclined to warn of things, impending changes like earthquakes, hurricanes. They do speak of the possibility of another war, but they say that war can be averted. That, of course, would be up to us.''

"Why don't they give us advice on how to find the cure for AIDS, on how to avoid violence, on how to avoid war?"

"This is kind of a dumb answer, but they said that in the case of AIDS, the disease has been around for centuries, maybe since the beginning of time. It's not anything new. They do say that it's a very intricate and complicated disease, and yet the answer for its cure is right under our noses, it's very simple. They did say the answer has something to do with protein. I've been told that. But again even if they try to communicate an answer to me, I'm not necessarily going to understand what they're saying.''

"What about war? They can't tell us how to avoid war?" I asked.

"They tell us that the way to avoid war is to learn to live together, but are we going to do it? We have the choice. In certain cases it may be destiny, but I think in others we have a chance to avert it. We just don't listen.''

"Does the other side give you any clue as to what the future will be, if people will be more understanding of the ability, more tolerant of it, more open to it?''

"Yes. As we progress toward the twenty-first century and the later years of this century, people will definitely be more open. Because people will be looking for answers and they will find that the answers are within themselves. As Dorothy said at the end of *The Wizard of Oz,* we don't have to look any farther than our own backyards.

"I want people to understand that life is everlasting. Everything that happens in your life has a purpose. There is no one you are close to who ever dies. Everyone just goes on to another stage of life that runs parallel to this one. Be at peace with yourself and fulfill your mission, knowing that your stay here is temporary, and that you are doing something here to fulfill your spiritual purpose. Tune in more to yourself. And understand more within yourself so that you can find your way easier. Don't place so much emphasis on life materially, place more emphasis on it spiritually. Death is not the end, it's the beginning. There is life everlasting, there is no such thing as death. That child, that husband, that wife, that loved one— they are all still very much alive. It's just as if they've moved to Outer Mongolia and you may not see them again for many, many years.''

"Anything you want readers to take away about you?''

"I'm just the instrument, for some reason I can't answer myself.''

Appendix I

Glossary of Psychic Symbols

Below are examples of some symbols George receives psychically and how they are interpreted in readings.

AIDS—the word appearing over a subject's head indicates either that the spirit passed from the disease or that he or she suffers from it.

an airplane—work-related (the subject or spirit works with airlines or travel) or future travel.

apples—ripe apples mean the subject is "ripe for a job change."

artist's easel—work or study of art.

black—when the subject appears to George to be surrounded by black, it means that someone close to him or her will pass on in the near future.

black spots—around an individual or around a particular area of the body usually indicate cancer, either past, present, or future.

blood—violence, a violent incident or death.

blood, seen bursting—a stroke or other vascular problem.

blood cells—a disease related to the blood cells, such as leukemia.

books, a hand writing—work, study, or strong interest related to writing; work around books, as in a library.

bread—abundance.

broken heart—romance gone bad, a broken love affair.

car wheel—auto accident or car trouble, either in the recent past or the foreseeable future.

cards—a large deck of playing cards indicates that the spirit of the reading had, or the subject will be making, a big deal in business.

classroom or school—the subject may be a student or is or will be learning something that will enhance his or her career.

clear water—usually in a glass or in a stream, a symbol of "clear going" in the future. A positive sign.

computers, electrical wiring, machinery—references to the careers of the subject or the spirit.

contracts—legal papers are being signed, either in the present or the future.

currency, piles of money—money coming to someone through an inheritance, job, or gift. May also mean that the subject or spirit works with or around money, as in a bank.

dog, or dog barking—indicates that the spirit was met and greeted on the other side by a deceased pet dog.

drink, on the rocks—indicates that the subject should exert caution in relationship ahead.

Empire State Building—New York City.

Felix the Cat—this cartoon character's appearance indicates that the subject will be hearing good news ahead.

a finger placed to closed lips—advises a subject to keep quiet about something.

glass of milk—relaxation is needed.

green fields—money or abundance.

gun—psychically seen weapons almost always indicate the means by which the communicating spirit was killed.

Sherlock Holmes—the subject or the spirit was involved with some kind of police or detective work, either in uniform or undercover. Also indicates that a situation calls for investigation.

horn of plenty—abundance ahead.

ice cubes—advises subject to "keep cool."

knife—see *gun,* above.

lemon—a large lemon on wheels suggests car trouble for the subject.

letters of the alphabet—a specific letter appearing psychically over the subject's head is a clue to a key word, such as the first letter of the spirit's name.

Lourdes water—sign of healing, related to the health condition of subject.

musical instruments—might indicate that the subject or spirit was a musician, disc jockey, songwriter, music teacher, or has a strong interest in music.

musical notes—see *musical instruments* above.

New York Stock Exchange—someone works at or with the exchange, or is or will be involved with investments.

nose—a large nose means that someone else is butting into the subject's marriage with future marital upset as the result.

palm trees—travel or a move to a southerly, tropical location.

piano—someone plays either the piano or some other percussion instrument.

priests, nuns, other clergy—indicates that the subject or the spirit was or knew others in religious service.

question mark—indicates some mystery or question around a situation.

rainbow—optimism, a new beginning ahead.

red light—George takes this as a psychic symbol to stop psychic reading, that he is in danger of overexerting himself.

rosary beads—generally means that the spirit, regardless of religion, is asking for prayers. When the subject or spirit is Catholic, it usually refers to the rosary of someone in particular, often identifiable, because George will be shown their color.

roses—white roses are a sign of congratulations or celebration from the other side. The roses may be offered by the spirit around the time of a celebration, anniversary, or birthday.

scales of justice—a legal situation in the subject's or the spirit's life.

sinking ship—a situation "rocked your boat."

skull and crossbones—negativity, friction.

Smith Brothers—the famous trademark pair found on boxes of cough drops indicates a subject's or spirit's surname is Smith.

spider's web—being trapped.

star—creativity.

Star of David—the spirit or subject was of the Jewish faith.

stripes on shoulder—promotion, as in military service.

suitcases—future travel.

swastika—sometimes seen with the screaming face of Adolf Hitler, coils of barbed wire, concentration camp victims, and the Star of David superimposed over the image. This symbolizes that the spirit or subject was a victim of the Nazis.

Switzerland—when George sees a map of this country, it means that the subject is being advised to stay neutral in a conflict.

towels, in knots—a short temper.

triangle—a love triangle, infidelity, adultery.

trumpets sounding—happy news.

uniforms—these symbols give clues as to the subject's or the spirit's occupation, and are distinguished by color. White for health and medical workers, blue for police, firemen, military, and so on.

washing machine—health difficulty related to kidney or adrenal malfunction.

wedding ring—a broken wedding ring indicates a marital breakup or discord in a romantic relationship.

windmill—someone has "been through the mill."

X—a large X shown over a scene, symbol, or word that George sees psychically means that it is incorrect, not what it seems to be, or that the subject is being advised not to take some action represented by that symbol. For example, an X over a vision of the floor of the New York Stock Exchange meant that the spirit was advising the subject not to invest money in a financial scheme.

yellow rings, murky—when these appear around a specific part of the human anatomy, they indicate illness or some malady affecting that area, in the future.

Appendix II
A Selective History of Mediumship

The nineteen eighties have brought forth a vast array of books, magazine articles, films, and other works on all types of unexplained phenomena. With this seeming newfound interest in these subjects comes the general public's perception that this is all new territory, and, unfortunately, that much of it is faddish or trendy. While our research with George is all original, we spent many hours exploring and discussing the history of mediumship. We were astonished to find that so many respected historical figures—from Socrates to Helen Keller—professed, based on their own experiences, to have been in contact with spirits. Why, we wondered, had we not learned of this in school? Probably for the same reason that few people know of séances in the Lincoln White House or Thomas Alva Edison's work on a machine to communicate with the dead. Were our attitudes toward all manner of psychic and unexplained phenomena formed by lack of information and misinformation? As we read further and listened to what friends and acquaintances had to say on the subject, we concluded that the answer was yes. For that reason we are including this history of mediumship in an attempt to trace the roots of prejudice and preconceptions. It is by no means complete—the topic could easily fill several books—but we believe it demonstrates that while mediumship may be uncharted territory, it is anything but unexplored and certainly not new.

Psychic phenomena and, specifically, communications with

the other side, have been recorded for thousands of years. Belief in life after death, discarnate survival, and communications between the deceased and the living, and the abilities of the spirits to help or guide the living are known in so many cultures and have been so widely accepted that they can be said to be universal. There is archeological evidence, derived from ancient burial areas, that preliterate humans embraced some concept of a continuing existence after physical death. These beliefs are further articulated and elaborated on in the many ancient religious texts devoted to the subject, such as *Bardo Thödol,* or the *Tibetan Book of the Dead* (believed to have been written in the eighth century, A.D., but no doubt passed down orally for generations before that), the various funerary writings that taken together comprise what is called the *Egyptian Book of the Dead* (parts of which may date as far back as 1580 B.C.), and the Hindu *Bhagavad-Gita* (which, coming from Hinduism, perhaps the oldest surviving religion, may have existed in oral form thousands of years B.C.). Although some of what these predominantly pre-Christian texts contain may sound to us like primitive superstition, thanatologists have noted in several published works the striking similarities between the texts' descriptions of the phases of death and dying and what we have learned in the past few decades from recent scientific research. Consider, for example, a description of the "classic" near-death experience and the English translation of the *Egyptian Book of the Dead*'s title: *pert em hru,* "coming forth by day" or "manifested in the light."

Historically, belief in the paranormal, particularly discarnate survival and guiding spirits, was widely accepted. Human faith in or knowledge of discarnate survival and communication are constant themes throughout most of recorded history. What those beliefs mean to a particular culture at a specific time, however, does change. A brief, selective history of mediumship reveals the sources of our knowledge and preconceptions about communications from the other side.

Socrates (469-399 B.C.) believed that he had been guided throughout his life by an entity whose purpose was to protect him. When sentenced to die by drinking hemlock, he said, "My approaching end is not happening by chance. I see quite clearly that to die, and thus to be released, will be better for me; and therefore the oracle [as he called the voice] has given me no sign [that it is not to be]."

His pupil and friend Plato believed not only in the soul's immortality but in several forms of psychic phenomena, including precognitive dreams and visions. His ideas were not considered odd, either. Clairvoyants were hired by Grecian and Roman governments, and the legendary oracles at Delphi, believed today to have been mediums who conjured the spirits while in a trance, were consulted for more than one thousand years. The ancient Greeks also diagnosed illness and prescribed treatment with information received through dreams, a process ostensibly similar to the work of twentieth-century psychic clairvoyant Edgar·Cayce, who diagnosed and prescribed cures in 9,000 documented cases. Despite what appears to be a full-fledged acceptance of some psychic phenomena, the ancient Greeks and Romans also sought to control certain forms of paranormal activities. The private practice of magic was illegal, and necromancy—calling up, or conjuring, the dead—was specifically prohibited. The Roman Twelve Tables proscribed witchcraft and set death as the penalty for anyone practicing it.

The Old Testament contains numerous references to prophetic dreams and dream interpretation (Jacob, Joseph, David), and in Deuteronomy (18) prohibits psychics, specifically mediums. However, the First Epistle of Saint John, in the New Testament (Verse 4), states:

Beloved, believe not every spirit, but try the spirits whether they are of God: because many false prophets are gone out into the world.

2. Hereby know ye the Spirit of God: Every spirit that confesseth that Jesus Christ is come in the flesh is of God:

3. And every spirit that confesseth not that Jesus Christ is come in the flesh is not of God: and this is that *spirit* of anti-christ, whereof ye have heard that it should come; and even now already is it in the world.

4. Ye are of God, little children, and have overcome them: because greater is he that is in you, than he that is in the world.

5. They are of the world: therefore speak they of the world, and the world heareth them.

6. We are of God: he that knoweth God heareth us; he that is not of God heareth not us. Hereby know we the spirit of truth, and the spirit of error.

Although Christianity's fundamental premise is the eternal life of the soul, not all Christians concur on the soul's fate. For example, some Christians assert that certain passages in the New Testament refer to reincarnation, but the majority reject that interpretation. Not surprisingly, the Christian positions on psychic phenomena and discarnate survival have been at times contradictory. To read the New Testament literally, one could conclude that Jesus Christ was perhaps the greatest psychic in history. Among the miracles he performed were healings, raising people from the dead (necromancy), discerning spirits (mediumship), his own resurrection, levitation, and other physical phenomena such as turning water into wine and multiplying the fishes and the loaves. Yet most believers elect to see miracles as proof of God's power and the province of only the extremely devout (the saints, for example) or the few great religious leaders. Why modern-day examples of psychic phenomena are not treated similarly is an interesting question for another book.

Few people today are aware that in sharp contrast to their descendants, the early Christians believed in reincarnation, as had the Hindus and Buddhists for many centuries before the birth of Christ. It was only after the Second Council of Constantinople denounced reincarnation in 553 A.D. that it was rejected by the Church. Though we are not concerned with the history of religions per se, the Council's decision is indicative of several things, namely organized religion's power to reinterpret, revise, and dictate religious doctrines and "facts" instead of reaching some consensus based on the experiences and observations of followers.

Between the fall of the Roman Empire in the fifth century A.D. and the end of the Middle Ages in the fifteenth century, the Church underwent a radical shift in attitude toward everything we would consider paranormal. It is generally believed that before the fifteenth century, people accepted various forms of psychic phenomena. Indeed, a number of saints exhibited, witnessed, or possessed psychic abilities, including levitation, bilocation, astral travel, healings, clairvoyance, clairaudience, and discerning spirits. Although it's safe to assume that their true understanding of these phenomena was no greater than our own, their acceptance of precognitive dreams as part of the human experience, for example, was less compromised by the limitations placed on these experiences in later years by science and the Church. In the ninth century A.D., the Church rejected most superstitions (which one might view as man's attempts to impose a theory and sense of order to a world he didn't fully understand) not because they were evil, but because they were pagan (which means "of the country") holdovers from earlier, non-Christian religions. In fact, anyone who believed in witches was "an infidel and a pagan," for belief in them was in opposition to the Church's position that they did not exist.

Although many people today associate all facets of the occult with evil and the devil, the Church did not attribute what is generally termed the practice of witchcraft (which we will define to include manifestations of psychic abilities, since many with psychic abilities were "found" to be witches or sorcerers) or any other demonstrations of psychic abilities until 1326, when Pope John XXII pronounced sorcery a crime. By the end of the fourteenth century the Inquisition was in high gear, and the practice of magic became, officially, all the more threatening. It was viewed not only as a product of the accused practitioner's alleged pact with the devil, but as a vast conspiracy against Christianity. The social and psychological forces fueling the mass paranoia that gripped Europe, England, and later America (although on a much smaller scale) between the mid-sixteenth and mid-eighteenth centuries are too complex to recount at length here. For the most part they seem very worldly—recurring, devastating outbreaks of the plague (which in some areas killed six men to every woman), a growing population of independent single women, and the Church's continuous quest for universal political domination. And, as author Kurt Seligmann points out, "witch prosecution soon became an industry. It employed judges, jailers, torturers, exorcists, wood-choppers, scribes, and experts . . . the abolition of the trials would have caused an economic crisis."

By the close of the fifteenth century, the discovery and execution of accused witches became an obsession of both the Church and the secular courts. Over the next four hundred years perhaps as many as 200,000 were tortured and executed, usually by burning at the stake, beheading, or died as a result of the torture itself. The first witches were mostly women—usually spinsters and widows—but with time virtually everyone, regardless of sex, age, or social position was fair game. It was at that point that any and all manifestations of the paranormal were lumped together, creating confusion and misunderstanding that continue today. In the grip of this hysteria, anyone who spoke of precognitive dreams, exhibited signs of clairvoyance, clairaudience, or any other psychic ability was assumed to be guilty of doing the devil's work and so was a threat not only to the Church as an institution—which ruled literally every aspect of one's life then—but to every Christian alive. So powerful did people perceive this threat that fears about any unexplained phenomena continued for hundreds of years after witch-hunting declined. But the persecutions never really stopped. The Salem, Massachusetts, witch trials of 1692 were particularly odious; most accusations were brought in the hopes that the accused's land or other assets would be freed upon his or her execution. Twenty people were executed. Ritual slayings of accused witches by the superstitious have been reported to have occurred in the present day.

The most famous victim of the witch-hunts was Saint Joan of Arc, who like many other saints had psychic abilities. And, like many who claimed or demonstrated those abilities, she was murdered for these "crimes." Joan was a thirteen-year-old peasant girl when she first heard the voices of Saints Michael, Catherine, and Margaret, all urging her to "go to the succor of the King of France" in 1425. At the time France was involved in the last few years of the Hundred Years' War, and the dauphin, Charles VII, had failed to wrest control of his country from the Duke of Burgundy and his English allies. In 1428, around the time the English began their siege of Orléans, the voices grew louder and more persistent. Within the year, Joan had met the dauphin and convinced him and his advisers that her voices were genuine, from God or godly sources. By May of 1429 she was leading the French army and, disguised as a man, helped free Orléans from the English. Also that year the dauphin was crowned king.

In May 1430, however, she was captured, betrayed by a Catholic bishop, and eventually sold to the English. Tricked into signing a confession, she was eventually tried, convicted of heresy, and burned at the stake in late May 1431. After her body had been entirely consumed by flames, her executioners examined the remains and found that her heart was still beating. After another three hours of trying to destroy the still living organ by fire, they concluded—much to their shock—that they had murdered a saint. Twenty-five years later, following a lengthy investigation, the Church retracted its condemnation of her. In 1920 she was canonized and is today the patroness of France.

There's no question that most of what was written on the subject of the paranormal prior to and during the Middle Ages was destroyed. It's amazing that we know anything about psychic phenomena in earlier ages. We can't assume that simply because there is no longer extant documentation of such things that they did not occur. Rather, consider the opposite: reports of unexplained experiences and so-called occult information must have been common and well known for any knowledge of them to have survived whatsoever.

In the centuries between the close of the Middle Ages and the mid-1800s, there were several well-documented cases of people with psychic abilities. Among the most famous was the Swedish scientist Emanuel Swedenborg (1688-1772), who in his later years actively studied psychic phenomena and in several documented instances proved to possess second sight. Swedenborg was one of the earliest scientists to explore the subject. Others, including Sir Isaac Newton, also believed the subject worthy of investigation but were censured by the Church or by their peers.

In 1846 a Scotsman named Daniel Dunglas Home (pronounced Hume) revealed his psychical abilities when he reported having had a precognitive dream of a friend's death. Home was then thirteen and living with relatives in the United States. He subsequently became internationally famous, toured the world, and gave countless demonstrations for, among others, Napoleon III and the Empress Eugenie, the Russian royal family, and Queen Sophia of the Netherlands. Home's career was not without its problems, many of which he apparently brought on himself. He was publicly criticized by famous contemporaries, including Robert Browning and Charles Dickens, but these attacks were inspired by their personal dislike of Home and not based on any exposures of his work. In fact, despite numerous rigorous tests, Home was never exposed as a fraud, nor did he ever accept money for his demonstrations. He not only received spirit messages, but he displayed physical mediumship and possessed extensive telekinetic abilities. In his presence, furniture moved about, tables rose from the floor, and multitudes of sounds were heard. These manifestations occurred in well-lighted rooms before, cumulatively, hundreds of witnesses. Unlike many self-proclaimed mediums of the latter nineteenth century, Home did not dictate the conditions under which he would be observed. In one remarkable sitting, he floated headfirst out a foot-high window opening and returned through another window. Impressive as his list of feats is, it represents only a fraction of Home's abilities. In 1863, while in France, he predicted the assassination of President Abraham Lincoln, which occurred in 1865.

Some modern researchers and writers agree that in the absence of "scientific" testing, Home's abilities must be accepted as genuine based on the sheer number of witnessed demonstrations. In 1871 he was observed by the physicist William Crookes (later Sir), who later cofounded the Society for Psychical Research. When Crookes published a report favorable to Homes, outraged fellow scientists attributed Crookes's conclusions to either his madness or Home's fraud. This wasn't the first or the last such reaction from the scientific community to the evidence of psi phenomena. In fact, it was quite typical: the Church had once seen the devil in every corner; science now saw a charlatan behind every paranormal event.

Unfortunately, this prejudice silenced people who had experienced or witnessed paranormal events and drove the subject— and its study—further underground. As a result, we really do not know how common any psychic phenomenon, especially discarnate communication, might have been. Those who believed it was the work of the devil held the most popular opinion, but at least they acknowledged that such phenomena existed. Even in the face of overwhelming evidence, as in Home's case, the possibility was rejected out of hand. In his excellent book *The Medium, the Mystic, and the Physicist,* Lawrence LeShan says of science and parapsychology, "The general refusal to deal scientifically with the material gathered in this field seems to be a phenomena *in itself demanding explanation*" [italics in original]. This statement seems no less true today—over twenty years since LeShan's book was first published—than back in 1871.

To understand mediumship's current status, we have to go back nearly a quarter of a century before William Crookes's report on Home, to upstate New York, where in 1847 John and

Margaret Fox and their children moved into a two-bedroom house in Hydesville. The house's previous tenant is said to have left because of the strange knocks and noises he claimed to have heard. Prior to moving to Hydesville, several members of the Fox family reported having psychic abilities, although we do not know exactly what these were, or how—or if—the family dealt with them. Whether or not the two youngest Fox sisters, Catherine, or Kate (b. 1841) and Margaretta, or Maggie (b. 1838)—knew of the earlier tenant's complaints or the family's unusual experiences is not clear. According to the family, on March 31, 1848, Kate and Maggie heard knocks emanating from the house. Their mother later stated that the girls asked the ''spirit'' questions, to which it replied by knocking a specific number of times for yes or no. Later, an older brother named David realized that the spirit could deliver more complex messages if someone present would recite the alphabet and stop when the spirit knocked, indicating that the letter was part of the message (sort of like a human Ouija board). Now the spirit's repertoire was unlimited. Not long after, the Foxes moved to Rochester, and an older sister, Leah Fish, joined them in their mediumistic pursuits.

Whether or not the rappings were genuine soon became a secondary issue. One fact about the Fox sisters is certain: they were in the right place at the right time. Upper New York State was in the midst of a wave of evangelical-style religious revivals, with new sects and cults—some quite extreme and bizarre, even by today's standards—cropping up everywhere. The sisters' youthful innocence, and reports that David Fox had discovered some unidentified human bones and teeth in the Hydesville house's basement (presumably those of a murdered peddler, now the rapping spirit, Charles B. Rosma), made their account seem all the more credible. And so spiritualism, the quasi-religious movement that preached life after death and spirit communication, was born.

Shortly after their move to Rochester, the three sisters became world famous. They had their defenders, some quite well known in their time, but skeptics voiced their doubts very early on. Finally, in August 1888, before a crowd at the New York Academy of Music, Maggie stated that it had all been a fraud. Katie, who was seated in the audience, backed her up. Maggie then demonstrated how she and her sister produced the knocks by popping their joints (they also claimed to have made sounds by dropping apples). But was the confession genuine? By then Kate and Maggie had both fallen on very hard times. Both were widowed, both drank; Maggie was suicidal. Maggie eventually recanted the original confession, but few noticed. She and Kate were dead by early 1893. In contrast, Leah, who had acted as something of a manager for her younger sisters, was a wealthy married woman who held psychic demonstrations for New York City's elite in her home.

In 1904 workmen called in to repair the Hydesville residence found parts of a human skeleton and a peddler's box. This discovery, made over fifty years after the raps began, lends some credence to the original story, while the fact that Maggie and Kate earned $1,500 for their 1888 "confession" casts doubt on its veracity. Could their claim to having had no psychic abilities have been the real hoax?

If the Fox sisters' "act" was a prank, it was a very influential one. The idea of spirit communication took the nation by storm. Magazines, pamphlets, and books on the subject were published. In 1854 Illinois Senator James Shields presented the United States Congress with a petition bearing 15,000 signatures, calling for the federal government to investigate communications from the dead. The Fox sisters' celebrity and wealth proved a real inspiration, for within two years of their discovery, there were one hundred known mediums in New York City alone. Were all of them frauds? Probably not. But with so gullible a public, and in the absence of unbiased scientific investigation, a little chicanery went a long way.

As the spiritualism craze grew, so did the charlatans' bag of tricks. Simple communications delivered in coded knocks or words scratched out on a slate would not suffice, so physical mediumship became popular. There were schools for mediums, and suppliers of items such as luminous paints, special shoes, and other props and tools for conducting the classic séance, did brisk business. Turning (or tilting) tables, making objects float or fly, or causing musical instruments to play without human assistance were all "evidence" of physical mediumship. The ultimate proof of spiritual contact was spirit materialization. Not surprisingly, phony materializations, usually of historical figures and fetching young girls, were popular and easily achieved. After all, the medium set all the rules, and in the darkened room, where witnesses could neither touch nor speak to the spirit, who could say it wasn't real? In fact, few who attended these séances would want to. For many, spiritualism, like most religions, was a matter of faith. (A stranger form of evidence was ectoplasm, which can best be described as a substance or otherworldly limb that emanates from the medium's body, usually while in trance. One classic form of ectoplasm was nothing more otherworldly than the medium's self-induced regurgitation of filmy fabrics or food. White was the preferred color for this product.)

From this era and style of mediumship—much of it clearly fraudulent and deliberately sensationalistic—we inherit many of the negative stereotypes we associate not just with mediumship but with all psychic and unexplained phenomena. But science is to blame as well. Just for argument's sake, let's say someone really did produce ectoplasm. We would never know. Perhaps if scientists had shown a greater interest in studying genuine mediumship and other parapsychological phenomena early on, this carny-style spiritualism might not have been so popular. Why the story of genuine mediumship appears as a footnote to what seems to be a catalog of hoaxes is simple: someone who produced a materialization of a beautiful woman or coughed up unearthly gobs of ectoplasm got much more attention than a person who delivered far less sensational messages from the other side.

Further complicating things for serious researchers were those cases of mediums who were genuine but not above resorting to trickery or other immoral acts. (Also, in the Victorian moral climate, the sexual possibilities presented by the darkened room and the "materialization"—while limited—were not totally absent.) The closely studied Eusapia Palladino of Italy and the founder of Theosophy, Madame Helena Petrovna Blavatsky were two mediums who were considered genuine but who were caught cheating. Depending on your point of view, exposure of such tricks proved either that some mediums were all too human or that all mediums were fakes. No wonder skeptics, and even the faithful, might doubt.

The educated men and women who investigated mediumship and other paranormal events generally fell into one of two clear-cut groups: believers and debunkers. But there were exceptions, people who studied the phenomena carefully and made honest attempts to learn from them. One of them was the great American psychologist William James, the leading figure in the field in his day. Brother of novelist Henry James and son of theologian Henry James, himself a Swedenborgian, James was a major philosopher as well. His strong interest in survival after bodily death, and specifically mediumship, led him to study, among others, the gifted medium Leonora Piper of Boston and to write extensively on the subject.

In 1882, Sir William Crookes, who studied Home, Katie Fox, Florence Cook, and others, cofounded the Society for Psychical Research (SPR) in London with a group of scientists and philosophers that included Sir Oliver Lodge (who in 1916 published *Raymond or Life and Death,* a book about his spirit communication with his late son Raymond, through Mrs. Osborne Leonard), F. W. H. Myers, Henry Sidgwick, and Edmund Gurney. The group's goal and attitude were reflections of the era's scientific optimism: to apply "rigid scientific criteria" to psychical research, "to examine without prejudice or prepossession and in a scientific spirit those faculties of man, real or supposed, which appear to be inexplicable on any generally recognized hypothesis." One of the founders' main goals was to end the debate between science and religion on the subject of discarnate survival. They sought to investigate "thought-reading [which today we would term telepathy], divination, psychic sensitivity, and hauntings" as well as what they termed "deathbed visions." The deathbed visions (which skeptics term hallucinations) were not seriously studied until 1961, when researchers began to compile statistics on them. (Anecdotal reports had been published as far back as 1878.) Perhaps the SPR's most important contribution to the study of psychic phenomena in general was its pragmatic approach: to examine them not as religious manifestations (which is basically what spiritualism was), but as events to be observed and recorded like any other natural occurrence.

Three years later the unaffiliated American Society for Psychical Research was established in the United States. Along with similar organizations in other countries, such as the Institut Métaphysique International, in Paris, and similar groups throughout Europe and Latin America, with varying degrees of success, documented genuine psychic occurrences.

As always, the questions psychic phenomena raised troubled some people. Just nine years after the Fox sisters went public,

Charles Darwin published his *Origin of Species*. It's not hard to imagine the impact of the theory of evolution on Darwin's contemporaries. Accepting Darwin's theory meant replacing a perfect God in whose image you were deliberately, divinely created, with the anatomical results of natural selection and an ape for an ancestor. Into this, parapsychology—if its research proved strange phenomena to be real—threatened to redefine man's very nature, abilities, and purpose. For if, indeed, people did possess "other abilities," then the current concept of humankind, religion, perhaps even God, would have to be changed, or at the very least reexamined.

Public interest in mediumship periodically rose and fell between the 1850s and the 1920s, peaking during times of crisis and attracting followers in all walks of life. President and Mrs. Lincoln held séances in the White House, in attempts to contact their deceased son Willie, who had died of typhoid at the age of twelve in 1862. There is also evidence that Lincoln may have received messages concerning the conduct of the Civil War through spirit channels. How deeply he believed in spiritualism is uncertain. His wife, Mary Todd Lincoln, was clearly more deeply involved than he. She was not a strong woman, and following Willie's death, she attended séances in the hope of communicating with Willie, whom she claimed visited her every evening at the foot of her bed. One medium, Nettie Colburn Maynard, conducted séances at the White House and later wrote of her experiences with the Lincolns (*Was Abraham Lincoln a Spiritualist*, 1891).

Though Lincoln may not have believed in mediumship, he experienced and accepted other paranormal events in his own life. He was, by his own admission, very superstitious. He believed in omens and the power of dreams, which he considered part of the "workmanship of the Almighty," to forecast events. It has been widely reported that in 1860, shortly after he was elected to his first term of office, he saw his image doubled in a mirror. One image appeared quite normal, but the second had what he described as "a deathlike pallor." He and his wife interpreted this to mean that he would die in his second term, which he did. In addition, just several days before he was assassinated, he dreamed of walking through the White House, where he heard sobbing and saw a body laid out on a catafalque in the East Room. In his dream, Lincoln asked one of the many soldiers in the room who had died, and the answer was, "The President. He was killed by an assassin." Lincoln was shot to death on April 14, 1865, and died the next day.

Following her husband's death, Mary Todd Lincoln sought further comfort with the spiritualists, even sitting for a "spirit photograph," essentially a photo of herself onto which a likeness of the President was superimposed so that it resembled his ghost hovering over her. Only the average person's unfamiliarity with the then-new technology of photography explains how such an obvious fraud could be accepted.

As bizarre as some of the events in the Lincolns' lives seem, it would be a mistake to conclude that their involvement with spiritualism was a rare example. For instance, Mrs. Lincoln was not the first President's wife to hold a séance in the White House. At some point during her husband's term of office (1853 to 1857) Mrs. Franklin Pierce invited the Fox sisters to the White House, hoping to hear from her late son Benjamin.

Spiritualism's last big boom came during the First World War. Not only was this war an international tragedy on a scale incomprehensible to most people—of 65 million men who served, 10 million were killed and probably twice that number wounded—but it was the war that marked what one historian called "the end of order." Many saw it as proof that man had fallen to an unredeemable state of moral degeneracy. In this atmosphere, millions turned to mediums (and, coincidentally, Ouija boards, which had been on the market in their current form since 1902). This unprecedented demand for mediums inspired countless frauds. As always, genuine mediums existed, Gladys Osborne Leonard among them, but with an almost infinite market to be exploited, they were outnumbered by charlatans. Mrs. Leonard became famous for bringing comfort to countless people who had lost loved ones in the war. Among those who sought her help was the British physicist Sir Oliver Lodge, who wrote in the introduction to Mrs. Leonard's 1931 autobiography, *My Life in Two Worlds,* "To communicate with the spirit world . . . [is] . . . not out of accord with the doctrines of modern physics."

The serious study of psychic phenomena and mediumship continued, but the topic was as controversial as ever. There are many possible reasons why progress in these studies seemed to have stopped. People with abilities may have feared or repressed them, and so went uncounted and unstudied. Science

lacked many of the tools—advanced theories in physics, scie
tific data on the near-death experiences and how they diffe
from hallucinations, psychology, and a range of diagnostic
tools that would not be invented for the next sixty years—to
show evidence of the existence of such phenomena. But the
most regrettable problems were caused by the prejudices—
both pro and con—of observers.

Two leading figures of the time—the master magician Harry
Houdini and the writer Sir Arthur Conan Doyle, creator of
Sherlock Holmes—clashed in a classic argument over the existence of spirit communications. Neither seemed to have taken a
serious interest in spiritualism until he experienced a personal
tragedy; for Houdini, it was the death of his mother, Cecilia
Weiss, in 1913; for Doyle, it was the loss of a son in 1915 and
a brother-in-law in 1916. Both believed that spirit communications were possible and devoted their energies to finding proof.
As a result of their mutual interest, the two became good
friends, but the intensity of their debate on the subject—cou-
pled with Lady Doyle's delivering what she claimed was a
message from Houdini's mother that she'd received through
automatic writing—ended their friendship.

By 1922, the year of Lady Doyle's message, Houdini had
spent about nine years sitting with mediums, none of whom
brought forth what he considered a genuine message from his
mother. He stated that until his mother's death, he rarely
thought about the possibility of receiving genuine messages
from the dead. However, his mother's passing changed all
that. In his own way, Harry Houdini stands as the first psychic
debunker, though it should be remembered that the true source
of his widely publicized disgust with all aspects of spiritualism
and the paranormal was not that he'd unearthed so many frauds
but that he had suffered such profound disappointment. He had
been unusually close to his mother. Houdini's investigations
and exposure of fake mediums were widely publicized, though
he was much less honest and much less successful in his quest
than popular myth suggests. Today many people believe that
Houdini exposed every medium he ever tested as a charlatan,
which is not true.

Not long after Lady Doyle's message, Houdini and Doyle's
private debates on the subject became quite public. For his
part, Doyle would never accept Houdini's claims that his feats

magic were simply tricks and illusions. Doyle was con-
nced that Houdini possessed some paranormal abilities, a
charge that infuriated the magician. In fact, Houdini's tricks
really were tricks. The brilliant escapes from locked safes were
accomplished with the help of locksmith's tools that either
Houdini or an assistant discreetly hid inside the safe while they
inspected it. To create the illusion that he could read his wife's
and his assistant Beatrice's mind, the two had developed a
subtle, elaborate set of signals that they used to communicate
to each other even offstage.

Doyle, whose drive to convince the world of the authenticity
of spirit communications and all manner of paranormal phenomena, was described by Sir Oliver Lodge as "missionary." He
wanted, desperately, to believe. When it came to intelligently
analyzing the evidence, Doyle's approach was completely opposite to that of his most famous creation; he simply didn't. He
even went so far as to publicly state that he believed in the
existence of fairies. The proof: crude photographs of young girls
staring at what are obviously pictures of fairies cut out from
books and placed on branches and lawns. Looking at the photographs, it's hard to imagine even a child being fooled by them.

Another reason why Houdini was so good at detecting fraud
in mediumship is that he had played the part of the medium in
phony séances, which he and his wife had staged for money as
far back as the late 1890s, a practice that stopped after his
mother's death. Though he claimed he was exposing fake mediums as a public service because they were preying on the
vulnerable, gullible bereaved, Houdini was actually obsessed
with his task. And, in at least one documented case, he used
trickery to discredit a medium.

In 1924 Houdini belonged to a committee formed by *Scientific
American* magazine to test and award a monetary prize to a
genuine medium. The committee had been testing a woman
named Mina Crandon, or Margery, as she was known publicly,
and was satisfied with the results of tests administered in
Houdini's absence. By the time he joined the committee, they
were on the verge of awarding her the prize, based on her
demonstrations of both physical and spiritual mediumship. Angry at having been excluded from the first tests, Houdini proceeded to re-create many of Margery's physical phenomena,
using props to create the illusion that the spirits were responsible

for things like table tilting. However, he was at a loss to disp..
her spiritual mediumship, which involved direct-voice cc..
munications from her late brother Walter. In desperatio..
Houdini instructed his assistant to conceal near Mrs. Crandon a
folding ruler, which once discovered, would lead others to
conclude that she had been using the ruler to move objects.

During a reading, Walter verbally abused Houdini. When
the ruler was discovered, Houdini and Mrs. Crandon both
denied placing it. The committee, apparently trusting Houdini
implicitly, decided against Mrs. Crandon, and Houdini seemed
to have won. But years after Houdini's death, the assistant
confessed to planting the ruler. One wonders how many other
genuine mediums were similarly discredited by Houdini's un-
scrupulous methods. Years before the assistant's confession,
some of Houdini's fellow committee members voiced suspicions about the magician's overzealousness and the real goal of
his participation in the tests.

Houdini died of peritonitis at the age of fifty-two on Halloween, 1926; Doyle died almost four years later. Ironically,
Houdini's place in the history of mediumship may or may not
have ended with his death. That he believed spirit communication was possible is undeniable. Not only did he state so in his
book on fraudulent mediumship, *A Magician Among the Spirits,* but he left his wife a secret message that he promised to
send to her after death. Only Beatrice knew what the message
was—a ten-word code that could be further distilled to a two-
word message: ROSABELLE BELIEVE.

By then, the spiritualism fad was waning, although the sales
of Ouija boards continued to soar. Maybe people still believed
in spirit communications, but not in self-proclaimed mediums.
One year after Houdini's death, Arthur Ford, perhaps one of
the greatest mediums of this century, made his public debut at
a lecture given by Sir Arthur Conan Doyle. Ford's messages
came to him through a spirit control he called Fletcher, a
pseudonym for the soul of a man Ford had known who was
killed in the First World War. On February 8, 1928, Ford
announced that Houdini's mother had come through to him
with a secret message that Beatrice would understand.
Houdini's widow confirmed the message and, following a séance with Arthur Ford in 1936, announced to the world that her
husband's spirit had delivered the secret message. It isn't hard

..agine the public's response to this news. Here the man ... made a reputation as the greatest debunker of alleged ...ony mediumship had returned with a message, delivered ...rough a medium and confirmed by the only person alive who would know it. If Houdini's spirit "proved" it, then spirit communications were possible.

There's no question but that the code was broken, the question is how. It's still a subject of controversy. There remains some question as to when the actual séance took place. What we do know, however, is that Mrs. Houdini announced to the world that her husband's spirit had delivered the secret message. She wrote that the message was "the correct message prearranged between Mr. Houdini and myself."

If the story had ended there, most of our ideas about mediumship might be very different, but it didn't. For reasons that have never been made entirely clear, Mrs. Houdini retracted the statement sometime later. Whether the retraction was the result of pressure from others—in the family, church, government—is unknown. If the message had not been delivered, why would she have lied? If it had, why risk the public humiliation and embarrassment of retraction? In the fifty-plus years since the incident, several possible scenarios have been offered, but none really satisfies.

This would not, however, be the last time that Arthur Ford made the news. Despite drug and alcohol problems, the results of a nearly fatal 1931 car accident that left him in severe pain, Ford continued his mediumship, often touring and lecturing on the subject. His most famous and controversial reading occurred in 1967. The Episcopal bishop of California, James A. Pike, having noticed some unusual occurrences in his home following his twenty-one-year-old son James's February 1966 suicide, contacted Ford. The medium's reading for Pike took place on Canadian television, and Pike acknowledged that he believed the messages Ford gave him came from his late son. The program was highly controversial and made Ford well known outside the realm of mediumship. The following year, Pike wrote a book about his experiences with Ford. Ford died in 1971, but, according to Ruth Montgomery, he has continued to communicate through her via automatic writing, or more specifically, typing.

Investigations into psychical abilities have progressed in the years since the Fox sisters heard their first raps, and are currently being conducted in universities and other private and government institutions. The focus of these studies, however, seems to be on the types of abilities that are reproducible, easily tested, quantifiable, and of some practical application (for example, telepathy and second sight for espionage). Unfortunately, instances of discarnate communications rarely meet any of these criteria. The sole exception might be the use of discarnate communications for police work, but instances of such involvement are rarely publicized.

Generally speaking, the study of the paranormal moved forward more rapidly in areas other than survival research or discarnate communication. Looking back, we find many instances of great scientists and thinkers exhorting others to embark on this search. In 1920 the inventor Thomas Edison gave a startling interview to *Scientific American* in which he stated, "Therefore, if personality exists after what we call death, it's reasonable to conclude that those who leave this earth would like to communicate with those they have left here." In his *Diary and Sundry Observations,* Edison wrote: "There has always been a certain amount of life on this world and there will be the same amount. You cannot create life, you cannot multiply life. . . ." "I do claim," he told *Scientific American,* "that it is possible to construct an apparatus which will be so delicate that if there are personalities in another existence or sphere who wish to get in touch with us . . . this apparatus will at least give them a better opportunity." Edison was working on such a machine in the years before his death, but he died in 1931 before it was completed.

The study of the paranormal made an important leap from the séance room to the laboratory when J. B. Rhine, a young professor of psychology at Duke University, began conducting scientific experiments on extrasensory perception, or ESP, in the 1930s. Rhine employed a series of cards which subjects were asked to describe without seeing them. He then kept statistics on rates of accuracy and probability. Rhine also worked with several mediums but decided that he had to "back away from the problem of postmortem survival and turn to things we could do experimentally with living people." He continued to test telepathy, clairvoyance, precognition, and later psychokinesis. Nonetheless, before his death at eighty-four in 1980, he called for further experimentation to learn about death and postmortem survival.

Were Edison and Rhine the only scientists to publicly discuss psychic phenomena? Hardly. In 1921 Sigmund Freud said, "If I had my life to live over again, I should devote myself to psychical research rather than to psychoanalysis." And Albert Einstein, in his introduction to Upton Sinclair's book on telepathy, *Mental Radio,* called on science to take such phenomena seriously. Ironically, some of the most extensive documentation of psychic phenomena was done by Edgar Cayce, the so-called sleeping prophet. His assistant carefully recorded his trance readings and prophecies—some 30,000—which are now kept and studied at the Edgar Cayce Foundation and the Association for Research and Enlightenment in Virginia Beach, Virginia.

In 1951 the Irish medium Eileen Garrett, who figured prominently in John G. Fuller's *The Airmen Who Would Not Die,* founded the Parapsychology Foundation in New York City. In 1967 the University of Virginia opened a division of parapsychology under the direction of Dr. Ian Stevenson, who had studied case histories of people who had experienced reincarnation.

The next milestone in survival research was laid in 1969 with the publication of Dr. Elisabeth Kübler-Ross's *On Death and Dying*. Although it did not deal specifically with postmortem survival, this book helped bring about a change in public attitudes toward death and the dying. With these subjects at last being approached openly, the question then followed of what happens to us after our physical deaths. In the mid-seventies, research into the near-death experience came to public attention with the publication of Dr. Raymond Moody's *Life After Life*. It should be noted that several others had studied this phenomenon before Moody (as far back as 1878), and that some have criticized his methods. Nonetheless, partially as a result of his and others' work, the near-death experience and research into discarnate survival have been rescued from the Twilight Zone and are currently being considered by researchers in a wide range of fields.

Bibliography

This bibliography lists books and references used to compile information on the history of psychic phenomena, science, and religion. Others are included as a matter of general interest to readers who wish to learn more about the subject.

Allen, T. G. *The Egyptian Book of the Dead*. Chicago: University of Chicago Press, 1960.

Ariès, Philippe. *The Hour of Our Death*. New York: Knopf, 1981.

Bradbury, Will, ed. *Into the Unknown*. Pleasantville, New York: Reader's Digest Associates, 1981.

Brandon, Ruth. *The Spiritualists*. New York: Knopf, 1983.

Brandon, S. G. F. *The Judgment of the Dead*. New York: Charles Scribner's Sons, 1967.

Brown, Slater. *The Heyday of Spiritualism*. New York: Hawthorn Books, 1970.

Cayce, Hugh Lynn, and Edgar Cayce. *God's Other Door and the Continuity of Life*. Virginia Beach, Virginia: A.R.E. Press, 1958.

Chinmoy, Sri. *Death and Reincarnation*. Jamaica, New York: Agni Press, 1974.

Christopher, Milbourne. *Mediums, Mystics, and the Occult*. New York: Thomas Y. Crowell Company, 1975.

_ovina, Gina. *The Ouija Book*. New York: Simon & Schuster, 1979.

Doyle, Arthur Conan. *The History of Spiritualism*. New York: George H. Doran Company, 1926.

Ebon, Martin, ed. *The Signet Handbook of Parapsychology*. New York: New American Library, 1978.

————. *Communicating with the Dead*. New York: New American Library, 1968.

————. *The Evidence for Life after Death*. New York: Signet/New American Library, 1977.

————. *They Knew the Unknown*. New York: World, 1971.

Evans-Wentz, W. Y., ed. *The Tibetan Book of the Dead*. New York: Oxford University Press, 1957.

Fodor, Nandor. *Between Two Worlds*. West Nyack, New York: Parker Publishing, 1964.

Ford, Arthur. *Unknown But Known*. New York: Harper & Row, 1968.

Fuller, Elizabeth. *My Search for the Ghost of Flight 401*. New York: Berkley Medallion Books, 1978.

Fuller, John. *Arigo: Surgeon of the Rusty Knife*. New York: Thomas Y. Crowell Company, 1974.

————. *The Ghost of Flight 401*. New York: G. P. Putnam's Sons, 1976.

Gaer, Joseph. *How the Great Religions Began*. New York: Dodd, Mead, and Company, 1929.

Garrett, E. J. *Many Voices*. New York: G. P. Putnam's Sons, 1968.

Greenhouse, Herbert B. *The Book of Psychic Knowledge*. New York: Taplinger Publishing Co., 1973.

Grof, Stanislav, M.D., and Joan Halifax, Ph.D. *The Human Encounter with Death*. New York: E. P. Dutton, 1978.

Hooper, Judith, and Dick Teresi. *The 3-Pound Universe*. New York: Dell, 1987.

Houdini, Harry. *A Magician Among the Spirits*. New York: Arno Press, 1972.

Hunter, Stoker. *Ouija: The Most Dangerous Game*. New York: Barnes and Noble Books, 1985.

Jackson, Herbert G., Jr. *The Spirit Rappers*. New York: Doubleday, 1972.

Jacobson, Nils O., M.D. *Life Without Death?* New York: Dell, 1973.

Jung, Carl. *Memories, Dreams, Reflections.* New York: York Books, 1963.

Keen, M. Lamar as told to Allen Spraggett. *The Psychic Maf*. New York: St. Martin's Press, 1976.

Kübler-Ross, Elisabeth. *On Death and Dying.* New York: Macmillan, 1969.

Langley, Noel. *Edgar Cayce on Reincarnation.* New York: Warner Books, 1967.

LeShan, Lawrence. *The Medium, the Mystic, and the Physicist.* New York: Viking, 1966.

McCaffery, John. *Tales of Padre Pio.* Garden City, New York: Image Books, 1981.

Meek, George W. *After We Die, What Then?* Franklin, North Carolina: Metascience Corporation Publications Division, 1980.

Midelfort, H. C. Erik. *Witch Hunting in Southwestern Germany.* Stanford, California: Stanford University Press, 1972.

Mitchell, Edgar, ed. *Psychic Exploration.* New York: G. P. Putnam's Sons, 1974.

Monroe, Robert A. *Journeys Out of the Body.* New York: Anchor Books, 1971.

Montgomery, Ruth. *Here and Hereafter.* New York: Coward-McCann, 1968.

———. *A Search for Truth.* New York: William Morrow, 1966.

———. *The World Before.* New York: Coward, McCann, and Geoghegan, Inc., 1976.

———. *A World Beyond.* New York: Ballantine Books, 1972.

Moody, Raymond A., Jr., M.D. *Life after Life.* Atlanta: Mockingbird Books, 1975.

———. *Reflections on Life after Life.* Atlanta: Mockingbird Books, 1977.

Osis, Karlis, Ph.D., and Erlendur Haraldsson, Ph.D. *At the Hour of Death.* New York: Avon Books, 1977.

Ostrander, Sheila, and Lynn Schroeder. *Psychic Discoveries Behind the Iron Curtain.* Englewood Cliffs, New Jersey: Prentice-Hall, 1970.

Pearsall, Ronald. *The Table-Rappers.* New York: St. Martin's Press, 1972.

Perry, Michael. *Psychic Studies: A Christian's View.* Wellingborough, Great Britain: The Aquarian Press, 1984.

Anna. *Devotions to the Saints*. Toluca Lake, California: International Imports, 1982.

oerts, Jane. *Seth Speaks*. Englewood Cliffs, New Jersey: Prentice-Hall, 1972.

————. *The Seth Material*. Englewood Cliffs, New Jersey: Prentice-Hall, 1970.

Rogo, D. Scott. *Miracles: A Parascientific Inquiry into Wondrous Phenomena*. New York: The Dial Press, 1982.

Seligmann, Kurt. *The History of Magic and the Occult*. New York: Harmony Books, 1975 (originally published New York: Pantheon Books, 1948).

Shepard, Leslie A., ed. *Encyclopedia of Occultism and Parapsychology*, vols. I and II. Detroit: Gale Research Company, Book Tower, 1979.

Sherman, Harold. *The Dead Are Alive*. New York: Ballantine Books, 1981.

————. *You Live after Death*. Greenwich, Connecticut: Fawcett Gold Medal Books, 1972.

Spraggett, Allen. *The Case for Immortality*. New York: New American Library, 1974.

Spraggett, Allen, with William Rauscher. *Arthur Ford: The Man Who Talked with the Dead*. New York: New American Library, 1973.

Springer, Sally P., and Georg Deutsch. *Left Brain, Right Brain*. San Francisco: W. H. Freeman & Company, 1981.

Stearn, Jess. *Edgar Cayce—The Sleeping Prophet*. New York: Doubleday & Co., Inc., 1967.

Stevenson, Ian. *Twenty Cases Suggestive of Reincarnation*. Charlottesville, Virginia: University Press of Virginia, 1974.

Sugrue, Thomas. *There Is a River: The Story of Edgar Cayce*. New York: Holt, Rinehart and Winston, 1942.

Swedenborg, Emanuel. *Compendium of the Theological and Spiritual Writings of Emanuel Swedenborg*. Boston: Crosby and Nichols, 1853.

————. *Heaven and Hell*. New York: Swedenborg Foundation, 1972. (Originally published in Latin, London, 1758.)

Targ, Russell, and Keith Harary. *The Mind Race: Understanding and Using Psychic Abilities*. New York: Villard, 1983.

Taylor, Ruth Mattson. *Witness from Beyond*. New York: Hawthorn, 1975.

Tietze, Thomas R. *Margery*. New York: Harper and Row, 1973.

White, John. *A Practical Guide to Death and Dying*. Whea⸱ Illinois: Quest Books, 1980.

Wilkerson, Ralph. *Beyond and Back: Those Who Died and Live⸱ to Tell It*. Anaheim, California: Melodyland Productions, 1977.

Wilson, Colin. *Mysteries*. New York: Perigee Books, 1978.

————. *The Occult*. New York: Vintage Books, 1973.

Winer, Richard, and Nancy Osborn. *Haunted Houses*. New York: Bantam Books, 1979.

The World Almanac Book of the Strange. New York: Signet/New American Library, 1977.

Zalasin, Paul. *Witchcraft: Its History, Philosophy, and Rituals*. West Hempstead, New York: Gemini Press, 1979.

In addition, George Anderson and Joel Martin are the subjects of a chapter in Sharon Jarvis's *True Tales of the Unknown* (New York: Bantam Books, 1985).

STORIES OF ENCOURAGEMENT AND FAITH

__ASHES TO GOLD Patti Roberts
   0-515-08976-1/$3.50
The heartbreaking true story of Patti Roberts' life with the son of Oral Roberts—and how she rebuilt her life and restored her faith after their "perfect" marriage failed.

__THE CROSS AND THE SWITCHBLADE
   David Wilkerson
   0-515-09025-5/$3.50
New York's most desperate ghettos had little hope—until a young country preacher arrived, and began preaching a message of renewal, miracles, and God's love.

__THE WIDER PLACE Eugenia Price
   0-515-09448-X/$3.50
The wider place...an eternal realm of faith, freedom, and spirit. Take the journey there with beloved author Eugenia Price.

__ALL THINGS ARE POSSIBLE THROUGH PRAYER
   Charles L. Allen 0-515-08808-0/$3.50
A practical guide to effective prayer that shows how you can change your life through faith.
